Introducing Needs Analysi
English for Specific Purpos

Introducing Needs Analysis and English for Specific Purposes is a clear and accessible guide to the theoretical background and practical tools needed for curriculum development in ESP. Beginning with definitions of needs analysis and ESP, this book takes a jargon-free approach which leads the reader step-by-step through the process of performing a needs analysis in ESP, including:

- How to focus a needs analysis according to the course and student level;
- The selection and sequencing of a wide variety of data collection procedures;
- Analysis and interpretation of needs analysis data in order to write reports and determine Student Learning Outcomes;
- Personal reflection exercises and examples of real-world applications of needs analysis in ESP.

Introducing Needs Analysis and English for Specific Purposes is essential reading for pre-service and in-service teachers, and students studying English for Specific Purposes, Applied Linguistics, TESOL and Education.

James Dean Brown is Professor in the Department of Second Language Studies at the University of Hawai'i at Mānoa. He has spoken and taught courses in places ranging from Brazil to Yugoslavia, and has published numerous articles and books on language testing, curriculum design, program evaluation, and research methods.

Routledge Introductions to English for Specific Purposes provide a comprehensive and contemporary overview of various topics within the area of English for specific purposes, written by leading academics in the field. Aimed at postgraduate students in applied linguistics, English language teaching and TESOL, as well as pre- and in-service teachers, these books outline the issues that are central to understanding and teaching English for specific purposes, and provide examples of innovative classroom tasks and techniques for teachers to draw on in their professional practice.

SERIES EDITOR: BRIAN PALTRIDGE

Brian Paltridge is Professor of TESOL at the University of Sydney. He has taught English as a second language in Australia, New Zealand and Italy and has published extensively in the areas of academic writing, discourse analysis and research methods. He is editor emeritus for the journal *English for Specific Purposes* and has co-edited the *Handbook of English for Specific Purposes* (Wiley, 2013).

SERIES EDITOR: SUE STARFIELD

Sue Starfield is Associate Professor in the School of Education and Director of The Learning Centre at the University of New South Wales. Her research and publications include tertiary academic literacies, doctoral writing, writing for publication, identity in academic writing and ethnographic research methods. She is a former editor of the journal *English for Specific Purposes* and co-editor of the *Handbook of English for Specific Purposes* (Wiley, 2013).

TITLES IN THIS SERIES

Introducing Business English
Catherine Nickerson and Brigitte Planken

Introducing English for Academic Purposes
Maggie Charles and Diane Pecorari

Introducing Needs Analysis and English for Specific Purposes
James Dean Brown

Introducing Genre and English for Specific Purposes
Sunny Hyon

Introducing English for Specific Purposes
Laurence Anthony

Introducing Course Design and English for Specific Purposes
Lindy Woodrow

Introducing Needs Analysis and English for Specific Purposes

James Dean Brown

Routledge
Taylor & Francis Group

LONDON AND NEW YORK

First published 2016
by Routledge
2 Park Square, Milton Park, Abingdon, Oxon OX14 4RN

and by Routledge
711 Third Avenue, New York, NY 10017

Routledge is an imprint of the Taylor & Francis Group, an informa business

© 2016 James Dean Brown

British Library Cataloguing-in-Publication Data
A catalogue record for this book is available from the British Library

Library of Congress Cataloging-in-Publication Data
Brown, James Dean, author.
Introducing needs analysis and English for specific purposes / James
Dean Brown.
pages cm
Includes bibliographical references and index.
1. English language—Study and teaching (Higher)—Foreign speakers.
2. English language—Business English—Study and teaching (Higher)
3. English language—Technical English—Study and teaching (Higher)
4. English language—Study and teaching (Higher)—Evaluation.
5. Education, Bilingual—Ability testing. I. Title.
PE1128.A2B7323 2016
428.0071—dc23
2015026495

ISBN: 978-1-138-80380-0 (hbk)
ISBN: 978-1-138-80381-7 (pbk)
ISBN: 978-1-315-67139-0 (ebk)

Typeset in Sabon
by Book Now Ltd, London
Printed and bound in Great Britain by
Ashford Colour Press Ltd

Contents

Contents

Figures

Tables

Preface

As the title says, this book is about needs analysis (NA) as it is applied to English for specific purposes (ESP). Examples of some of the different types of ESP include English for academic purposes, engineering purposes, business purposes, and so forth. The aim of the book is to provide language teachers and teachers in training with the theoretical background and practical tools they will need to perform NA at the initial stages of ESP curriculum development. As such, the writing style has intentionally been made clear and accessible by minimizing jargon, by clearly defining any jargon that is necessary, and by reducing the number of cryptic academic conventions (for example, e.g., i.e., cf., and so forth).

Relationship to other books

At this point in time, NA and ESP are well-established subfields. For example, in preparing for this project, I reviewed dozens of books. Some books were published on second language curriculum development (Brown, 1995; Clark, 1987; Dubin & Olshtain, 1986; Finocchiaro & Brumfit, 1983; Graves, 2000; Johnson, 1989; Munby, 1978; Nation & Macalister, 2010; Nunan, 1988, 1991; Pennington, 1991; Richards, 2001; Tickoo, 1987; White, 1988; Yalden, 1987). Typically, these curriculum books have included a chapter or section on NA. I have also found books explaining NA in general educational contexts with no particular focus on English language teaching (Altschuld & Witkin, 2000; Craig, 1994; English & Kaufman, 1975; Goldstein & Ford, 2002; Gupta, Sleezer, & Russ-Eft, 2007; Johnson, Meiller, Miller, & Summers, 1987; Kaufman, Rojas, & Mayer, 1993; McClelland, 1995; McKillip, 1987; Queeny, 1995; Soriano, 1995; Stufflebeam, McCormick, Brinkerhoff, & Nelson, 1985; Tobey, 2005; van Hest & Oud-De Glas, 1990; Witkin, 1984; Witkin & Altschuld, 1995).

Another category of related books included edited collections on *language for specific purposes* (or LSP), often with no particular focus on English, but sometimes including a chapter or section on NA (Bowles & Seedhouse, 2007; Freudenstein, Beneke, & Ponisch, 1981; Mackay & Palmer, 1981; Parker & Reuben, 1994; Pugh & Ulijn, 1984; Trace, Hudson, & Brown, 2015).

In ESP, a number of books included sections on NA. Some were single author books about doing ESP (Basturkmen, 2006, 2010; Dudley-Evans & St. John, 1998; Harding, 2007; Hutchinson & Waters, 1987; Robinson, 1980, 1991), others were edited collections on research perspectives in ESP (Belcher, 2009; Belcher, Johns, & Paltridge, 2011; Holden, 1977; Mackay & Mountford, 1978; Paltridge & Starfield, 2013), and still others were case studies in ESP (Master & Brinton, 1998; Orr, 2002; Richterich, 1983a; Richterich & Chancerel, 1977, 1987; Swales, 1985)

I was already familiar with books covering the development and teaching of specific types of ESP including *English for academic purposes* (Benesch, 2001; Flowerdew & Peacock, 2001; Hyland, 2008; Jordan, 1997; Strain, 2006; and Tarone & Hanzeli, 1981), *business English* (Donna, 2000), *workplace English* (Pratt, 1982), and *English for science and technology* (Richards, 1976; Trimble, 1985; Trimble, Trimble, & Drobnic, 1978).

I was also familiar with five books published on using NA in teaching of English as a Second/Foreign Language (ESL/EFL) (that is, ones not focused on ESP). Three of the five were very short and dated, one was a 46-page pamphlet focused on ESL NA (Buckingham, 1981), and two were short treatments of NA for the languages (including EFL) covered in the Council of Europe project of the 1980s (Richterich, 1985; Richterich & Chancerel, 1987). The others provided substantial treatments of NA in language teaching: one was an up-to-date edited collection (Long, 2005b), rather than a how-to book on doing NA; the other provided a narrowly defined learner-centered approach to NA (Tarone & Yule, 1989). In any case, none of the NA books in this paragraph focused on ESP.

In short, I found that there were many books in language teaching, ESL, and EFL that included some discussion of NA, and there were five books that focus on NA in language teaching. One other recent book is worth mentioning because it centers on NA in ESP (Huhta, Vogt, Johnson, Tulkki, & Hall, 2013). This last book is theoretically sound and practical. However, like several of the books above, it focuses too narrowly (in this case, on what it labels the holistic approach to ESP) and is only directly relevant to teachers working within the Common European Framework of Reference (CEFR) with most of the examples drawn from sources related to CEFR.

The present book

In examining all of the above published books, I felt that what was missing was an up-to-date entry-level book that introduces a wide range of theoretically sound approaches and practical options for actually performing ESP NA in the real world. I hope that the present book will serve those purposes.

To those ends, the book is organized into three parts and seven chapters that correspond to the three stages and seven steps that must be included when doing any ESP NA well (see Table of Contents). The chapters cover those seven steps in considerable depth with ample examples drawn from the literature and from my own ESP curriculum development experience.

Getting ready to do an ESP needs analysis

Chapter 1 is designed to define NA in ESP. To that end, the chapter addresses issues like: what NA is, what ESP is, the different types of ESPs, and how *specific* ESP should be. The chapter also examines the initial options in an ESP NA—ones that need to be sorted out before the process can begin—by exploring what *needs* means in *needs analysis* and what *analysis* means in *needs analysis*.

Chapter 2 is about focusing the ESP NA. Thus the chapter begins by suggesting two ways to grapple with the important issue of finding the right level of specificity: (a) by narrowing the scale of the population of students that ultimately must be served by the NA and then (b) by reducing the scope of the NA in terms of the purpose and content of the target ESP course or program. The chapter then discusses a wide variety and number of situational, stakeholder, and theoretical constraints—ones that will tend to limit an NA to what a course or program can realistically provide for students. The chapter ends by expanding the discussion of syllabuses and how important they are as the basic units of analysis for focusing an ESP NA.

Chapter 3 covers the issues involved in selecting and sequencing ESP NA data-gathering procedures. The chapter starts by examining the characteristics of NA as well as factors that affect information-gathering choices. The chapter then describes 32 different procedures that ESP needs analysts may want to use. The chapter ends with a discussion of several strategies that may prove useful for combining and sequencing multiple procedures in an NA.

Doing the ESP needs analysis

Chapter 4 is focused on helping needs analysts do information/data gathering by suggesting: (a) questions that they can ask themselves and strategies they can use to sequence data-gathering activities; (b) strategies for conducting NA interviews and meetings, observing classes, and meeting with learners; (c) developing and administering questionnaires (including Likert items); and (d) collecting NA data on actual oral and written ESP use.

Chapter 5 examines different ways to analyze and interpret NA results. The quantitative analyses that are explained include simple statistics like frequencies, percentages, means, and standard deviations, while the qualitative analyses that are explained include how to use matrices to understand non-numerical data and doing corpus analyses to understand oral and written ESP language use. The chapter also includes explanations of: (a) what triangulation is, why it is useful in an NA, and nine different types of triangulation; (b) strategies for enhancing the quality of NA results and interpretations; and (c) mixed methods research (MMR), the seven MMR techniques that are available, and why applying MMR may be important in an NA.

Using the needs analysis results

Chapter 6 explores ways to effectively use the results of an NA, especially in interpreting the NA results in terms of what they mean for student learning outcomes (SLOs). The chapter defines SLOs and then describes three different types: precisely defined, embedded, and experiential SLOs. The chapter goes on to explain strategies for writing effective SLOs, revising and organizing SLOs, getting teachers to accept and use SLOs, and using those SLOs as a bridge from the NA to all the other curriculum elements.

Chapter 7 is about reporting on an NA project. To that end, the chapter describes ways to organize an NA report and ideas about potential audiences for an NA report. Then the chapter discusses ways to describe the NA process, to report quantitative, qualitative, and mixed methods results, and to format the SLOs that the NA suggests might prove useful. The chapter also covers some of the issues involved in publishing an NA report. The chapter ends with a discussion of strategies to use in accounting for the many viewpoints that surface in any NA.

In addition, each chapter provides clear, concise, simple-to-read, and easy-to-understand information, tools, and practical examples in each of the core areas of NA by tentatively including all of the following:

1   a list of questions to which you will find the answers in the chapter (providing an initial preview of the chapter);
2   background (explaining key concepts and why they are important);
3   key issues on this topic (key issues from the literature);
4   examples of real-world practical ESP NA applications;
5   personal reflection tasks (to help readers understand how the material fits into their professional experiences);
6   tasks (to help readers organize and internalize the material);
7   graphic organizers (including figures and tables that illustrate, organize, and summarize key concepts).

Some parting thoughts

I would like to end with one important suggestion. The fact that this book is arranged in a step-by-step manner is a bit deceptive. True, when in doubt, the steps outlined here will indeed prove useful to follow. However, having been part of many such projects, I have recognized that they are much more recursive and holistic than these steps imply. What I am saying is that you may start out with these steps, but you will soon find yourself circling back or wishing that you had known something from the outset that you only learned in the last step. For example, knowing that the ultimate goal of most NAs is to create a sound set of student learning outcomes can help in all the earlier steps. Thus reading Chapter 6 first might help with all the other chapters. However, the same is true of other aspects of NA. So it probably makes no sense to read the book backwards. A better strategy might be to get a fairly good take on all aspects of NA before you begin any actual NA process in the real world. What I am suggesting is that you read the whole book through before doing an NA, and then you will know what sections to refer to in the relevant chapters as you move step-by-step through your actual ESP NA.

Although there are many books that discuss NA, none focuses on how to do ESP NA following these seven steps. Nor do any of those books provide the breadth of NA options that this book provides, options written about by an author with the authority of being a long-time and currently recognized practitioner of ESP NA and curriculum development.

In short, the book you are holding is an entry level text that has long been missing—one that introduces a wide range of relevant topics integrated into a step-by-step guide to doing needs analysis that is at the same time up-to-date and authoritative.

Aloha![1]

J.D. Brown
Kaneohe Bay, Hawai'i
January 15, 2015

Note

1 FYI, *Aloha* is an ancient Hawaiian word that, in this context, essentially means: I live in Hawai'i and you don't, ha ha!

Part I

Getting ready to do an ESP needs analysis

Needs Analysis   Brown (2016 p.3)

(1) – process of determining
the needs for which a
learner or group requires
a language

(2) Needs according to
priorities

Defining needs analysis in English for specific purposes (ESP)

In this chapter, you will find answers to the following questions:

- What is a needs analysis (NA)?
- What is English for specific purposes (ESP)?
- How specific should ESP be?
- What does the word *needs* means in *needs analysis*?

What is needs analysis?

This is a book about needs analysis, so I will begin by pointing out that the phrase *needs analysis* is used interchangeably with the phrase *needs assessment*, and as far as I am concerned they mean the same thing. Conveniently, both can be abbreviated as NA. But what is NA? According to one dictionary, it is

> the process of determining the needs for which a learner or group of learners requires a language and arranging the needs according to priorities. Needs assessment makes use of both subjective and objective information (eg data from questionnaires, tests, interviews, observation) ...
> (Richards & Schmidt, 2010, p. 389)

Unfortunately, this definition leaves out a great deal.

However, definitions can go overboard in the other direction by trying to include too much detail. For example, in an earlier book, I provided a very elaborate, detailed, and formal definition in which I tried to include everything by combining a number of other definitions I had found in the literature. The result was a definition that was too inclusive and consequently rather ponderous: NA is the systematic collection and analysis of all subjective and objective information necessary to define and validate defensible curriculum purposes that satisfy the language learning requirements of students within the context of particular institutions that influence the learning and teaching situation.

(Brown, 1995, p. 36)

Perhaps if I break that definition apart a bit, it will become clearer. Consider the following relatively uncomplicated definition of NA: the systematic collection and analysis of all information necessary for defining and validating a defensible curriculum. That is fairly clear and straightforward.

However, to make it even clearer, I explain three concepts:

1   *Stakeholders* are people who have a stake or interest in the curriculum (for example, teachers, students, administrators, and parents).
2   A *defensible curriculum* is one that satisfies most of the language learning and teaching requirements of the students and teachers within the context of the particular institution(s) involved in such a way that it can be successfully defended to and accepted by all stakeholder groups.
3   The *necessary information* for defining and validating a defensible curriculum includes any and all types of quantitative and qualitative information from all relevant stakeholder groups that turn out to be available and appropriate in the particular NA.

In addition, before moving on, I must clarify one other key concept not directly related to the definition of NA, but nonetheless central to any NA project: the *needs analyst(s)*. Throughout this book, when I refer to the needs analyst or analysts, I mean whoever is actually doing the work of the NA including planning, gathering, analyzing, interpreting, and using the data, as well as writing the report. That may be a single hard-working teacher focusing on her class, one person put in charge of the NA for a multi-section class or program, or a team of people doing an NA for a multi-section class, program, institution, state, country, or international organization. Thus, I am referring throughout the book to the role of needs analyst(s), not to any particular set of arrangements.

What is English for specific purposes?

Having clarified what NA is, the next question I need to address is: What is *English for specific purposes* (ESP)? Again turning to a dictionary, ESP is defined as "the role of English in a language course or programme of instruction in which the content and aims of the course are fixed by the specific needs of a particular group of learners" (Richards & Schmidt,

2010, p. 198). That definition seems to work fairly well. Notice that ESP is fundamentally linked to "the specific needs of a particular group of learners," or put another way, if there is no *needs analysis*, there is no *ESP*.

Another way to define ESP is to consider what ESP is *not*. ESP is *not* what has been snidely called TENOR (Teaching English for No Obvious Reason, after Abbott, 1981) or ENOP (English with No Obvious Purpose). For example, when international students arrive in the United States for university studies, many of them have studied eight or more years of ENOP, during which time they probably learned a great deal of grammar, vocabulary, pronunciation, and perhaps something about classical American or British literature. However, when they try to communicate with American people, they make the disconcerting discovery that most Americans do not want to talk about grammar, vocabulary, pronunciation, or the small subset of classic literature they have read. And when such students start their studies at the university, they suddenly realize that they have trouble talking with their teachers and fellow students, have difficulties following lectures, have trouble keeping up with the assigned readings, and so forth. The problem may be that they have learned English for no obvious purpose.

If they had studied *English for academic purposes* somewhere along the line, they might have been better prepared with the English needed to deal with their teachers, fellow students, academic lectures, and readings. In short, if these students had studied the English that they needed for their own purposes, academic English in this case, they would probably have been much better prepared to use the language when they arrived in the United States.

At this point, you have no doubt recognized that *NA and ESP are inextricably intertwined*. Recall that the definition I cited above for ESP was "the role of English in a language course or programme of instruction in which the content and aims of the course are fixed by the specific needs of a particular group of learners." Given that definition, how can ESP exist without knowing what the learners' "specific needs" are? And, how can anyone know what those "specific needs" are without doing an NA? ESP and NA are also intertwined from the opposite direction: why would any organization do an NA for their students if that institution was not interested in shaping English instruction for their specific purposes?

In order to bring this section on ESP to a close, I will pose another question: why are you, the reader, interested in ESP? Is it because your institution or colleagues in other fields are pressuring you to teach your students the English of their particular field? Is it because you have realized that teaching students the specific English they will need in order to study or work in a particular field might be more motivating for them than learning general English? Is it because you recognize that learning all of English takes much more time and effort than most people are willing to invest, so you have decided to narrow the amount of English your students will need to learn to manageable proportions? Is it because you have come to the conclusion that learning general English (whatever that is) has no particular purpose beyond the mere exercise of learning grammar, vocabulary, and pronunciation for the intellectual challenge? Is it because you feel your students might be more highly engaged in studying English if they understood the purpose of doing so? Given that you have read this far in this book, I feel fairly confident that you are at least moderately interested both in NA and ESP and that one or more of the reasons listed in this paragraph are behind your interest. So let us continue our exploration by considering the different types of ESP that you can choose from.

Personal reflection

Think about any second or foreign language that you have studied (or would like to study). Aside from meeting some academic requirement, why did *you* want to study that language? What was your purpose? Frame that as a language for specific purpose (for example, *French for studying abroad purposes*). If you had no purpose, try to think of one that might have been valid for you personally.

What are the different types of ESP?

In your personal reflection above, I asked you to consider your purposes for wanting to learn a foreign language. Earlier, I also discussed students needing to learn English for academic purposes in order to survive in an American university, but those are only two, out of many reasons why students might need to learn English. While most students study *general English* or *ENOP*, if they have any real needs for the language (that is ESP), their purposes for learning the language will typically be considerably more specific. Books and articles on the topic of ESP often roughly subdivide those purposes or needs into *English for academic purposes* (EAP) and *English for occupational purposes* (EOP). Figure 1.1 shows this division of ESP into the two EAP and EOP main categories.

EAP[1] can also be further divided into third-level categories of English for science and technology, English for social sciences purposes, and English for humanities purposes (see Figure 1.2). Similarly, EOP can be divided into various categories, like English for medical purposes (which could be even further subdivided into specializations like doctors, nurses, emergency

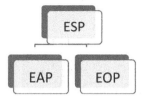

Figure 1.1 Two primary categories of ESP.

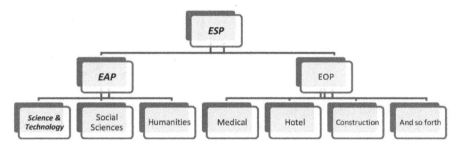

Figure 1.2 Third-level subcategories of ESP.

medical technicians, eldercare, and X-ray technicians), hotel purposes (which could be even further subdivided into jobs like maids, reception desk, concierge, and bell hops), construction purposes (which could be even further subdivided by industry or job titled), and so forth (again, see Figure 1.2).

The third level of English for science and technology (EST) shown in Figure 1.3 can also be divided and subdivided into English for hard sciences and engineering (with engineering further subdivided into civil, mechanical, electrical, chemical, aeronautical, and so forth). The result is that Aeronautical English is a subcategory of Engineering English, which is in turn a subcategory of EST, which is one type of EAP in ESP. Clearly, if I were to try to create a figure that included all types of ESP in five levels, it would be enormous. There are two additional problems raised by this way of thinking about ESP: (a) it makes these categories look like they are independent and mutually exclusive and (b) it raises the problem of how *specific* an ESP should be.

Are these ESP categories mutually exclusive?

Figures 1.1–1.3 show one system for categorizing and understanding the relationships among various levels of ESPs. Unfortunately, in the process,

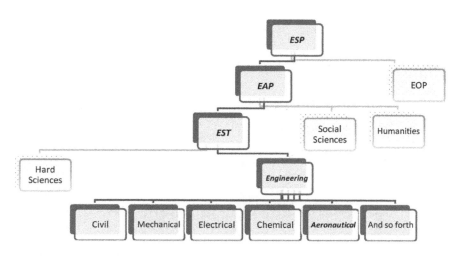

Figure 1.3 Further subdividing EST.

they make it appear that all of these ESPs are mutually exclusive, which is not entirely true. Consider Figure 1.4, in which I have shown how EST, English for social sciences, and English for humanities might all have a *common core*[2] of EAP. These three subcategories each have their own distinct rhetorical structures, organizational principles, grammatical structures, vocabulary items, and other features. However, as Figure 1.4 also shows, reality can be even more complicated because some of the characteristics of these three subcategories may or may not overlap with other subcategories. For instance, social sciences English shares a host of features with EST (consider all the statistical forms of logic and attendant conventions like $p < 0.01$, *null hypotheses*, and *random assignment*) and some with the humanities (especially literary and philosophical analyses, for example, the postmodern terminology in some of the social sciences research like *agency*, *identity*, *power*, and *critical analysis*). My point is that sometimes it is useful to think of the various English purposes as distinct and different (as shown in Figures 1.1–1.3), while other times, especially in light of increasing interdisciplinarity in the academy, it is useful to think about how the English used to serve those different purposes may draw on a common core or overlap with the English of other specific purposes.

At this point, I must confess that there are certainly other ways to categorize ESPs. For instance, Huhta (2010) divides ESP up into three main orientations: academic (including general EAP and discipline-specific), professional (including business, technology, law, and professional purposes), and vocational (including entry level and field-specific) with all the subcategories

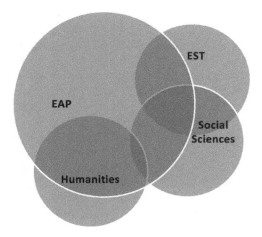

Figure 1.4 Venn diagram of common core and overlaps in EAPs.

in parentheses further subdivided as well. The point isn't so much that any particular system of categories is correct or wrong (the categories of ESP explained here happen to work well for me), but rather that, no matter which system is used, such categories can be helpful in finding that level of specificity which will best serve the *specific* ESP needs of a particular group of students.

Personal reflection

Think about a group of students that you teach English to (or students you would like to teach some day). What is their purpose for studying English (whether it is officially recognized or not)? Is that purpose an EAP or an EOP? Can you be more specific in labeling it? If there is no such existing purpose, what are some possibilities?

How specific should English for *specific* purposes be?

Working out what the specific purpose is for a particular ESP course will inevitably involve working out just how *specific* that purpose can realistically be defined as. In a perfect world, a specific plan of study would be worked out for the exact purposes for which each individual student needs to learn English. However, realistically, it is not possible to tailor most teaching to that degree. Thus, it is usually necessary to work out the most specific level of English that all (or most) of the students in a course will need in common.

In an EST program that I once worked in, we had about 225 Chinese scientists of different kinds including physical scientists (for example, chemists, physicists, and geologists), life scientists (for instance, botanists, zoologists, and medical doctors), and engineers (for example, civil, mechanical, electrical, and civil). We soon discovered that physical sciences, life sciences, and engineering are only very rough categories, and that even subcategories like chemistry, physics, and geology are only very rough groupings of somewhat similar specializations. For instance, we had physicists who were interested in cosmic scale astrophysics, but also some who were interested in the much smaller scale particle physics. We had medical doctors who were general practitioners, but also one doctor who specialized very narrowly in controlling pain in heart surgery with acupuncture. And worse yet, it seemed like engineers were often narrowly confined to specializations that were not even remotely similar. For example, I specifically remember one engineer who specialized in *cement* (as opposed to *concrete*, which was apparently an important distinction to him).

So how specific should an ESP program be? And, how should all such variations in specializations be handled? In the China program, we chose to use two strategies to deal with this issue of having students with varying specific purposes within our EST program. First, in the general classroom activities, we felt that the only way to address the needs of most students at any given time was to teach *common core EST*, that is, the EST common to all scientists and engineers. Figure 1.5 attempts to show how EST is the general category overlapping considerably with the three subcategories of physical science, life science, and engineering. It was at the level of that general EST that we built many of our materials.

Second, in a number of the individual activities, we encouraged students to delve into the English of their specialization. For example, in one of our reading courses, we had five extensive reading assignments that required the students to search out English language articles in their area of specialization. We had a fairly complete set of *Scientific American* magazine in our library. We simply assigned the students to locate five different articles in their specialization (or as close as they could find) and write brief summaries in English that their English teacher could understand. We felt that this assignment allowed students to do reading in their specialization, but also to practice the important skill of summarizing information from their specialization for educated lay people. More importantly, this assignment helped students find and learn the English of their specialization within a curriculum that was mostly based on the more general and widely applicable common core EST.

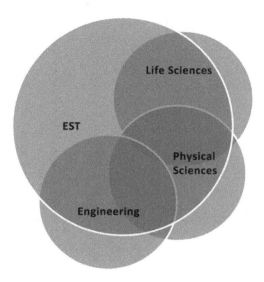

Figure 1.5 Venn diagram of common core and overlaps in ESTs.

In most cases, this pair of strategies should help you deal with the issue of having students with varying specific purposes within an ESP. To summarize, it involves two steps:

1   Find the right common core ESP that is shared by most of the students (EST in the example above).
2   Then work out activities that will allow the students to search out and delve into the more specific English of their own specialization within that common core ESP.

Task 1.1 Abstract from Wozniak (2010, p. 243) – Recognizing the Purpose of the English in an NA

This paper gives a detailed account of an analysis carried out at the French National Skiing and Mountaineering School from August 2008 to June 2009 to assess the language needs of French mountain guides. A targeted literature review highlighted two main points to be taken into account in the design of this language needs analysis: target situations and insiders' expert knowledge. Then,

(Continued)

(Continued)

one hypothesis and two research questions were identified. Data gathering methods including unstructured interviews, nonparticipant observation of the foreign language certification process and a questionnaire allowed testing of the questions via triangulation (by sources and methods) to validate the results.

The two research questions were: "What are the language needs of French mountain guides? In a context of international mobility, what type of "English" should be taught?" (p. 245).

Read the above abstract and the research questions just below it. Then, working in pairs (if possible), answer the following questions and compare your answers:

1   What purpose does the English have in the needs analysis that Wozniak is describing?

    English for _____ *and* _____
    purposes

2   Would this NA fall into the broader category of EOP or EAP?
3   If the program was for skiing, mountaineering, travel guides, and tour coordinators, what might that more general ESP be called?
4   If the program was only for *mountain guides*, what would it be called?

Initial options in ESP needs analysis

Over the years, I have met a number of teachers and researchers who seemed to feel that what we are looking for when we do an NA is the *truth* about what the students need to learn. Such a notion is absurd on the face of it from my point of view, probably because I have actually done needs analyses. In my experience, different groups of stakeholders in a program are likely to hold different views of what the students need to learn. Indeed, individuals within those groups are likely to disagree among themselves about those needs (more about dealing with these differences among people in Chapter 7). In the rest of this chapter, I will consider these differing views in more detail by examining what the word *needs* in *needs analysis* means to various people as well as how different people interpret the word *analysis* in *needs analysis*.

What does *needs* mean in *needs analysis*?

One early problem often faced in doing NA is that the word *needs* means so many different things to different people and in different contexts. Indeed, all of the following words can and do serve as synonyms for *needs* in one way or another: *wants, desires, necessities, lacks, gaps, expectations, motivations, deficiencies, requirements, requests, prerequisites, essentials,* the *next step,* and *x + 1* (where *x* is what students already know, plus the next step, or *1*). Since different groups of stakeholders or even individuals within those groups may have different definitions/conceptualizations of *needs,* anyone doing an NA should put some thought into this issue at the beginning of the process. Definitions/conceptualizations of *needs* seem to fall into at least four different categories. As shown in Table 1.1, these points of view on needs, or what I will call *needs viewpoints,* include at least: (a) the democratic view: whatever the most people want, (b) discrepancy view: whatever is missing, (c) analytic view: whatever logically comes next, and (d) diagnostic view: whatever will do most harm if missing.[3]

Democratic view: Whatever the most people want

In the narrow definition of the *democratic view of needs,* students' needs are whatever elements of the ESP the majority of students want. Thus from this perspective, needs analysts should be interested in the students' *wants, desires, expectations, requests,* and perhaps their self-described *motivations.* This narrow definition is probably too restrictive. For example, consider a group of students who have studied English and other languages in the grammar-translation tradition all their lives. Though they are destined to go to the UK next year to study marketing, such students will tend to want, desire, expect, and request more grammar and translation because those are what the students are used to and comfortable with. However, these people are already good at grammar and translation because they have been practicing those things for years. As a result, the teachers and administrators may think the students need something quite different like English for marketing purposes taught using marketing simulations.

This difference between what the students want and what other stakeholder groups think the students may need poses a problem – a problem that can be corrected fairly simply by broadening the definition of needs to include people other than the students, that is, *needs are whatever elements of the ESP majorities of all stakeholder groups* (teachers, administrators, and so forth) *want, desire, expect, and so forth.* This broader definition still allows needs to be framed around what the students need, but from various stakeholders' viewpoints, which will generally shape the needs into much more than just what the students want.

The democratic view of needs has three primary benefits. First, it involves important groups of stakeholders in the process of determining the needs that will be addressed in the ESP program. Since people like to be consulted in any such process, they are more likely to buy into whatever the

Table 1.1 Four viewpoints on needs

Needs viewpoints	Definition of needs	Related synonyms
Democratic view	Whatever elements of the ESP majorities of all stakeholder groups want	Wants; desires; expectations; requests; motivations
Discrepancy view	The difference or discrepancy between what they should be able to do in the ESP and what they currently can do	Deficiencies; lacks; gaps; requirements
Analytic view	Whatever elements of the ESP students should learn next based on SLA theory and experience	Next step; x + 1
Diagnostic view	Whatever elements of the ESP will cause harm if they are missing	Necessities; essentials; prerequisites

needs analysis reveals if they have been asked about it. Second, given that a variety of different points of view will no doubt exist in any program, it is usually wise to gather as many good ideas as possible. After all, 2, 10, 50, or 100 heads are usually better than one. Third, doing an NA that will successfully lead to a defensible curriculum can depend in great part on knowing what people are thinking about the English language, ESP, language learning, and language teaching. This last point is true whether those people agree or not. Indeed, when there is disagreement, it may be more important than ever to understand the thinking of the various stake-holder groups, so that negotiations among them can proceed early and successfully.

Discrepancy view: Whatever is missing

Within the *discrepancy view of needs*, students' needs are the difference or discrepancy between what students should be able to do in the ESP and what they currently can do. From this perspective, needs analysts would typically be interested in the students' *deficiencies*, *lacks*, *gaps*, and *requirements*. The discrepancy view often leads needs analysts to investigate and describe where the program wants the students to end up with regard to their ESP knowledge and skills, where they currently are in their ESP learning, and what the discrepancies are between the two.

This discrepancy view of needs provides three benefits. First, this view encourages needs analysts to start early thinking about and formulating the programs goals and student-learning outcomes (also known as *instructional objectives*). Second, as a result, this viewpoint naturally promotes the creation of targets for the instruction and a sense of how far the students need to progress to get to those targets. And third, this way of looking at needs encourages the needs analysts to think about the whole ESP course as a single package, from the beginning to the end and all the steps along the way. However, the discrepancy viewpoint alone is probably too narrow and can lead to disaster if the needs analysts simply outline the target outcomes and discrepancies, but fail to democratically consult with all the groups of stakeholders as discussed in the previous section. I actually witnessed this happening in an *English for petroleum purposes* needs analysis that was conducted for a Middle Eastern company I was working with. This needs analysis cost millions of dollars and absorbed a great deal of very talented energy, but ultimately the program based on the needs analysis failed because not a single student or teacher was consulted during the NA.

Analytic view: Whatever logically comes next

Within the *analytic view of needs*, students' needs are whatever elements of ESP they should learn next based on the best available second language acquisition (SLA) theory and experience. From this point of view, needs analysts would usually be interested in the *next step* for the students in the hierarchy or process of language learning; this next step is sometimes referred to as $x + 1$. In more detail, the needs analysts should first learn what the SLA field knows about the hierarchy of learning English (or the steps involved in the process).Then, they should interpret what that means for learning the specific ESP in question, particularly for their students in terms of where the students currently are in the hierarchy or process of learning the ESP.

I find this understanding of needs to be fairly problematic because it presupposes that our field understands the hierarchy of learning points and order of processes involved in learning English. While we clearly do understand some aspects of how English is learned, I personally believe that we are far from having a comprehensive understanding of the hierarchy or steps in the learning process. I also have doubts that any such hierarchy or process would be the same across different language groups learning English, or even across different individuals within those language groups. However, some teachers do take the analytic view seriously, perhaps because they have more faith in our understanding of these hierarchies or processes. Such teachers may quite rationally choose to define the needs of their ESP students analytically within the framework of that SLA knowledge.

Diagnostic view: Whatever will do most
harm if missing

Within the *diagnostic view of needs*, students' needs are whatever elements of ESP will cause the most harm if they are missing. From this perspective, needs analysts will tend to be interested in the students' *necessities, essentials,* and any *prerequisites* (that they need to fulfill before moving on). This view will typically lead needs analysts to investigate the ESP situations that the students are likely to encounter, and then, based on what is known about the students, the needs analysts will first identify potential student needs, then prioritize those needs that are likely to have the most negative consequences if not addressed, then include less crucial needs if there is sufficient time. The diagnostic view of needs is very commonly used in English for immigrant survival purposes programs, where the students are not likely to attend regularly or for long periods of time, so identifying and addressing their most pressing needs first is a matter of efficiency and maybe even of survival. However, in any ESP program where the needs must be prioritized for more efficient teaching, the diagnostic view of needs may prove useful.

Combining different conceptualizations of needs

Coming back to the question at the top of this overall section (What does *needs* mean in *needs analysis*?), I feel compelled to make one very important point: be careful not to seek the *truth*. Notice that I have not used the word *truth* anywhere in this discussion and that the word *truth* does not appear in my list of synonyms for needs. Needs may be many things, but they should never be thought of as the *truth*. The problem is that the truth is likely to be different for various people. Hence, needs can at best be said to be sets of judgments and compromises justified by observation, surveys, test scores, language-learning theory, linguistics, or otherwise. In other words, what needs analysts learn in any NA can at best be considered their CBS (Current Best Shot) at a *defensible curriculum*, but never the *truth*.

How can an NA create the most defensible CBS? That is basically what this book is about. But for the moment let me answer at the level of defining what *needs* are. Given that the 14 synonyms for *needs* that I listed above are not all the same, they must be expressing different facets of needs – facets that may require attention in an ESP curriculum. Notice that my explanations of the four needs viewpoints implied that different sets of the 14 synonyms are associated with specific viewpoints. Thus, when needs analysts select only one of the four viewpoints, they are clearly favoring certain facets of *needs*. In the democratic view, needs are most likely associated with the *wants, desires, expectations, requests,* and *motivations* of students, teachers, and administrators. In the discrepancy view, needs are the *deficiencies, lacks, gaps,* and *requirements* for the students. In the analytic view, needs may consist of the *next step* or *x + 1* in the hierarchy of language learning or language learning processes as they are applied to ESP. And, in the diagnostic view, needs are the *necessities, essentials*, and *prerequisites* for using the ESP that will prove the most harmful if they are missing.

To capture the maximum number of facets (synonyms) for *needs*, needs analysts may find it useful to include two, three, or even four of these needs viewpoints in their thinking about and planning for an NA. The best advice I can give is to consider all four viewpoints as options (along with the many facets of *needs* they represent) and then combine and use them as they turn out to be useful and appropriate at different stages of the needs analysis process.

Task 1.2 Abstract from Spence & Liu (2013, p. 97) – Recognizing the viewpoints in an NA

The global high-tech industry is characterized by extreme competitiveness, innovation, and widespread use of English. Consequently, Taiwanese high-tech companies require engineers that are talented in both their engineering and English abilities. In response to the lack of knowledge regarding the English skills needed by engineers in Taiwan's high-tech sector, this paper presents an English needs analysis of process integration engineers (PIEs) at a leading semiconductor manufacturing company. Based on English skills for engineers and professionals in Asia–Pacific countries, online survey-questionnaires and semi-structured interview questions were developed and administered to PIEs. Results show that engineers face numerous English communicative events similar to other Asia–Pacific nations, including highly frequent writing and reading events such as email, reports, and memos, while common oral events include meetings, teleconferences, and presentations. Findings also indicate that the need for English increases in tandem with the engineer's career, with oral skills being in particular demand for customer visits and relationship building. Moreover, considering the scope of the communicative events PIEs face, Taiwanese learning institutions, ESP instructors and course designers should endeavor to include authentic training in specific areas such as genre-specific writing (i.e., email vs. reports vs. memos), CMC communication (i.e., telephony and teleconference), and delivering presentations.

Read the above abstract. Then, working in pairs (if possible), answer the following questions and compare your answers:

(Continued)

(Continued)

1   What purpose does the English have in the needs analysis that Spence and Liu are describing?

   English for _____ *purposes*

   Based on the abstract alone, what needs viewpoints do you think the authors held and were applying? Please explain why you think so in each case.

   Democratic?
   Discrepancy?
   Analytic?
   Diagnostic?

2   How would you apply all four needs viewpoints if you were in charge of this needs analysis? Again, please explain.

   Democratic?
   Discrepancy?
   Analytic?
   Diagnostic?

What does *analysis* mean in *needs analysis*?

Now that the word *needs* in *needs analysis* is clearer, what does the word *analysis* in *needs analysis* mean? At least eleven *analysis strategies*[4] are available to ESP needs analysts. These analysis strategies are ways of examining, investigating, exploring, and yes, analyzing information to determine what the current needs are for a defensible curriculum in a particular ESP learning–teaching context. As shown in Table 1.2, these eleven are: target-situation use analyses, target-situation linguistic analyses, target-situation learning analyses, present-situation analyses, gap analyses, individual-differences analyses, rights analyses, classroom-learning analyses, classroom-teaching analyses, means analyses, and language audits. Let's reflect on each analysis strategy in more detail.

Target-situation use analyses

Target-situation use analyses investigate what the students should be able to do in the ESP at the end of instruction. These analyses often begin by examining how the language is used in the particular ESP by creating or finding existing *corpora* (collections, often computer databases, of written or oral samples of actual language use) of the language used in the particular

Table 1.2 Eleven analysis options

Analysis options	Analysis of what?	What information will the NA typically examine?
Target-situation use analyses	What the students should be able to do in the ESP at the end of instruction	The language uses in the particular ESP and exemplars of those language uses
Target-situation linguistic analyses	What linguistic features the students will need to know and use in the ESP	The specific linguistic characteristics of the ESP (for example, vocabulary, discourse markers, pragmatics, and genres) in the exemplars gathered above
Target-situation learning analyses	What the features of learning and continuing to learn are in the ESP community	Information about the target situation in terms of the sorts of learning that students will need to do in target ESP situations at various stages
Present-situation analyses	What the students' ESP abilities are at the beginning of instruction	What the students can do with the language of the particular ESP at the outset of instruction (with respect to target-situation use, linguistics, and/or learning) – using tests or other observational techniques
Gap analyses	What the disparities are between the students' current abilities and what they need to be able to do in the ESP	The disparities between what the students can do at the beginning and the end of instruction with regard to the ESP – typically based on analysis of test scores or other observational techniques
Individual-differences analyses	What students' individual preferences are with regard to learning processes	Students individual preferences in learning strategies, learning styles, error correction, group sizes, amount of homework, and so forth

(Continued)

Table 1.2 (Continued)

Analysis options	Analysis of what?	What information will the NA typically examine?
Rights analyses	What the key power relationships are in the situation and how they are resisted	The ways power is exerted and resisted within the ESP-teaching institution (in terms of teaching, materials, curriculum decisions, governing rules, and so forth), between that institution and other entities, or within the target ESP community
Classroom-learning analyses	What the classroom-learning situation is or should be	The selection and ordering of course content, teaching methods and materials that will be used in learning the ESP, and so forth (often requiring negotiations among stakeholder groups)
Classroom-teaching analyses	What the classroom-teaching situation is or should be	The selection and ordering of course content, teaching methods and materials that will be used to teach the ESP, and so forth *from the teachers' perspectives*
Means analyses	What the contextual constraints and strengths are	The availability of funding, facilities, equipment, materials, and other resources; cultural attitudes that might affect instruction; and the teachers' proficiency levels in English, training, and teaching ability – all in terms of both constraints and strengths
Language audits	What global strategic language policies should be adopted	Aimed at regions (like the European Community), countries, companies, professional groups, and so forth, such analyses typically ignore the needs of students in particular ESP situations, but can nonetheless inform local ESP NAs

ESP and then analyzing them. Investigating the *language use* might lead to gathering information about the specific ways people understand and use language in the *discourse community*[5] of the particular ESP, or what I would simply prefer to call an *ESP community*. For example, for an English for science and technology (EST) course, the NA might look for general information about the language used in common EST language events (for instance, listening to science lectures and participating in science seminars and labs, as well as conversing in student/teacher conferences, writing emails, and writing reports in scientific departments). The analysis might then gather *exemplars of those language uses* in the form of recordings (for instance, recordings of lectures, seminars, labs, and student/teacher conferences) and photocopied texts (for example, photocopies of lecture notes, emails, and reports).

Target-situation linguistic analyses

Target-situation linguistic analyses examine what linguistic features the students will need to know and use in the ESP to accomplish the language uses found in the target-situation use analysis. These analyses often describe and analyze the specific linguistic characteristics of the ESP as found in the exemplars collected above. The linguistic characteristics of interest might include vocabulary, collocation, grammar, morphology, pronunciation, connected speech, levels of formality, discourse markers, pragmatics, genres, or other language features. The features selected for a particular NA will have something to do with the knowledge and interests of the needs analysts, but also should be determined in large part by the characteristics found to be most important for understanding and using the particular ESP in question. For instance, for an EST course, an NA might look for information about the linguistic characteristics of the (a) ESP vocabulary in science lectures (by say, listing and calculating the frequencies of scientific *technical vocabulary* specific to each scientist's specialization, *subtechnical vocabulary* known by all scientists, and *non-technical vocabulary* known by all academics), (b) prominent scientific abbreviations in readings (such as *e.g.*, *i.e.*, *cf.*, *etc.*, but also H_2SO_4, S^2, and $p < 0.01$), (c) salient spoken functions in science seminar discussions (for instance, *defining*, *describing*, *giving an example*, and *clarifying*), (d) written genres in science reports (for example, narrative, description, and suasion), and (e) discourse markers in scientific texts (for example, *in addition*, *furthermore*, *however*, *nonetheless*, *therefore*, *as a consequence*, and *for instance*).

Target-situation learning analyses

Target-situation learning analyses investigate what the features are of learning and continuing to learn in the ESP community. This means that the NA should gather information about what people must be able to learn and continue learning in the particular ESP community. This whole idea is based on the observation that knowing how to learn the content of each field is often a very important aspect of succeeding at various stages of assimilating into an ESP community – an aspect that is sometimes quite independent from the specific language use and linguistics involved. Such stages of learning in a particular ESP might include steps like initial orientation, pre-service and in-service training, and re-certification. For example, for an EST course, needs analyses might look for information about initial orientation (where people learn things like classroom and laboratory procedures, university rules and regulations, and common practices in publishing scientific articles), pre-service and in-service training (where people learn things like accepted procedures, common practices, traditions, and philosophies of science), and re-certification (where people learn things like new facts, procedures, policies, and practices in their field).

Present-situation analyses

Once the target-situation analyses are well underway, *present-situation analyses* might be a logical next step. These analyses typically examine the students' ESP abilities at the beginning of instruction (in terms of the relevant target-situation use, linguistic, and/or learning abilities). Such analyses include investigating what students can do with the language of the particular ESP at the outset of instruction using test scores or other observational techniques (like interviews, corpora of learner-produced writing samples, and class observations). For instance, in an EST program, present-situation analysis might mean using established tests to gather general proficiency information about the students like their strengths and weaknesses in terms of the four skills. More specifically, in the EST program where I worked in China, we tested all students using the Michigan Placement Test, and we also gathered writing and taped interview samples. We discovered that the students had extraordinary knowledge of grammar and vocabulary, that is, they knew a lot *about* English. However, they could not actually *do* much with that knowledge in terms of speaking, listening, reading, or writing English effectively. Despite the fact that the students wanted us to teach more of the grammar and translation that they were so comfortable with, we were able to analyze the present situation using test scores and other observations, and thereby argued that the last thing they needed was more grammar and translation. Indeed, we found that their needs broadly were to learn to fluently *use* what they knew to help them speak, listen, read, and write. As this same EST program developed, we created specific course tests based on our target-situation use, linguistic, and learning analyses. We were then able to use those tests to regularly do *present-situation analysis* as each new group of students started their courses.

Gap analyses

Gap analyses examine the disparities between what the students need to be able to do at the end of instruction (target-situation use, linguistic, and learning abilities) and what they currently can do in the ESP (present-situation). Thus this type of analysis combines the three target-situation analyses (use, linguistic, and learning) and the present-situation analysis to investigate what students will need to learn to get from where they presently are to where they need to be at the end of instruction. This form of analysis is clearly related to the discrepancy view of needs discussed above. Thus, it inevitably requires that the NA should look for deficiencies, gaps, or lacks in current abilities in light of the students' target-situation ESP needs. Gap analysis is also clearly dependent on the existence of both present-situation and target-situation (use, linguistic, and learning) analyses. For example, in an EST program, once the target-situation use, linguistic, and/or learning analyses are done, the students' abilities to perform those aspects of the ESP can be tested or otherwise observed (for example, using role plays, interviews, or meetings) at the beginning of instruction (present situation) and end of instruction (target situation), and then the gaps between the two can be isolated.

Individual-differences analyses

Individual-differences analyses explore what students' preferences are with regard to learning processes. These analyses often examine students' preferences in learning strategies, learning styles, error correction, group sizes, amount of homework, and so forth. For instance, for an EST course, information could be gathered using questionnaires about differences and expectations with regard to students' preferred learning styles (for instance, preferences based on biological and developmental traits like extraversion and introversion; visual, aural, kinesthetic processing preferences; and field dependence and independence), preferred learning strategies (like strategies for memorizing, metacognitive strategies, and social strategies for successful learning), and culturally conditioned beliefs (for instance, automatic acceptance of ideas written by authorities vs. critical approaches to all texts, and student beliefs that they should listen and not talk vs. the Socratic method[6]).

Rights analyses

Rights analyses investigate what the key power relationships are in the situation and how they are resisted. Or as Benesch (1999, p. 313) put it in more detail, "Rights analysis examines how power is exercised and resisted in various aspects of an academic situation, including the pedagogy and the curriculum." For example in an EST program, the analyses could be focused solely on power relationships (and how they are resisted) within the ESP teaching institution (perhaps investigating how administrators create policy that the students resist, and how teachers can mediate between the two groups). To broaden the definition a bit, the analyses could additionally examine the power relationships between the ESP teaching institution and other entities (perhaps examining ways the EST program can effectively resist the insistence by the national ministry of education that the program focus on TOEFL preparation), or indeed, the power relationships in the target ESP community (perhaps studying how and why engineers with MS degrees feel they are treated poorly by scientists with PhD degrees). (For more on the related topic of identity roles in ESP, see Belcher & Lukkarila, 2011, and on critical ethnography and ESP, see Johns & Makalela, 2011.)

Classroom-learning analyses

Classroom-learning analyses investigate what the classroom learning situation is or should be. This means examining issues like the selection and ordering of the course content, the teaching methods that will be employed, the types of activities students will engage in, and the materials that will be employed. For instance, in an EST program, based on the target-situation linguistic analysis, the NA might conclude that the greatest need is for students to learn common scientific abbreviations, salient spoken functions in science, and written genres in science. Classroom-learning analyses could then be used to determine which abbreviations, functions, and genres should be taught (perhaps based on the target-situation linguistic analysis), what order to teach them in (for instance for abbreviations, it might make most sense to teach general academic abbreviations first, then chemical notations, and then statistical symbols), what teaching methods to use (perhaps lectures for the abbreviations, role-play demonstrations for the functions, and analysis of video-recorded lectures for text genres), and what activities the students should engage in (perhaps rote memorization for the abbreviations, pair-work tasks for the functions, and group-work analysis of example genre texts with guided worksheets). For those who take a democratic view of needs, this process of deciding on materials, teaching methods, activities, and other learning-oriented analyses will very often require needs analysts to guide negotiations between and among various groups of stakeholders who may have very different ideas about learning-oriented issues.

Classroom-teaching analyses

Classroom-teaching analyses investigate what the teaching situation is or should be. Like the classroom-learning analyses, this form of analysis typically examines information about the selection and ordering of the course content, the teaching methods that will be employed, types of activities students will engage in, and the materials that will be employed – *but from the teachers' perspectives*. These analyses often involve gathering information about how teachers prefer to teach, which might involve information about the teachers' preferred teaching styles and teaching strategies, as well as how those preferred teaching styles and strategies relate to the students' preferred learning styles and strategies. For example, for an EST course, an NA might examine information about the teachers' preferred teaching styles (that is, ways of doing things in the classroom that are comfortable for the teacher(s) and engaging for the students like using simple English, providing clear explanations, telling stories to illuminate concepts, and using humor effectively) and teaching strategies (for instance, creating a pleasant learning environment, using student-centered activities, correcting errors, and getting students to participate).

Means analyses

Means analyses explore what the contextual constraints and strengths are. This usually means that the analyses examine issues like the availability of funding, facilities, equipment, materials, and other resources, as well as cultural attitudes that might affect instruction, and the teachers' proficiency in English, training, and teaching ability. For example, for an EST course, an NA might look for information about the institutional context (for example, audio-visual and computer equipment availability, previous and in-service faculty training, and teaching abilities) and the cultural environment (for instance, the attitudes of students, parents, and the public toward learning in general, toward EST learning in particular, and toward native English speakers more generally). But be careful: investigating these sorts of considerations tends to focus the NA on the negative aspects or the weaknesses of the institutional context and cultural environment, which is why it is important to also consciously pay attention to the institutional and cultural strengths of the context. Indeed, attending to such strengths may prove very important for insuring (pedagogically and politically) that the NA and resulting ESP program will have credibility and be able to capitalize on those strengths.

Language audits

Language audits tend to be used in more global and large-scale NAs that investigate strategic language policies for regions like the European Community, countries, companies, and professional groups. Though such analyses, by definition, ignore the needs of small, well-defined groups of students in particular ESP teaching situations, they can nonetheless inform local ESP NAs. It is unlikely that you will ever be involved in language audits, but it is important that you recognize the existence of these sorts of NAs because they can provide useful information that can be adapted to your local needs. Be careful though: language audits are sometimes used to promote and justify the imposition of top-down and bureaucratic language policies, standards, common frameworks, and the like.

Combining analysis strategies

I have listed eleven analysis strategies here that can be used singly or in combination in doing an NA. Each of these provides a way for analyzing ESP needs, but they tend to work better in combination. In every NA that I have been involved in, I have found myself initially using at least target-situation use analysis, target-situation linguistic analysis, target-situation learning analysis, present-situation analysis, and gap analysis. But then, in later stages, I have found myself using various combinations of the other forms of analysis, especially classroom-learning analysis, classroom-teaching analysis, individual-differences analysis, rights analyses, and means analysis.

Task 1.3 Abstract from Kaur and Khan (2010, p. 1) – Identifying NA strategies

Students studying Art and Design courses need to have good proficiency in English in preparation for today's globalised work contexts. This study evaluated the perceptions of 47 final year diploma Art and Design students and 10 members of staff about the current English Language course in a private college in Penang, Malaysia. This study used both quantitative and qualitative methods to collect data from the students and the academic staff. The data gathered from the questionnaires were analyzed in terms of frequency counts and percentages whereas data collected from the interviews were analyzed based on the responses provided. The findings of this study revealed that the 96% of students perceived the speaking skill to be important for their Art and Design courses and their career whereas the listening skill was rated the second most important skill by 95% of the respondents. Reading and writing skills in English were regarded as 'fairly important' by 80% of the respondents. The findings also revealed that the students were 'moderately satisfied' with the current English language course in their college. The results of the study indicate that a new ESP course focusing on speaking and listening skills should be developed at this college. The ESP course should include workplace-based oral presentations, specialised vocabulary activities and course materials and topics relevant to students' area of specializations. Language teaching strategies such as games, puzzles and riddles could also help improve the ESP students' proficiency in the English language.

Read the above abstract. Then, working in pairs (if possible), answer the following questions and compare your answers:

1   What purpose does the English have in the needs analysis that Kaur and Khan are describing?

English for _____ *and* _____ *purposes*

Based on the abstract alone, what analysis strategies (Target-situation use, Target-situation linguistic, Target-situation learning, Present-situation, Gap, Individual-differences, Rights, Classroom-learning, Classroom-teaching, Means analyses, or Language audits) do you think the authors applied? Please explain why you think so in each case.

2   How would you apply at least four of these analysis strategies if you were in charge of this needs analysis? Again, please explain.

Summary and conclusion

To review briefly, this chapter on defining NA in ESP, addressed a number of issues including what an NA is, what ESP is, the different types of ESPs, and how *specific* ESP should be. The chapter also explored the initial options in an ESP NA (that need to be sorted out before the process can begin) in terms of what *needs* means in *needs analysis* and what *analysis* means in *needs analysis*. These options are summarized in Table 1.3.

Why do these various views of needs and the strategies for analysis matter? As I pointed out several times above, the problem is that different participants in an NA may have quite different views of what *needs* and *analyses* are. Since it is probably foolish to ignore such fundamental disagreements about what *needs* are, it is important to discuss and decide in advance whether to consider democratic, discrepancy, analytic, diagnostic needs, or some combination of the four. Similarly, it is crucial to consider at an early stage whether the NA will include target-situation use analysis, target-situation linguistic analysis, target-situation learning analysis, present-situation analysis, gap analysis, classroom-learning-oriented analysis, classroom-teaching-oriented

Table 1.3 Defining the purpose of an NA: options for defining needs and analyzing them

What are needs?	*How should we analyze them?*
Democratic view – whatever the most people want	Target-situation use analysis
Discrepancy view – whatever is missing	Target-situation linguistic analysis
Analytic view – whatever logically comes next	Target-situation learning analysis
Diagnostic view – whatever will do the most harm	Present-situation analysis
if missing	Gap analysis
	Individual-differences analyses
	Rights analyses
	Classroom-learning analyses
	Classroom-teaching analyses
	Means analysis
	Language audits

analysis, individual-differences analysis, means analysis, and language audits, or more productively, some combination of these analysis strategies. Clearly, all of these options must be carefully considered at the outset and needs viewpoints and analytic strategies should be identified, negotiated, and agreed upon in advance in ways that will be acceptable to a majority of the participants in each of the central stakeholder groups so that ultimately a consensus can be built around the findings that result from the NA. More importantly, the needs viewpoints and analysis strategies must be carefully related to the purposes of the NA because the outcomes of the NA itself may be predetermined to some extent by how the needs are conceived of at the outset and how the analysis strategies are initially selected by the needs analysts.

Notes

1 For much more on EAP, see Charles and Pecorari (2016).
2 Please note that, while the notion of a common core is sometimes useful conceptually, it is not without controversy. Is the EAP common core the same everywhere? Or is it different depending on location and dialect (for example, the UK and North America)? Is the common EAP core based only on native-speaker English? If so, what is a native speaker? And, so forth.
3 These four viewpoints on needs have been adapted considerably from Stufflebeam, McCormick, Brinkerhoff, and Nelson (1985) and Brown (1995, pp. 38–39, 2009, pp. 271–272).
4 This list was adapted considerably from Brown (2009, p. 272), which itself was combined and adapted from West (1994, pp. 8–12) and Jordan (1997, pp. 23–28).
5 A discourse community is

> a group of people involved in a particular disciplinary or professional area (e.g., teachers, linguists, doctors, engineers) who have therefore developed

means and conventions for doing so. ... The concept of discourse community thus seeks to explain how particular rhetorical features of texts express the values, purposes, and understandings of particular groups and mark membership in such groups.

(Richards & Schmidt, 2010, p. 175)

6 In the *Socratic method*, teachers model reasoning and the critical thinking by asking questions, promoting discussion, and encouraging further questioning, rather than by lecturing and giving answers.

Focusing the ESP
needs analysis

In this chapter, you will find answers to the following questions:

- How does scale restrict what I need to accomplish?
- How does scope limit what I need to do?
- What situational constraints will I have to contend with in my NA work?
- What stakeholder constraints will I have to deal with in my NA work?
- What theoretical constraints will I encounter in my NA work?

The specificity of the needs analysis

The specificity of NAs can vary in terms of what I will call their scale and scope. The *scale* of an NA has to do with how broadly it is targeted, or more precisely how broad the student population is that the NA must analyze and serve. The *scope* of an NA has to do with what you will teach and how specifically or narrowly you will focus that content.

The scale of the NA

Figuring out the *scale* of an NA requires that you consider how broad or narrow the student population is that you will be serving with your ESP curriculum. Obviously, NAs can range a good deal in scale from very broad to very narrow. For example, an NA on an international scale is obviously very broad, aiming to serve all the potential students in some clearly defined international context, while an NA for one of the courses you teach is obviously very narrow, aiming to serve only the students that you teach – or perhaps other students like them that you may teach in the future. In theory, NAs can be conducted to include students internationally, nationally, at a state or province level, for a county or school district, across multiple programs, for an entire English program, at the classroom level by individual teachers, for one group within a single class, or even for an individual student. This range in scale from international to individual student represents a wide span indeed.

A number of examples of large-scale international and multi-language NAs occurred in the last few decades of the twentieth century due to Council of Europe efforts to identify adult foreign language learners' needs (including needs for English) in Conseil de la Coopération Culturelle (2000), Council of Europe (2001), Richterich (1980, 1983a, 1983b, 1984, 1985), Richterich and Chancerel (1977, 1987), Trim (1973, 1978, 1980), Trim, Richterich, van Ek, and Wilkins (1980), van Ek (1975, 1984), and van Ek and Trim (1998a, 1998b, 2001). Other NAs have been large scale, but not as ambitious as those listed above. For instance, Brecht and Rivers (2005) described an NA at the national level in the United States; Lett (2005) reported on a large-scale NA for the US military; and Coleman (1988) did the same for a large university. Clearly an NA can be large in scale, but such efforts typically need to be funded by governments, large-scale grants, or sizable institutions, and require considerable organizing.

Probably as a result, NAs are most frequently performed on a much narrower scale in local situations. For example, I am very familiar with a number of English for academic purposes (EAP) needs analyses that were performed for the English Language Institute (ELI) at my home base at the University of Hawai'i at Mānoa (UHM). The ELI serves the EAP needs of matriculated undergraduate and graduate students at UHM who have sufficient English (usually based on the TOEFL iBT scores) to be admitted but need further training before they graduate. I encouraged, instigated, and helped write a number of needs analyses while I was director of the ELI (from 1986 to 1991) for courses in academic listening (for example, see NAs reported in Kimzin & Proctor, 1986, and Alexandrou & Revard, 1990), academic reading (for example, Asahina, Bergman, Conklin, Guth, & Lockhart, 1988), and academic writing (Koh, Michaelis, & Wichitwechkarn, 1990), and even for a course we developed for developing the oral language skills of what are now called international teaching assistants (Brown, Chaudron, & Pennington, 1988). Notice that all of the above were essentially in-house documents that served our EAP curriculum development purposes, but were not published. I wonder how many such needs analyses have been conducted around the world, but never been published. I know I have taken part in many such unpublished NAs myself over the past three decades. However, as you will see in the next section, there have also been many NAs that were published, often with titles containing the defensive phrase "case study" somewhere in the title. Many of these have appeared in the *ESP Journal*, but also in *System* journal, or in other local or in-house journals.

Personal reflection – What is the scale of your ESP NA?

Think about a group of ESP students that you teach (or ESP students you would like to teach some day). What would the *scale* of the NA for those students be? Would you describe that NA as international in scope? National? State or provincial? County or school district? Across multiple programs? An entire English program? Multiple sections of a single course? A single class and teacher? A group of students within a class? An individual student? And, how will that scale affect your NA?

The scale of a particular NA must be decided in the early stages of any such efforts, but that is only one aspect of the specificity of an NA, though a crucial one. Another important aspect of deciding on the specificity of an NA has to do with the content and scope, as you will see next.

Scope of the NA

The *scope* of an NA is related to the types of NAs that were discussed in the previous chapter, which, by-and-large, had to do with what the purpose and content of the ultimate course or program was likely to be as well as the degree of specificity with which you will need to present that content in order to adequately serve the students' purposes. As pointed out in the previous chapter there are various types of ESP, which means that there are various content areas or purposes that ESP programs can address. Typically the issue of content is easy to decide because that decision was a part of the decision to set up the ESP program as a matter of general policy. For example, an institution might set out to create a program that teaches science English, or social science English, or humanities English. In those cases, at least in general, the content area has been delineated. However, deciding on one of those general content areas, say the English of science, is just the first step. It is then necessary to start the harder work of deciding how specific the English of science needs to be for the particular program involved. In a sense, you can decide this at the beginning of an NA, but it is important to recognize that you are just making an estimate and that as you gather more information about science English, about the students and teachers, and about their abilities and opinions, your judgement about the scope of what you can practically teach of science English is likely to change.

As shown in Figure 1.1 of the previous chapter and Table 2.1 here, ESP is often further divided into two main general types, one for *occupational purposes* (EOP) and the other for *academic purposes* (EAP). Table 2.1 also shows specific categories within those two main types as well as a number

Table 2.1 Examples of the diversity of NA studies within EOP and EAP

General type	Specific category	Situation-specific English NA examples
English for occupational purposes (EOP)	Workplace	General Workplace (Holmes, 2005) Post University Workplace (Lambert, 2010; Lehtonen & Karjalainen, 2008) Coffee Shop Workers (Downey Bartlett, 2005) Factory Floor (Garcia, 2002) Food Servers (Decamps & Bauvois, 2001) Footballers (Kellerman, Koonen, & van der Haagen, 2005) Hajj Guides (Abdellah & Ibrahim, 2013) Hotel Workers (Jasso-Aguilar, 1999, 2005) Mountain Guides (Wozniak (2010)) Textile & Clothing (So-mui & Mead, 2000) Tourism (Afzali & Fakharzadeh, 2009)
	Business	Advertising (Tanaka, 2001) Banking (Chew, 2005; Edwards, 2000) Industry (Cowling, 2007; van Hest & Oud-De Glas, 1990) Journalism (Gilabert, 2005) Petroleum Industry (Holliday, 1995)
	Healthcare	Healthcare (Bosher & Smalkoski, 2002; Lepetit & Cichocki, 2002; Uvin, 1996) Nursing (Cai, 2012; Cameron, 1998; Gass, 2012; Hussin, 2002) Medical (Chia, Johnson, Chia, & Olive, 1999; Eggly, 2002)
English for academic purposes (EAP)	Skills	General EAP (Akyel & Ozek, 2010; Braine, 2001; Chan, 2001; Jordan, 1997; Kim, Kong, Lee, Silva, & Urano, 2003; Shing, Sim, & Bahrani, 2013; Waters, 1996) Writing (Casanave & Hubbard, 1992; Hale, Taylor, Bridgeman, Carson, Kroll, & Kantor, 1996; Huang, 2010; Leki, 1995; Matsuda, Saenkhum, & Accardi, 2013) Reading (Holme & Chalauisaeng, 2006; Bosuwon & Woodrow, 2009) Oral/aural (Ferris, 1998; Ferris & Tagg, 1996a, 1996b; Kim, 2006; Teng, 1999)
	Content areas	Art & Design (Kaur & Kahn, 2010) Business (Bernbrock, 1977; Barbara, Celani, Collins, & Scott, 1996; Crosling & Ward, 2002; Grosse, 2004; Huh, 2006; Louhiala-Salminen, 1996; Poon, 1992; St. John, 1996; Wu, 2012) Engineering (Kaewpet, 2009; Shamsudin, Manam, & Husin, 2013; Spence & Liu, 2013) English philology (Moreno, 2003) Environmental Studies (Matsuda, 2010) Information (Atai & Ogholgol, 2011) Law (Deutsch, 2003)

of situation specific examples. While probably fairly comprehensive, this list was developed to provide examples of needs analysis studies that have been conducted, rather than as an exhaustive list of situation specific examples or even specific categories.

I also ran across one other category of ESP NAs that does not fit neatly into the EOP versus EAP dichotomy: English for survival English purposes for immigrants (for example, Cathcart, 1989; Nunan, 1990; Winn, 2005). In one sense, such studies probably denote very low entry-level English students, but a careful look at the two examples will reveal that the English involved clearly had a specific purpose.

How specific should the scale and scope be?

Dovey (2006) said the following about *specificity*:

> Central to the idea of specificity is the notion that literacies are situated within sociocultural contexts and have socially defined purposes. It is implied that a relatively homogeneous purpose can be identified for any context, and that the genres by which this purpose is achieved can be identified and taught.
>
> (p. 388)

That would seem to be a general statement of what the specific in ESP is (yes, that irony was intended). More precisely, Hyland (2002) looked at the issue of specificity as follows: "Put most simply, this resolves into a single question: are there skills and features of language that are transferable across different disciplines and occupations, or should we focus on the texts, skills and language forms needed by particular learners?" (p. 385). In some ways, Hyland has pinpointed a central conundrum in ESP. Naturally, if you are teaching a single student, you can tailor the instruction to the very specific and even personal needs of that student. In contrast, if you are teaching large groups of students, you may necessarily have to look for more general communalities that will serve the greatest number of students, at least partially.

From a practical standpoint, in looking at Table 2.1 with its many examples of real ESP studies of many different kinds, you may have noticed that there are general types of ESP and even specific categories of ESP, but, even the most specific of these categories may not be specific enough with regard to time frames. For example, some of the students in a given course may be studying the ESP *before* engaging in the work or schooling that requires that they have that knowledge; other students may be studying the ESP *while* they are working or studying at school and using that knowledge; on occasion, still other students may be learning the ESP *after* working or studying at school and needing that knowledge (as pointed out by Basturkmen,

2010, p. 6), each of which would cast the NA in a very different and more specific light.

My point is that, in reality, ESP NAs are conducted at the situation specific level of content and scope. Or as Cheng (2011)[1] put it, "ESP teaching is context-specific teaching that always occurs in a specific social milieu" (p. 49). For example, when I was working at the University of California at Los Angeles (UCLA) with a group of teachers setting out to create a new English for Science and Technology (EST) program in China, the scale of the program was decided by the contract that had been negotiated with the Ministry of Education, which said that we would train 225 Chinese scientists at any given time from all parts of China, that these scientists would need a TOEFL score of 400 or higher to be admitted to our program, and that they would have a score of 550 when they finished (see Chapter 3 for more on these negotiations). So, even though this NA was very large in scale, that is, on a national scale drawing from all of China, the NA was delimited in scale by the fact that only accept 225 students at a time were to be accepted and even then, only those with TOEFL scores between 400 and 550. The NA was also delimited in content and scope by the fact that the curriculum was designed only for scientists needing to learn EST *before* going to English-speaking studies for postgraduate work. I should add that those "scientists" included a variety of different types of engineers, medical doctors, biologists, chemists, physicists, and mathematicians, which meant that much of the time our EST was pitched at a fairly general level that would be useful to most of our students. I hope you can see from the foregoing the sorts of real-world considerations that had to be taken into account and how they shaped the specificity of the NA and ultimately everything else about that EST program.

The bottom line, as Hyland (2002, p. 394) put it, is that "effective language teaching in the universities involves taking specificity seriously. It means that we must go as far as we can." Put very simply, ESP can only be as specific as it can be, but we need to make it as specific as is practically and reasonably possible. In this context, then, each ESP NA should be as specific as possible, but only as specific as it needs to be given the institutions and people involved and even given the specific era in which it is performed.

In a sense, the classifications in Table 2.1 provide an important illustration of this specificity issue. Yes, there are EOP and EAP categories of NA, and yes, there are more specific categories like workplace, business, and healthcare subdivisions shown for EOP. But when I labeled the column furthest to the right *situation-specific English NA examples*, I did so conscious of the fact that each and every NA is unique unto itself. Consider the Business-specific category under EOP. That includes situation-specific English NA examples for Advertising, Banking, Industry, Journalism, and Petroleum Industry. The second of those, *Banking*, has two example NAs, Chew (2005) and Edwards (2000). The Chew (2005) NA examined the

English needed by 16 newly graduated employees in various departments of four Hong Kong banks. A main finding was that Cantonese language was used dominantly in spoken discourse, while English was used in written, though both languages were clearly needed. Consider how different the Chew (2005) NA probably was from the one reported in Edwards (2000), which looked at the English needs of three German banking employees for a three-week course (that eventually lasted for a year). Both studies were for banking English, but they differed considerably in where they were done, how they were conducted, what they were looking for, and what they found.

One question you might ask is why I put these two NAs under EOP rather than in the EAP Business content area. True, either of these could inform an undergraduate curriculum designed to prepare such graduates, but in both cases that was not their *purpose*. Instead, they were conducted in *banking workplaces for purposes of training employees*.

The nine studies in the Business content areas under EAP were even more varied. These nine were put in this category rather than under EOP Business because their focus was on designing courses for academic institutions. Bernbrock (1977) reported on an NA for business English at a Catholic college in Thailand. St. John (1996) examined the available research and materials available at that time in terms of the language, skills, business knowledge, and cultural issues needed by people learning business English. Crosling and Ward (2002) was conducted in an ESL situation in Australia for purposes of understanding the oral communication needs and making recommendations for an undergraduate English curriculum in a business and commerce program. Similarly, Huh (2006) was conducted in an ESL situation, but in the US and for the purpose of designing a business English course at a US university for students from various language backgrounds. Barbara, Celani, Collins, and Scott (1996) studied the relative needs in national and international business settings in Brazil for English and Portuguese. Grosse (2004) examined the distance-learning business English needs for a class in Mexico. Louhiala-Salminen (1996) examined the communication needs (especially written communication) for Finnish business people. Poon (1992) was designed for business studies majors at a school for commerce in Hong Kong, while Wu (2012) was for a college business English course in China. I think my point is clear: each and every one of these EAP business English NAs was different from all the others in terms of location, NA methodology, purpose, and findings.

More precisely, Table 2.2 shows how Huh (2006) summarized the business English tasks that she identified by reviewing key studies like St. John (1996), Louhiala-Salminen (1996), Barbara et al. (1996), Grosse (2004), and Chew (2005). Notice how the tasks identified across these five studies differed. This table is interesting from several perspectives. First, except in one case, Huh identified different business English studies from those I put

Table 2.2 Business English tasks identified through literature review (adapted from Huh, 2006, p. 15)

	St John (1996)	Louhiala-Salminen (1996)	Barbara et al. (1996)	Grosse (2004)	Chew (2005)
Correspondence	Telephoning Writing correspondence	Letters Faxes Telexes Email	Telephone calls	Letters Faxes Phone call Email	Email (request) Faxes
Writing a document	Report writing	Reports Official documents (e.g., contracts)	Reports Memos Prospectuses Proposals Projects Meetings Presentations		Minutes, letters, memos Review report, requests Procedural guides Proposals, daily commentary Contracts and agreements Writing rules and regulations Opinion letters Internal newsletter Press releases and invitations Research analysis reports
Business meeting	Presentations Meetings Negotiating		Seminars Teleconferences	Meetings Negotiation Conference Products exhibition Presentation	Seminar presentations Meetings Conferences Road shows
Business trip Attending foreign guests Translation		Translating	Visits Dealing with guests	Business trips Reception of visitors	Translating (customers' opinions, reports)
Readings related to the job		Prof. journals Other publications		Prof. readings	
Others	Socializing	Revising English text	Interviews Purchasing	Internet Face-to-face interaction Training programs	Reviewing and updating clients files Spread sheets (charts and tables) Reading manuals Credit reviews research Oral command to colleagues

in Table 2.1. And second, while there is considerable overlap among tasks identified as important in the five studies in Table 2.2, there are also large differences. All of which is to say that, regardless of the scale, scope, or categorization, "all needs assessments are *situation-specific*" (Purpura et al., 2003, p. 9; italics in original).

Personal reflection – What is the scope of your ESP NA?

Think about a group of ESP students that you teach (or ESP students you would like to teach some day). In terms of the *scope* of the content, what sort of ESP are you thinking of designing for your students? Is that a type of EAP or EOP, or something else altogether? Can you be more specific in labeling it, at least in terms of some of the situation specific possibilities shown in Table 2.1? Do any of the example studies shown in Table 2.1 sound similar in content to what you are thinking of doing? Would you expect to identify the same sorts of language points or tasks that students should learn as other needs analysts have?

Constraints on ESP NA

A number of forces within any institution may tend to delimit what can be accomplished. Naturally, this is true of an ESP project as well. Such factors may serve as constraints[2] on what can be accomplished in an NA so they should at least be considered early in the NA process. As shown in Figure 2.1, such constraints seem to naturally fall into three categories: situational, stakeholder, or theoretical constraints.

Situational constraints

As also shown in Figure 2.1, *situational constraints* may arise in an NA because of issues in the general society in which the institution is situated, because of politics and policies in the entire chain of command above that institution, because of restrictions on funding and resources, or because of issues within the curriculum of the institution itself. Let's consider each of these four sources of situational constraints in turn.

Society constraints

The society in which an NA is being conducted can impose very real constraints on what can be accomplished, and this differs from society to society.

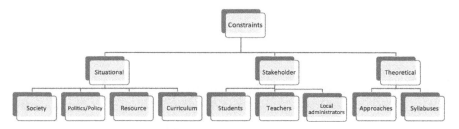

Figure 2.1 Main categories of constraints on ESP NA.

For example, I have been actively involved in various aspects of curriculum development in ESL settings in Los Angeles and Honolulu. I have also been involved in doing or evaluating curriculum in China; Saudi Arabia; Tunisia; Fiji; Cyprus; Turkey; Saipan; and other places. In all of these different societies, I have found constraints, but interestingly, there were different sorts and combinations of constraints at work in each case.

The sorts of constraints that you may find yourself dealing with at the societal level include things like the society's general attitudes toward education or more specifically general attitudes toward language learning and its role in life. Such attitudes may focus on the relevance of language learning to other subjects in the educational setting, or the potential of language learning to help students with future employment, income, or career opportunities. Other societal constraints may result from teaching and learning traditions in the society or the status of teachers generally, and English teachers more specifically. Such factors should not be dismissed lightly. They can deeply shape what is possible in any given society.

Politics/policy constraints

Related to society but also distinct is the area of politics and policy, which can impinge greatly on what can be accomplished in an NA. Such political and policy concerns may be national or even international, provincial, or local. For example, government language policies about the importance of learning foreign languages or which foreign languages should be studied may emanate from national, provincial, or local government or politicians. Other political and policy issues may have to do with traditions at all levels with regard to how much latitude there is toward change, specifically as that latitude is related to change in the form of curriculum development. Political and policy constraints may come from the way the ESP program is organized or how it is related to other ESL or EFL programs. For example, at UHM, there are three ESL programs, two of which are in the Second Language Studies Department: the English Language Institute

(ELI, a full-fledged EAP program for matriculated students at UHM) and the Hawaii English Language Program (HELP, a pre-EAP program to prepare students for university level studies). The third program, the New Intensive Course of English (NICE, a flexible program that offers a variety of relatively low-level ESL and ESP courses) is housed in the Outreach College at UHM. Different constraints arise because of where these three programs are housed and how they relate to each other.

Other political and policy constraints may largely be a concern within the specific ESP program. These may take the form of policies for supporting lead teachers or coordinators, class sizes and control over class sizes, the availability of rooms for classes, how and when scheduling of classes is done, and so on.

Resource constraints

One of the most tangible results of the impact of societal or political/policy constraints will be resource constraints from lack or withdrawal of funding. This may be a general trend for education in the country or state, or generally for an entire school, or be a particular problem for the ESP program involved. For example, for most of my 30 years at UHM, there have been consistent budget cuts or hiring freezes (for all departments other than athletics) year after year. These are general cuts that have had profound effects on the resources available for curriculum development efforts in our EAP program, and especially for NA. We have managed to circumvent these resource cuts by relying on (dare I say abusing) the good nature and high motivation of our MA and PhD students and encouraging them to do NAs and curriculum development projects as their term projects for their graduate courses, scholarly papers, theses, and dissertations.

Even more tangible evidence of resource constraints in a teacher's everyday life may take the form of unavailability of crucial teaching tools. Such tools may include audio–video–computer equipment or software. Or, there may be constraints on the availability of student textbooks, in-class teaching materials, or other supplemental materials like course assessment materials, student class evaluation forms, and so forth. In some situations, all of the items in this paragraph may be available, but must be carried to class because equipment is lacking in the classrooms.

Curriculum constraints

A combination of some or all of the above may have their greatest impact in terms of policies, decisions, and rules that I can only call curriculum constraints. These may have to do with the duration of courses in terms of the number of weeks/months available for instruction. Other constraints may arise from the intensity of instruction (usually discussed in hours per week) or lack thereof. Another related factor is the total number of contact hours available for students to study English start-to-finish.

Still other curriculum constraints may have to do with existing curriculum including things like the adequacy of existing course syllabuses, the quality of program goals/mission statements, the quality of course objectives (also known as student learning outcomes), and the adequacy of the placement testing system in terms of both accuracy and appropriateness (especially for the ESP involved).

Another way of looking at curriculum constraints is in terms of political and resource support for classroom assessment, materials selection and ordering, materials development as necessary, in-class teacher observations (administrative, self, and peer), teacher professionalization (workshops, conferences, degree pursuit), course evaluation, and program evaluation.

Stakeholder constraints

Much will depend in any NA on the characteristics or the people involved, who are also known as the *stakeholders*. Each NA will involve different groups of stakeholders, for example, students, teachers, administrators, teaching assistants, parents, future professors in content area courses, future employers, and politicians. However, the groups that most regularly turn out to be key stakeholder groups are the students, teachers, and local administrators.

Students

The students are not only the largest stakeholder group in most settings, but also the group that might be called the customers of our language teaching institutions, or at least the targets of our NAs. Students can vary in a number of important ways that can dramatically affect an NA. The most obvious ways that they can vary are things like gender, language backgrounds, nationalities, and ages. Imagine, for example, if the students in an EAP NA are all female 18- to 22-year-old L1 Spanish speakers from Colombia and Peru learning English in California. Can you picture the impact of those factors on how the NA might progress? Now compare that to a situation in which the students are mixed-gender 55- to 78-year-old immigrants learning English for survival purposes on the Big Island of Hawai'i.

Other more academic characteristics can also have an impact on an NA. For example, academic status (for instance, undergraduate or graduate students at university) might turn out to be important. The students' major fields of study will generally also have a strong bearing on any ESP NA, especially the degree to which their majors are related to the specific purpose of the ESP, but also the degree to which the students' majors are homogeneous with regard to that ESP. For instance, it is very different to do an English for medical professionals NA for students who are all registered nurses, than it is to do one for practical and registered nurses, paramedics, and doctors combined.

Other issues related to the students' language backgrounds include whether they are now studying or are going to study English as a foreign or second language, whether they are heritage learners of English (that is, have a parent or other influential relative who is a native speaker of English), and whether they have been part of a bilingual or immersion program. Other language exposure issues may turn out to be critical – things like the amount of time students have spent abroad away from their home countries, or more specifically, the amount of time they have spent in English-speaking countries.

Yet another key characteristic that deserves special attention is their English proficiency in terms of overall levels, but also specifically in reading, writing, listening, speaking, culture, pragmatics, and so forth. With regard to proficiency, it is particularly important to think about it in terms of the range from lowest to highest abilities because proficiency limits (high and low) will tend to put upper and lower bounds on what the ESP course or program (and therefore the NA) can address.

Still other student characteristics that may affect a particular ESP NA are things like work experience, socio-economic status, the educational level of their parents, their own personal purpose(s) for learning English, their attitudes and motivations toward learning English, the place of English in students' long-term plans, their preferred teaching and learning styles, and their beliefs about what approaches and syllabuses are appropriate for learning English (see explanation below).

The list seems to go on and on. Yet, each of the factors listed above is important in its own right. You should probably consider each in terms of what the general trend among your students is, but also in terms of the degree to which the students are homogeneous or heterogeneous with regard to each of these characteristics (an issue discussed in more depth by Peck, 1979).

Teachers

The teachers are another stakeholder group in most NAs that *must not be ignored*. Teachers can vary in a number of interesting ways that can affect any NA (this discussion is much expanded from Richards, 2001, p. 99). Some of the most obvious ways teachers may vary are in terms of their professional backgrounds with regard to professional training as ESL or EFL teachers, professional qualifications (degrees or certifications), professional development (for instance, in terms of papers published, conferences, and workshops presented), expertise in different aspects of the second language teaching field (for example, materials development, language testing, curriculum development, and computer assisted language learning), and others.

At a more individual level, teachers can vary in terms of their English proficiency levels, teaching skills, teaching experience, motivation levels, and preferred teaching styles. Another issue that is sometimes important in an ESP program has to do with how teachers can vary in terms of their knowledge of the content area and language conventions of the SP in the ESP involved. For example, a teacher who did an MA in TESOL after a BA in engineering would certainly have a fair amount of knowledge of the content and language conventions needed in an English for engineers program, while a teacher with the same MA in TESOL, but a BA in English literature would not. In addition, teachers can vary in their willingness or abilities to access the language of the SP of the ESP. When I left to teach in the English for science and technology program in China in the early 1980s, I had an MA in TESL and was working on my PhD dissertation in Applied Linguistics. However, because I had also finished most of a BA in geography, had an odd personal interest in the philosophy of science, and had intense training in statistical analyses for educational and psychological research during graduate school, I may have been more willing and able to access the language conventions of the sciences that we were teaching than say a teacher with a BA in English literature major and an MA in TESOL.

Looking at teachers more generally as a group, it may also be important to consider issues like the proportions of full-time, part-time, and volunteer teachers on staff because of differences in what and how much it may be reasonable to expect these three very different types of teachers to contribute to an NA or curriculum development more generally. Another important group dynamic issue may be the proportions of native English speaker teachers who are monolingual and bilingual teachers of English (especially those who speak the mother tongue of the students). Other issues that may be equally important to the teachers as a group are whether they are unionized, their security in the job (that is, whether they have tenure or not), their pay scale and equality of pay, their satisfaction with their working conditions, and their general morale.

A final way in which teachers can vary is in terms of how they relate to the curriculum and the institution. For example, they may vary in their beliefs about which approaches and syllabuses (see below) or which combinations of approaches and syllabuses are appropriate for English teaching generally or for ESP teaching in particular. Teachers can also vary in terms of their willingness to cooperate in an NA project, or any curriculum development for that matter. Teachers may also vary in their attitudes toward change and/or their personal willingness to change, especially when applied to their teaching practices, materials, and tests. Another issue may have to do with teachers' readiness to relinquish the sovereignty that they have always enjoyed over their students and classrooms (that is, whether they will be willing to let needs analysts and/or curriculum developers into their classrooms). A final set of concerns has to do with how well teachers get along with their coordinators, needs analysts, curriculum developers, and administrators generally.

Administrators

The last stakeholder group that I will consider here is whoever constitutes the local administrators, by which I mean any administrators who can have a direct impact on the NA and curriculum development in an ESP program. These people may go by many titles, but typically they are the program director, the assistant director, program coordinators, or other such people. It is almost always a mistake to ignore or not include administrators in an NA.

Administrators can vary in a number of interesting ways that can affect any NA. For instance, they can vary in terms of competence, leadership ability, leadership style, effectiveness at getting things done, readiness to work hard, and willingness to delegate important tasks or leadership roles. Administrators can also vary in terms of attitudes toward clerical employees, instructors, and students, as well as in willingness to change. Administrators can also vary in important ways with regard to personality especially with regard to sense of openness, friendliness, self-importance, egotism, arrogance, ambition, empathy, and introversion/extroversion. I have also noticed that administrators who are interested in being promoted up the chain of command are more likely to take care of their own interests at the expense of other stakeholder groups. In contrast, administrators who are on the verge of retiring or who want to return to the teaching ranks are much more likely to look out for the interests of students and teachers.

Other stakeholder groups

Clearly, much of what happens in an NA will depend on the characteristics of the stakeholders involved. I have argued that students, teachers, and local administrators almost always turn out to be key stakeholder groups for any NA. However, other potential groups of stakeholders should be considered if they turn out to be important to the success of the NA. To forget a crucial group may prove fatal. So yes, be sure to include students, teachers, and administrators, but also consider other potential stakeholders like teaching assistants, parents, future professors in content area courses, future employers, politicians, or any other pertinent group in your situation. These groups can vary tremendously in importance depending on the context. For example, including the parents in our EST NA in China would have been very strange (especially since our students were 35 to 65 years old). However, in an EAP NA for a local public intermediate school in Japan, the parents might be a crucial stakeholder group, because, without knowing what they think and indeed without their cooperation, the EAP course might fail altogether, regardless of how much effort was put into it.

Theoretical constraints

Theoretical constraints do not stand alone in the same way that situational and stakeholder constraints do. Nor do they have direct impact on an NA on their own. The theoretical constraints that I am referring to are *approaches* (that is, sets of beliefs about language and language learning) and *syllabuses* (that is, sets of principles used to organize the teaching/learning process). These approaches and syllabuses only impact an NA through the various stakeholder groups involved, who will often believe strongly, even fervently, in different approaches and who will often argue strongly, even fervently, for organizing around different syllabuses. Let's look a bit deeper into these two concepts.

Approaches

Constraints may arise when the language teaching and learning approaches that various stakeholders believe in differ. Anthony (1965) and then Richards and Rodgers (1982) discussed the issues involved in a language teaching approach. Indeed, according to Richards and Rodgers, "Approach encompasses both theories of language and language learning. All language teaching methods operate explicitly from a theory of language and beliefs or theories about how language is learned" (p. 155). Brown (1995, p. 5) defined *approaches* more from a teacher's perspective as "ways of defining what and how the students need to learn", then listed five such approaches:

1   classical approach
2   grammar-translation approach
3   direct approach
4   audiolingual approach
5   communicative approach.

No doubt other ways of defining what and how language students need to learn exist around the world (one that pops to mind immediately is the cognitive approach). In doing ESP NA, one of the first issues that may arise is that different administrators, teachers, and students have very different ways of viewing what and how the students need to learn the ESP. Based on my experience in the field, I would even propose that it is rare to find any two teachers in an ESP program that believe in precisely the same approach or combination of approaches. I am certainly not arguing that some of these approaches are right and some wrong. Indeed, there are parts of me that believe that all five of the approaches listed above plus the cognitive

[handwritten note: Not types - but specific ways - of organizing the course & material]

[handwritten note: 12 specific syllabuses]

rtant to understanding what and
re also crucial to understanding
e thinking, that is, understanding
how various groups of stakehold-
g with regard to what and how

labuses that various stakeholders
s of organizing the course and
re certainly nothing new. Indeed,
ypes of syllabuses for years. For
veen *synthetic syllabuses* that are
description of the language"(p. 3)
organized in terms of the purposes
he kinds of language performance
that are necessary to meet those purposes" (p. 13). In contrast, White (1988) distinguished *Type A syllabuses*, which organized instruction in terms of "what is to be learnt?" from *Type B syllabuses*, which organized instruction in terms of "how is it to be learnt?" (both quotes are from p. 44).

Based on McKay (1978), Brown (1995) discussed syllabuses not as types but as specific "ways of organizing the course and materials" (p. 5) and listed the following seven specific syllabuses (pp. 6–14):

1 structural
2 situational
3 topical
4 functional
5 notional
6 skills-based
7 task-based.

Since then, other syllabuses have naturally gained prominence. Based on reading in the English as an international language literature, Brown (2012a) extended that list of seven syllabuses to include five additional syllabuses:

8 lexical
9 pragmatic
10 genre-based
11 discourse-based
12 communicative strategies.

And of course, other syllabuses will probably arise in the future.

It is important to remember that the approaches and syllabuses discussed here have dramatic impact on an NA insofar as the various stakeholder groups disagree in terms of what they believe and how they think things should be organized. Put another way, if the needs analysts, all the students, all the teachers, and all the administrators agree 100 percent about the approach(es) they believe in and the syllabus(es) they want to organize around, then there will be no problem. How likely do you think that is in any real-world ESP program?

In addition, because they furnish the basic units of analysis in any NA, the theoretical constraints imposed by syllabuses often turn out to be very important. As such, I will come back to them with additional explanations and examples later in this chapter.

Interaction of all of the above constraints

Making life even more complicated is the fact that the situational, stakeholder, and theoretical constraints have a tendency to interact, which is to say that they are seldom completely independent of each other. Consider the overall effects of a situational resource constraint like funding. Funding tends to not be a problem when it is plentiful, but when it is lacking, that aspect alone can dominate the issues an NA must overcome. For example, I worked in the early 1980s in association with an ESP program in an oil-rich country in the Middle East where money was plentiful. The quality of the physical buildings, the amount of classroom space, the availability of teachers, the quantity and quality of supplies, textbooks, and equipment were superb. However, the stakeholder characteristics were more problematic. For example, even though the students were all high-school graduates and were being paid a salary to attend classes, they were not terribly motivated to learn English for petroleum industry purposes, and they indicated that unwillingness in their general attitudes and by eagerly walking out of class whenever there was a call to prayer. In addition, the teachers came from many different nations including the US and UK, Canada, New Zealand, Australia, the Philippines, and all of the Middle Eastern countries. They were hard working, often exhausted by teaching six or more hours per day, but their morale appeared to me to be very low.

In contrast, in the EST program in China where I worked from 1980 to 1982, the quality of the physical buildings left much to be desired, the amount of classroom space though adequate was very uncomfortable and noisy, and the quantity and quality of supplies, textbooks, equipment were always a problem that we had to overcome (largely because "hard" currency was nearly impossible to come by). However, the stakeholders' characteristics were in many respects a boon. The initial batch of 225 students was made up of very talented, hardworking, and bright 35- to 65-year-old practicing scientists, who were clearly the cream of the crop in a country of over a billion people. The Chinese teachers, though coming from a grammar-translation background, were hard working, conscientious, and willing to try our communicative ways. Clearly then, characteristics and circumstances can vary dramatically from situation to situation with dire consequences for any NA, especially if the situational, stakeholder, and theoretical constraints are ignored.

While the bewildering array of constraints I have discussed here may at first seem discouraging to any group of needs analysts, I would suggest that setting reasonable goals for the NA will help and that it will also help to always keep in mind the benefits of maintaining a "balance between 'what is needed' and 'what is possible'" (Singh, 1983, p. 156), or put another way, a balance between the ideal and the realistic.

Personal reflection – Specifically, what constraints will you face?

Think about a group of students that you teach ESP to (or ESP students you would like to teach some day). What situational, stakeholder, and theoretical constraints do you expect to encounter in doing an NA for them? Go ahead and jot down half a dozen in each of the three categories. How might some of those different types of constraints interact with each other? How will you overcome them?

The twelve syllabus types revisited

If syllabuses are "ways of organizing the course and materials," there is an implication that *things* are being organized. Indeed it is these things that actually distinguish between the various syllabuses. For example, in a structural syllabus, the things that are being organized are typically the phonological and syntactic structures of English, or put another way, the pronunciation and grammar points are serving as the basic units of analysis that are being organized into a structural syllabus. In a situational syllabus, the things being organized are situations, so they serve as the basic unit of analysis in such a syllabus. And the same is true for all twelve syllabuses listed in this chapter.

Sequencing of the elements of a given syllabus (that is, ordering the basic units of analysis) refers to the order in which they will be presented. Sequencing is typically based on ideas of easiness, frequency, salience, chronology, or logical hierarchy. For example, a *structural syllabus* might be sequenced from the easy grammar points to the difficult ones. Or, when the futility of the easy-to-difficult organization becomes clear, the sequence might better be based on teaching the grammar items found most frequently in a particular ESP first, then less frequent ones, and so on.

The twelve syllabuses in more detail

A *structural syllabus* would be organized around the grammatical structures of the language. For example, successive chapters might focus on the simple present tense, the copula, articles, the future tense, prepositions, the simple past tense, and so forth. The rationales given for ordering the structures are often that they go from relatively simple to difficult, relatively frequent to less frequent, or relatively useful to less useful.

For a *situational syllabus*, the organization could be based on geography where situations occur on campus or on some sense of when they occur in the semester or day. For example, an EAP situational syllabus might start with the following situations: in the advisor's office; at course registration; at the bookstore; in the first-day class; at the cafeteria; and at the professor's office.

A *topical syllabus* might be organized into logical hierarchies, perhaps with macro-topics and micro-topics. For example, for an English for general science course the macro-topics might be biology, chemistry, physics, and mathematics with each further divided into micro-topics (micro-topics for the biology macro-topic might be zoology, microbiology, and molecular biology).

A *functional syllabus* could be organized around things we do with the language. For an EAP course, functions (like greetings, seeking information, giving information) might be presented sequentially, as in we say hello to people (greetings) before we ask about them (seeking information), and then tell them about ourselves (giving information). These functions might be taught giving the students the skill to do them in a formal register, but then recycled later while illustrating how to perform the same functions in less formal or even colloquial ways.

A *notional syllabus* is based on abstract concepts, called notions, like linear measurement, volume, weight, density, and shape. These are often sequenced more or less like topical syllabuses into macro-notions and micro-notions. For example, the macro-notion of linear measurement might be subdivided into micro-notions like length, width, and depth.

A *skills-based syllabus* is based on skills that can be learned in class and further developed even after the course is finished. In an EAP course, such skills might include: finding a book in the library, taking notes on a book, and so forth or guessing vocabulary from context, using Greek and Roman prefixes, stems, and suffixes to figure out vocabulary, and using a dictionary (as a last resort).

A *task-based syllabus* is organized around duties, responsibilities, errands, chores, and so forth that are typically a necessary part of using a particular ESP. For example, in an English for medicine syllabus, tasks might include the main syllabus tasks shown in Table 2.3 below: taking a History 1, taking a History 2, and examining a patient. These syllabuses tend to be organized round some sense of chronology as in we usually take a patient's history before examining them.

A *lexical syllabus* is typically organized round semantic categories and/ or in terms of frequencies. For example, semantic categories like birds, mammals, and reptiles could clearly be organized into subcategories with the appropriate animals for each. At the same time, those categories which appear most frequently in the lexicon of English or a particular ESP could be presented first with less frequent categories taught next.

A *pragmatic syllabus* is organized around particular speech act categories in which we know pragmatics play a key role. For instance, an ESP course could be organized around speech acts like requests, refusals, and apologies, for each of which the following issues could be taught: power, status, social distance, and degree of imposition.

A *genre-based syllabus* is organized around relatively broad categories that define the purpose of communication. For example, an EAP writing course might be organized as follows: describing, narrating, reporting, giving instructions, comparing, arguing, critiquing, and evaluating. Notice how the purposes of the writing are sequenced from the relatively simple describing, narrating, and reporting to the much more difficult arguing, critiquing, and evaluating (for an overview of the place of genres in ESP, see Paltridge, 2013).

A *discourse-based* syllabus involves having students do discourse analysis; it is therefore organized around spoken or written texts (sometimes based on genres) sequenced in terms of what they reveal about discourse. For each text, the analyses that students will be doing could be include cohesion, coherence, speech act analysis, implicature, and interactional analysis. Naturally, the students will need to be taught whatever discourse analysis techniques are chosen.

A *communicative strategies syllabus* is based on strategies for coping with mistakes, errors, difficulties, and breakdowns in communication. Such a syllabus might be structured around strategies like avoidance, abandonment of the message, circumlocution, approximation, and use of gestures, each of which might be exemplified, explained, and practiced in sequence.

Given our growing understanding and sophistication with regard to what language is and how people learn it, it is not surprising that new ways continue to be developed for thinking about the language-learning processes, which in turn lead to different categories that can be used for organizing any English course, and therefore for sequencing ESP materials and teaching.

Examples of how syllabuses combine in practice

To make all of this information about syllabuses a bit clearer, I would like to draw on a few examples from ESP textbooks to show first that such

Table 2.3 Partial Table of Contents from *English in Medicine* (Glendinning & Holmström, 2008, p. v)

Table of Contents

...

Unit 1   Taking a history 1
1   Asking basic questions
2   Taking notes
3   Reading skills: Scanning a case history
4   Case history: William Hudson

Unit 2   Taking a history 2
1   Asking about systems
2   Asking about symptoms
3   Reading skills: Noting information from a textbook
4   Case history: William Hudson

Unit 3   Examining a patient
1   Giving instructions
2   Understanding forms
3   Reading skills: Using a pharmacology reference
4   Case history: William Hudson

And so forth ...

syllabuses exist, but also how they can operate singly, or in combinations that are layered or alternating, or both.

For example, Table 2.3 shows part of the Table of Contents from an English in medicine textbook (Glendinning & Holmström, 2008). Notice first how multiple syllabuses are operating at the same time. The main syllabus represented by the chapter headings appears to be a *task-based syllabus* (that is, Taking a history 1, Taking a history 2, and Examining a patient). Layered below that main task-based syllabus, there appear to be two other syllabuses alternating with each other in the same pattern in each chapter – a *functional syllabus* (for example, asking basic questions, taking notes, asking about systems, asking about symptoms, giving instructions, and understanding forms) and a reading *skills syllabus* (for instance, scanning a case history, noting information from a textbook, and using a pharmacology reference) – as well as a recurring and evolving case history (Case history: William Hudson). The effect of using these layered and alternating syllabuses is that the materials are well organized, but at the same time provide a variety of ways to approach the material so that it stays interesting.

Another example of how syllabuses can combine is shown in Table 2.4, which was taken from Ibbotson (2009), an engineering English textbook. This Table of Contents (p. 4) is presented as a *scope and sequence chart* (a chart that illustrates the sequence of units or chapters and repeated elements that appear in each unit or chapter as columns), which makes it

Table 2.4 Table of Contents as scope and sequence chart (from Ibbotson, 2009)

	Skills	Language	Texts
UNIT I Technology in use (page 6)	Describing technical functions and applications Explaining how technology works Emphasizing technical advantages Simplifying and illustrating technical explanations	Words stemming from use (allow, enable, permit, ensure, prevent) Verbs to describe movement Verbs and adjectives to describe advantages Adverbs for adding emphasis Phrases for simplifying and rephrasing	Listening GPS applications Space elevators Advantages of a new pump A guided tour Reading Space elevators Otis lift technology Pile foundations
UNIT 2 Materials and technology	Describing specific materials Categorizing materials Specifying and describing properties Describing quality issues	Common materials Categories of materials (consist of, comprise, made of, made from, made out of) Properties of materials Phrases for describing requirements Compounds of resistant Adverbs of degree	Listening An environmental audit Specialized tools High performance watches Reading Materials recycling Regenerative brakes Kevlar
Etc. ...	...	...	...

relatively easy to identify the syllabuses involved. In this case, the units and their topics are listed down the left side and the repeated elements (labeled across the top) are skills, language, and texts. Notice again how multiple syllabuses are operating at the same time. In this case, the main syllabus appears to be a *topical syllabus* (that is, the unit topics: Technology in use, and Materials and technology), and layered below that main syllabus are three other syllabuses: a *task-based syllabus* (labeled as "skills" including: Describing technical functions and applications, Explaining how technology works, and so forth), a *structural syllabus* (labeled as "language" including: Words stemming from use..., and Verbs to describe movement), and a *skills-based syllabus* (labeled as "texts" including: Listening and Reading with texts listed under each). Again, the effect of these layered syllabuses is to make the materials appear well organized with a variety of approaches that make the materials more interesting.

The importance of syllabuses to NA

Why are syllabuses important for NA? Ultimately, any NA should end with suggestions for what should be taught in the course. Those suggestions will likely take the form of a set of tentative objectives or students' learning outcomes (SLOs). Such SLOs will necessarily reflect the basic units of some syllabuses. The two examples shown in Tables 2.3 and 2.4 illustrate that point clearly.

Also important is the fact that the people doing an NA, the needs analysts, would be well advised to recognize early on what syllabuses they want to use for two reasons. First, needs analysts tend to find that students need to learn language points that fit into the syllabuses they believe in (for example, needs analysts who believe in a structural syllabus are very likely to find that the students need to learn *grammar points A, B,* and *C,* while needs analysts who believe in a task-based syllabuses will tend to find that the students need to learn how to do *tasks X, Y,* and *Z*). Second, if the needs analysts do not agree among themselves what syllabuses they eventually want the curriculum to follow, many disagreements and delays may result.

In addition, if the syllabuses that an NA suggests are not acceptable to key stakeholder groups, those syllabuses will either need to be modified so that the stakeholders can buy into them, or will need to be explained and sold to those groups so they can come to accept them. For instance, when I was helping to develop the EST program in China, all of our NAs indicated that our EST students already had high abilities in English grammar and vocabulary, and that what they really needed was to learn how to put their existing abilities to work so they could use English for their future science or engineering studies and professional activities. However, because they were already very comfortable with learning grammar and vocabulary by rote, they wanted more of the same. Seeing the folly of that, we gathered NA information and used it to convince them that they did not need more grammar and vocabulary (we were able to show them that they generally had very high test scores in those areas) but rather needed more skills development in reading, writing, listening, and speaking (again, we were able to show them that they had very low scores in those areas). We further explained and argued that they especially needed to develop their *fluency* in reading, writing, listening, and speaking because they would soon be in the US or other English speaking countries where they would need to *use* the language to get things done. Ultimately, we explained, argued, begged, and cajoled to get them to do things our *communicative* way, and when they saw the results and understood what we were trying to do, the vast majority of the students joined us in the effort. But the important thing is that we did not try to impose our beliefs and thinking on this important stakeholder group, but rather we respected them enough to explain why we thought the way we did and to use our NA information to try to convince them to do it our way. It is fortunate for us that it worked, given that we were considerably outnumbered.

In short, using syllabuses can help to focus an ESP NA because syllabuses contain and organize the basic units of analysis and thus can be used to narrow the options, but at the same time syllabuses express the very needs that the students and other stakeholders will need to accept. In addition, syllabuses can then serve as a foundation that will support all the other curriculum building blocks (SLOs, materials, tests, teaching, and course or program evaluation) that will follow out of the NA.

Task 2.1 Partial Table of Contents from Glendinning, E., & Howard, R. (2009) – Recognizing Syllabuses in Real ESP Materials

Contents

INTRODUCTION

BASICS

1   Health and illness
    A   Asking about health
    B   Sickness
    C   Recovery

2   Parts of the body 1
    A   Parts of the body
    B   Referring to parts of the body
    C   Describing radiation of pain
    ...

MEDICAL AND PARAMEDICAL PERSONNEL AND PLACES

5   Medical practitioners 1
    A   Practitioners
    B   Specialties
    C   Choosing a specialty
    ...

9   Hospitals
    A   Introduction to a hospital
    B   Outpatients
    C   Inpatients
    ...

EDUCATION AND TRAINING

11 Medical education 1
    A   Medical education in the UK
    B   Extract from an undergraduate prospectus
    C   A student's view
    ...

Read the above Table of Contents. Then, working in pairs (if possible), answer the following questions and compare your answers:

1   What type of syllabus is the main syllabus (Health and illness, Parts of the body 1, Medical practitioners 1, Hospitals, Medical education 1, and so forth)?
2   What other sorts of syllabuses do you see at work at the A, B, C levels? Are they layered or alternating?
3   What function do the section headings (BASICS, MEDICAL AND PARAMEDICAL PERSONAL AND PLACES, EDUCATION AND TRAINING, and so forth) serve?
4   Would this NA fall into the broader category of EOP or EAP?
5   Specifically what sort of ESP does this Table of Contents represent? What sorts of students would likely benefit from such an ESP course?

Summary and conclusion

To review briefly, this chapter is about focusing the ESP NA. The chapter began by covering the issue of finding the right level of specificity by narrowing the scale of the population of students that ultimately must be served by the NA and then by limiting the scope of the NA in terms of the purpose and content of the ESP course or program that will ultimately result from the NA. The chapter next discussed a wide variety and number of situational, stakeholder, and theoretical constraints that will tend to temper an NA by revealing what the course or program can realistically provide to students. This chapter ended with an expansion of the discussion of syllabuses because only with syllabuses can an ESP NA focus on and organize the basic units of analysis.

Careful consideration of the scale, scope, and constraint issues discussed in this chapter before and during an NA can help needs analysts avoid wasteful and irrelevant work by revealing much of what cannot and need not be addressed. In a sense, needs analysts are like sculptors in that they start with a block of marble (all the ESP possibilities) and carve away until the statue (a realistic needs-based ESP curriculum) gradually emerges – revealing itself in greater and greater detail as time goes by.

Notes

1 Note that this quote is drawn from an interesting broader discussion in Cheng (2011) of the impact of specificity on "social milieu, learning objectives, input materials and output activities, methodologies, and assessment of student learning" (p. 48).
2 Note that this entire section was inspired by Singh (1983), though it is much expanded from that discussion.

Chapter 3

Selecting and sequencing ESP needs analysis data collection procedures

In this chapter, you will find answers to the following questions:

- What are the key characteristics of successful ESP NAs?
- What factors are likely to affect my information-gathering choices?
- Why do types of information matter?
- What data-gathering options do I have for my ESP NA?
- How can my ESP NA procedures be sequenced?
- How can I use the case study approach in my NA?

Characteristics of successful ESP NAs

Purpura et al. (2003) describe four characteristics of NA: NA should be situation-specific, learner-centered, pragmatic, and systematic (pp. 9–11). These four characteristics are key to selecting and creating data collection procedures for an NA because the procedures: (a) must end up being appropriate for the specific situation involved; (b) should be centered on the learners (though all other stakeholders should also be considered); (c) must be practical within the constraints found in the particular situation; and (d) should be systematic so the results will function well and lead to defensible NA conclusions.

Thus, in choosing data collection procedures, you will want to select or create procedures that are *appropriate for your situation* in that the procedures are likely to work in that situation and will generally be accepted in that particular context. To do otherwise will be inefficient, wasteful, and perhaps futile.

You will also want to select or create procedures that *focus on the learners*. Even if surveying or interviewing faculty or administrators is important, and it usually is, most of the questions and answers that will emerge from those data will be about what the *students* need in order to learn – and thus the data will be student-centered.

You should also think in terms of selecting and creating procedures that are *practical* in that they will not take unreasonable amounts of money, time, and effort to administer, score, code, analyze, and interpret. Again, to do otherwise is likely to prove inefficient, wasteful, and perhaps futile.

Finally, you should think in terms of selecting and creating procedures that are *systematic* so they will function well in themselves, but also so they will work systematically together. If the procedures are planned well they should not be redundant except in the sense that the strengths in one procedure help to compensate for weaknesses in other procedures. For example, interviews can gather exploratory and in-depth data, but they are difficult and time consuming to conduct and the results may not be very generalizable because of the small numbers of people involved. Fortunately, procedures like questionnaires can be used to compensate for those weaknesses: they are easier and less time consuming to administer; they can be based on what was leaned in-depth in the more exploratory interviews; and they are likely to produce results that are much more generalizable because everyone affected in an NA can be surveyed. Thus, if done well, the systematic combination of these two data-gathering procedures to compensate in each for the weaknesses in the other can lead to generally more defensible NA conclusions (much more about these ideas in Chapters 5 and 6).

Personal reflection – What are the characteristics of your ESP NA?

Think about a group of ESP students that you teach (or some you would like to teach). In terms of the characteristics listed by Purpura et al. (2003), will your NA be appropriate for the specific situation involved? Will it be centered on the learners while still considering all of the other stakeholders? Will it be practical within the constraints of your particular situation? Will it be systematic so the results will function well and lead to defensible NA conclusions? And in terms related to this chapter, how will your answers to these questions affect your choices and sequencing of NA data-gathering procedures?

Factors that affect information-gathering choices

In conducting an NA, you will probably need to decide at least tentatively on what types of information you want to gather and what procedures you will need to select or create to do so. Stufflebeam, McCormick, Brinkerhoff, and Nelson (1985) suggested five *factors that affect choices* of information-gathering procedures: (a) characteristics of the information source;

(b) situational characteristics; (c) type of information needed; (d) technical measurement criteria; and (e) level of accuracy desired. Let's consider each of these factors in turn.

Characteristics of the information source

Three characteristics of information turn out to be particularly important in NA and fairly obvious: relevance, practicality, availability. The most important consideration for decisions about what information to gather and how to gather it is the *relevance of the information*. Obviously, if information is irrelevant to the NA at hand, it should not be gathered even if it is practical and available. For example, if information is available on how students feel about the fact that they are getting older, that is probably not relevant. Hence the aging information could be ignored in favor of attending to more relevant information, say the students' English proficiency. However, once relevance has been established, the practicality and availability become important. For example, in the China EST program that I worked in, we felt that knowing the students' range of proficiency levels would be very helpful. So we inquired about getting their TOEFL scores. We were told that the TOEFL was not administered in China at that time and that it was not practical to require students to travel abroad to take the TOEFL. Relevance was clear to us, but getting TOEFL scores for the students presented both availability and practicality problems. So we had to choose other means (our own home-grown test in this case) to find out about their proficiency range.

Clearly, the *practicality of the information* is very important to consider early on. Is it practical to develop the information-gathering procedure, administer it, collect the data with it, code the data, and analyze the data? Some procedures are easier to deal with in these senses than others. But there are often trade-offs one way or another that must be considered. For example, doing interviews is relatively difficult from a practicality perspective because they are typically conducted face-to-face one person at a time. Then, the data which are typically audio-recorded need to be transcribed and coded for analysis, and the analysis itself is time consuming. In contrast, other procedures may seem easier to deal with like, for instance, questionnaires, which are easier to administer to large numbers of people, and produce lots of data without transcription and coding. In addition, the analyses can be done in a spreadsheet with relative ease (unless you happen to be math-phobic). What I have listed here are characteristics that need to be considered for interviews and questionnaires in deciding on their relative practicality. But one person's practical may be another's impractical as indicated by my parenthetical comment about math-phobia above. So deciding on the relative practicality of information sources will depend on the context and the people gathering the data. All I can do here is describe the various procedures that are available in as much detail and as clearly as possible so you can make these decisions for yourself.

The *availability of the information* is the third consideration. If information is simply not available, it does not matter how relevant and practical it might be, that information is not going to be obtainable. For example, it might be useful to have access to students' medical records to help determine if there are any students with hearing or vision problems that might require special treatment. However, if such records are not available because they are not systematically kept, or because of privacy issues, gathering that type of information will clearly be impossible.

However, availability should also be considered from another angle. Information may be so available that that becomes a problem. For example, information that is already gathered and readily available (as in information that already exists in institutional records or student files) might be quite attractive. Such information should certainly not be overlooked simply because it is readily available, but there is a danger that this sort of salient and easy-to-obtain information will serve as an attractive distraction from the real purpose of the NA. Hence, any such information must only be considered if it is relevant to the purpose of the NA.

While relevance, practicality, and availability are clearly interrelated, I discussed them in that order for several good reasons. Clearly, relevance is the most important criterion. If information is irrelevant, there is no point in gathering it. In addition, if information is not practical to gather or is simply not available, either an alternative practical method needs to be devised or the effort must be abandoned.

Situational characteristics

I discussed at some length in the previous chapter the constraints that can be imposed on NA and curriculum processes in three categories: situational constraints (including those related to society, politics and polices, and resources); stakeholder constraints (including students, teachers, administrators, and others); and theoretical constraints (approaches and syllabuses). Since these will differ widely from NA context to NA context, I will only say here that, in view of the fact that these constraints can affect the relevance, practicality, and availability of information-gathering choices in an NA, they should be revisited and considered with regard to these choices.

Type of information needed

Berwick (1989) discusses six ways of *planning* educational systems, each of which is based on a different type of information: (a) organized body of knowledge; (b) specific competencies; (c) social activities and problems;

(d) cognitive or learning processes; (e) feelings and attitudes; and (f) needs and interests of the learner (pp. 49–51).

Organized body of knowledge information focuses on the existing knowledge and how it is organized. Consider Biology, which is organized into separate taxonomies for botany and zoology, with hierarchical classifications for kingdom, phylum, class, order, family, genus, and species. It is not hard to imagine an NA for English for biology that would need to gather information about that body of knowledge and how it is organized.

Specific competencies information involves finding out about the abilities (or competencies) that members of a particular speech community, say biologists, need to perform in English. For example, an NA might set out to explore what biologists need to be able to do (in English) in different contexts, like out in the field, in a laboratory, in a classroom, in keeping a lab notebook, and in writing a research report.

Social activities and problems information centers on finding out what sorts of social interactions and social problems people encounter in their work and how they deal with those in English. For instance, an NA for biology English might focus on describing the discourse interactions of biologists in talking in the field or in a laboratory, examining successful communication, and documenting communication breakdowns.

Cognitive or learning processes information tends to be about how people learn and what those processes are like. A strategy-based biology NA might need to gather information about how biology students learn their field (in English) including what equipment-handling lab skills they need to develop (in English), what (oral English) skills they need to communicate with lab partners, and what skills (in written English) they need to keep a well-regarded and accurate lab notebook.

Feelings and attitudes information centers on the thoughts, views, emotions, attitudes, opinions, and evaluations of the stakeholders. As odd as it may at first seem, in most NAs that I have been involved in, this sort of information has been key to success in the sense that it has led to an understanding of what all the stakeholders are thinking/feeling about the ESP program and helped manage the analysis of the needs of these *human beings*.

Similarly, gathering information about *the needs and interests of the learners*, though different in focus from the feelings and attitudes information, can help with knowing what various groups of stakeholders want, appreciate, aspire to, require, and value. Again, this sort of information has proven key to the success of programs I have been involved in because it has led to understanding in what directions the stakeholders would like to see the ESP program go, which in turn has helped in analyzing the needs of these *human beings*.

The second language studies literature is filled with discussions that might pull you in one direction or another in deciding what types of information to gather in an NA. For example:

- Should you focus on the students' goals for learning the language or the processes by which they do so (Widdowson, 1981, p. 2)?
- Should you investigate the language content of the ESP or the learning content (Brindley, 1984, pp. 31–32)?
- Should you examine the content of what you will teach the students or the methodology with which you will do so (Nunan, 1985)?
- Should you focus on the linguistic content of the ESP or your students' learning processes (Brown, 1995, p. 41)?
- Should you study the language needs of your students or focus on their situation needs (Brown, 1995, p. 40; Richards, 2001, pp. 90–91)?
- Should you examine the belief systems that underlie the learning processes or the syllabuses that you need to use in organizing the teaching (Brown, 1995, pp. 4–14)?

Answers to these questions will depend on different types of information. And again, some combination of these various alternative types of information may best serve any given NA.

Indeed, each of the 11 NA options (from the NA literature) displayed in Chapter 1 (see Table 1.2) and explained in the associated text may depend on gathering particular types of information. Recall that they were target-situation use analyses, target-situation linguistic analyses, target-situation learning analyses, present-situation analyses, gap analyses, individual-differences analyses, rights analyses, classroom-learning analyses, classroom-teaching analyses, means analyses, and language audits. Not only should you consider each of these 11 needs analysis options in terms of the particular information types they might require (as described in the last column of Table 1.2), but also, you would probably benefit from thinking about the six different types of information described in this section and using those that will be most useful in your particular NA situation.

For example, a target-situation use analysis (see Table 1.2) for an English of biology course would tend to focus on what the students should be able to do in English in biology at the end of instruction, which in turn would typically involve examining the language uses in biology and exemplars of those language uses. However, such an approach would no doubt be enriched considerably by also gathering information about the organized body of knowledge in biology, the specific competencies involved in doing biology, the social activities and problems faced by biologists, the cognitive or learning processes that biologist need and use, as well as the feelings, attitudes, and interests of the learners. And, that is only taking into consideration Berwick's (1989) six suggestions.

Technical measurement criteria

Much has changed since Stufflebeam et al. (1985) suggested that there are five factors that affect choices of information-gathering procedures. One major change in our field has been the development of major traditions of quantitative, qualitative, and mixed-methods research theory and practices. In 1985, a discussion of quantitative research measurement validity issues would have been the focus of the technical measurement criteria for selecting information-gathering procedures. Today, the qualitative research concept of *credibility* needs to be added to the discussion as do certain mixed-method researcher concepts. These concerns will be addressed much more fully in Chapter 5.

Level of accuracy desired

Similarly, in 1985, a discussion of quantitative research measurement reliability issues would have been the focus of any discussion of the levels of measurement accuracy desired in selecting information-gathering procedures. Today, qualitative research concepts related to *dependability* need to be added to the discussion as do the related concerns in mixed-method research. Again, these issues will be addressed at length in Chapter 5.

Personal reflection – How do various factors affect the procedures you will choose?

Think about a group of ESP students that you have taught, are teaching, will teach. In terms of the Stufflebeam et al. (1985) five factors that affect choices of information-gathering procedures, what will the characteristics of the information sources be in your NA? What situational characteristics will be important to consider? What types of information will you need? What will your technical measurement criteria be? What level of accuracy will you need? And in terms related to this chapter, how will your answers to these questions affect your choices and sequencing of NA data-gathering procedures?

Data-gathering options for ESP NAs

A number of authors have listed the procedures that needs analysts have at their disposal for gathering data. For example, Buckingham (1981) remarked over three decades ago that "a great variety of assessment instruments and processes are available, and the use of more than one means of assessment is desirable" (p. 15). Hutchinson and Waters (1987) provided more detailed suggestions for NA data-gathering procedures including questionnaires, interviews, observations, data collection (by which the authors meant *gathering texts*), and informal consultations with learners and sponsors (p. 58). Jordan (1997) provided a longer list as follows:

"documentation, tests, questionnaires, forms/checklists, interviews, record-keeping and observation." Jordan particularly emphasized advance documentation, language testing at home, language testing on entry, self-assessment, observation and monitoring, class progress tests, surveys, structured interviews, learner diaries, case studies, final tests, evaluation/ feedback, and follow-up investigations (pp. 30–38).

Perhaps the most complete and systematic lists of such procedures are supplied in Brown (1989, 1995, 2001) and Long (2005a). For example, Brown (1995) lists 24 distinct procedures in six categories, then briefly describes each procedure (pp. 45–55). Long (2005a) went one step further with his list, and it turned out to be somewhat different from the one supplied by Brown. In addition, Long not only described each procedure, but also cited examples of papers that used each along with references to help readers find further information.

Table 3.1 shows a list of NA data-gathering procedures compiled from Brown (1995, 2001) and Long (2005a). When these lists are combined, they provide a much wider perspective on the many procedures available for gathering information in an NA, including 32 different possibilities (of at least eight different types: existing information, tests, observations, interviews, meetings, questionnaires, target language analyses, and intuitions). Clearly, trying to use all of them or even half of them in a particular NA would be insane. Hence, careful and reasoned selection of procedures early in the NA process will be crucial in most cases. Naturally, you should select those procedures that are relevant, practical, and available, as well as those that will best serve the purpose, scale, focus, approaches, syllabuses, and other constraints involved in your particular NA. However, you should also select procedures with an eye to ending up with a set that will work well together.

For example, you may decide that you want to try to achieve a balance between qualitative and quantitative data. Notice in Table 3.1 that I have created two columns on the right side that indicate whether the data coming from a particular procedure tends to be qualitative, quantitative, or both. Note also that by far the majority of the procedures listed in the table tend to produce qualitative data (25 to be precise), while only 16 typically produce quantitative data (nine of which can produce both qualitative and quantitative data).

Nonetheless, it will still be useful to consider each of the data-gathering procedures listed in Table 3.1 in much more detail, a task to which I will now turn. In fact, I will dwell on this topic because these options and choosing among them are crucial to any NA.

Existing information

Existing information is attractive as it means that you will not need to develop or administer procedures. The information may exist in local

Table 3.1 Procedures for needs analysis (compiled from Brown, 1995, 2001; Long, 2005a)

Types	NA procedures	Definition	Qual.	Quan.
Existing information	Records analysis	Examination of files that are kept for students or teachers or various reports that are automatically generated within the institution, and so forth	×	×
	Systems analysis	A bit broader analysis of existing records that looks at different organizations or systems, often comparing them	×	×
	Literature review	Examination of the NA work that has gone before, usually as reported in the NA literature on NA methods or actual NAs that have been performed	×	
	Correspondence	Contacting NA experts or other people doing NA by email, phone calls, letter writing, and so forth	×	
Tests	Aptitude	Tests of examinees' general abilities to learn languages (with no specific language in mind), usually to select those with the highest chances of success		×
	Proficiency	Tests of examinees' general abilities in a specific language (English in this case), usually for purposes of deciding on admissions to a program		×
	Placement	Tests of the examinees' English abilities within the range found at a particular institution, usually for purposes of placing those examinees in levels of study		×
	Diagnostic	Tests of students' performance of course SLOs at the beginning of the course for purposes of giving feedback on students' strengths and weaknesses		×
	Achievement	Tests of students' performance of course SLOs at the end of the course for purposes of determining the degree to which they had achieved the SLOs		×
Observations	Personal records	Diaries, journals, logs, or blogs for stakeholders to record observations, events, experiences, and reflections in their workplaces, classrooms, and so forth	×	
	Participant observations	An *insider* in a situation watches, experiences, makes notes, and analyzes the language in use, what is going on in the ESP classroom, and so forth (*emic*)	×	
	Non-participant observations	An *outsider* to a situation watches, makes notes, and analyzes the language in use, what is going on in the ESP classroom, and so forth (*etic*)	×	
	Inventories	Counts of people, places, and material goods that are likely to be important for the success of an ESP course	×	×

(Continued)

Table 3.1 (Continued)

Types	NA procedures	Definition	Qual.	Quan.
Interviews	Individual interviews	Question-and-answer sessions with single individuals who are stakeholders, or potential stakeholders	×	
	Group interviews	Question-and-answer sessions with groups of people who are stakeholders, or potential stakeholders	×	
Meetings	Advisory	Advisory meetings are designed to get advice from the group of stakeholders at the meeting	×	
	Review	Review meetings are designed to get the group of stakeholders to review, give feedback, critique, and revise something developed for the NA	×	
	Curriculum component	Curriculum component meetings are designed for help stakeholders working in a particular area of curriculum work together on common issues	×	
	Focus group	Focus group meetings are usually led by a moderator who follows a plan to help stakeholders interact to address a particular issue or set of issues	×	
	Interest group	Interest group meetings are designed for help stakeholders with a particular position on an issue to develop arguments in favor of that position	×	
	Conflict resolution	Conflict resolution meetings are designed to help stakeholders with different positions on an issue develop compromises that resolve their disagreements	×	
Questionnaires	Biodata items	Questionnaire items that seek background information about the respondents		×
	Opinion items	Questionnaire items that ask respondents about their ideas, views, and opinions	O-R	C-R
	Self-ratings items	Questionnaire items that ask respondents about how they rater their own abilities, knowledges, or skills	O-R	C-R
	Judgmental ratings items	Questionnaire items that ask respondents for judgments (feedback) on very specific aspects of the NA that they can look at	O-R	C-R
	Q sort items	Questionnaire items that ask the respondents to rank or prioritize aspects of the NA		×

	Procedure	Description		
Target language analyses	Written data analysis	(also known as *text analysis*) seeks to understand the structure and other features of written texts collected as writing samples from the particular ESP		×	×
	Spoken data analysis	(also known as *discourse analysis*) seeks to understand the structure and other features of spoken English collected as speaking samples from the particular ESP		×	×
	Interactional data analysis	(also known as *conversation analysis*) seeks to understand the structure and other features of the language in real-life ESP conversational interactions		×	
	Computer-aided corpus analysis	Analysis of corpora, which are databases of written or transcribed spoken language, typically stored in a written form that can be analyzed by computers		×	×
Intuitions	Expert intuitions	Insights that stakeholders with expertise in ESP teaching (especially teachers, needs analysts, and administrators) come up with		×	
	Non-expert intuitions	Insights that stakeholders with no expertise in ESP teaching (especially students, parents, employers, and so forth) may come up with		×	

Note: × = qualitative or quantitative tendency of each procedure; O-R = open-response: C-R = closed-response.

records, in larger systems databases, in the literature, or in other institutions that you can contact. Let's consider each of these options in more detail.

Records analysis

Records analysis focuses on examining files that are kept for students or teachers, or various reports that are automatically generated within an institution. These may take many forms. For instance, when I became director of an EAP program called the English Language Institute (ELI) at the University of Hawai'i at Mānoa (UHM), my first instinct in analyzing needs was to go to the office and talk with the secretaries. They explained (patiently, because as we all know, professors are a bit dim) where the students' and teachers' records were kept, and I spent the rest of the afternoon looking through those records. I then asked the secretaries if they had any other information that would be useful, and they produced semester by semester enrollment figures, breakdowns of the student population by nationality, and summary information about each semester's placement results. It was on that day that I learned that virtually all of our students fell between 500 and 600 on the old paper-and-pencil TOEFL test (because the University required 500 and the ELI exempted those with 600 from further EAP training). I also discovered, contrary to my preconceptions (that the ELI was made up largely of students from Japan), that the vast majority of our students (roughly 85 percent) were speakers of various Chinese dialects from the People's Republic of China, Hong Kong, Taiwan, and Singapore. Thus one afternoon of records analysis revealed much to me. I have always felt that that was an afternoon well spent.

Systems analysis

A slightly broader form of records analysis looks at systems, often comparing them. Along with the records analysis for the EAP program at UHM, I investigated the other ESL programs on our campus to see how all of the programs fit together and to understand the entire system. It turned out that (a) the Hawaii English Language Program (HELP), controlled by the College of Continuing Education, was a pre-academic program for students preparing to enter US universities and trying to get their TOEFL scores up to about 500 and (b) the New Intensive Course of English (NICE),[1] controlled by Summer Sessions, was designed to deliver eight-week courses in grammar and conversation mostly to Japanese students. Notice that the ELI was made up predominantly of various groups of Chinese students, who were fully matriculated students, while HELP appealed to Japanese students who were more-or-less interested in touring Hawai'i. The fact that I am able to write this section off the top of my head attests to the importance of my initial systems analysis in helping me to understand how our sister ESL programs were related to what we were doing in the ELI.

Literature review

There is absolutely no point in reinventing what already exists. Thus, it is always wise to examine the NA literature for work that has gone before you. You have already started that process by reading this book. However, I have already referred to and will continue to cite a number of other books and articles about doing NA that you might find useful.

Alternatively, you may want to search the literature for articles reporting NAs directly related to your particular ESP. One strategy you could use would be to look at the NA studies cited in Table 2.1. If you happen to be doing an NA in an area listed in that table, it would be silly not to have a look at the NAs by people who have done them before you. For example, if you are doing an EOP NA for healthcare English to help train nurses, it would be wise to check out the four citations given in Table 2.1 for nursing (Cai, 2012; Cameron, 1998; Gass, 2012; Hussin, 2002). Who knows, you might get some good ideas from those authors for your NA; you might find that they have already done some of your work for you; you might discover citations that they make to other NA studies that are also pertinent to your work; you might find a questionnaire in one of their appendixes that you can adapt for your NA; you might find a useful quote that you want to use in your NA report; or you might find the name of an ESP expert you would like to contact for more information.

Correspondence

I have also found that it is particularly useful to contact ESP experts by email, phone, or letter writing. For example, before leaving for China to set up the EST program, one name emerged because it appeared repeatedly in the ESP and EST literatures: Karl Drobnic, who was one of the "biggest names" in EST at that time. When he was contacted, it turned out that he was more than willing to help us. He sent us sets of in-house EST course objectives and materials, an edited book published at his university on EST (Trimble, Trimble, & Drobnic, 1978, which was very valuable to us in 1980), and back copies of the *ESP Newsletter* that he was editing. Our program ended up cooperating in a number of ways with him including guest editing two issues of the *ESP Newsletter* (full of articles about our program). So Karl Drobnic turned out to be very helpful indeed to our EST NA and indeed to all of our program efforts once it was developed.

Tests

Tests come in many flavors including at least aptitude, proficiency, placement, diagnostic, and achievement tests. These labels are used rather loosely in the testing world, especially in language testing, but the definitions and uses I am referring to are those in Brown (2005a). There is much that could be said about tests with regard to NA, but here I will zero in on what we can learn from tests that will specifically serve as NA information.

Aptitude

Aptitude tests are designed to measure examinees' general abilities to learn languages (with no specific language in mind). Aptitude information is useful where entrance to a program is competitive and the administrators need to select those with the highest chances of success. ESP programs are seldom that selective, but sometimes companies or government agencies are interested in selecting only those examinees with high chances of success, and so aptitude testing may make sense. For example, in 1966 on my second day in the US Army, I was made to take a test called the Defense Language Aptitude Test. I apparently did fairly well because the army felt that I was worth investing in for language training and offered me the opportunity to study Vietnamese (which incidentally, I turned down). If your NA is for a company or governmental agency, aptitude test scores might provide you with readily available and useful information.

Proficiency

Proficiency tests are designed to assess examinees' general abilities in a specific language. For English, proficiency tests include the internet-based *Test of English as a Foreign Language* (iBT TOEFL), the *Test of English as an International Language* (TOEIC), the *International English Language Testing System* (IELTS), and others. These tests are designed to test students' English abilities ranging from virtually zero English to educated native-speaker. For example, before I left for China with the UCLA group, an agreement was negotiated and signed with the Ministry of Education. Among other things that agreement said that the Chinese scientists we trained would leave our program with a TOEFL score of 550, but nothing was said about their proficiency level when they arrived. Essentially, we had agreed to train all comers (even if the TOEFL told us they had zero English) in 30 weeks to a level of 550, which I know to be impossible. In response, we used statistical analyses to develop a way to predict TOEFL scores from the English as a Second Language Placement Examination (ESLPE) at UCLA. We then asked all applicants to take the ESLPE and only accepted scientists who already had a predicted minimum of 400 on the TOEFL. Thus, thinking about proficiency scores in the initial stages of this NA helped us to limit the range of student proficiency levels we would have to deal with to those above 400 on the TOEFL. I hope it is clear how important such a real-world consideration was, how we took it into account in our NA, and how it ultimately shaped everything else in our EST program.

Placement

Once the 225 students were enrolled in the China EST program, it was necessary to divide them into three levels (cleverly labeled A, B, and C from bottom to top) of about 75 in each level of the five skills that we taught (reading, writing, listening, speaking, and culture). Placement tests are designed for just such purposes. They are not as broad in terms of the range of abilities tested as proficiency tests because placement tests need only distinguish among students found within a particular institution. Thus, our placement tests helped us decide who among our students would take what skill area course at what level, which turned out to be very important information indeed for the NA.

Diagnostic

Diagnostic tests are typically linked directly to the *student learning outcomes* (or SLOs, which are also called *objectives*, are statements of what the students will be able to do at the end of training in a particular course or program). Diagnostic tests based on SLOs are administered at the beginning of that course or program for purposes of giving feedback to students and teachers about where the students' strengths and weaknesses are. While this can be done on a macro level with the placement tests skill by skill, course-level diagnostic tests can detect the students' strengths and weaknesses SLO by SLO. In China, the initial NAs indicated tentatively what SLOs might be appropriate for a given course, then a diagnostic test (with, say five items per SLO) was developed and administered at the beginning of each course and students (and their teachers) were provided immediate feedback about their scores on each SLO. For example, a student would get scores like the following: 100 percent on SLO 1, 20 percent on SLO 2, 60 percent on SLO 3, and so forth. That student would then know that SLO 1 was not a problem for her, but she needed to work very hard on SLO 2, put some effort into SLO 3, and so forth. Thus the students knew exactly what the SLOs of each course were and how they stood on each. In addition, this diagnostic information was very useful for determining which of the perceived needs (as expressed in the SLOs) were really needs. For example, an SLO on which all students scored 80 percent or higher might not be a need at all, since they could already handle it at the beginning of the course, while another SLO on which the average was 27 percent was clearly more crucial. We were able to eliminate some SLOs in this way (even though they had initially been perceived as needs) and devote more time and energy to SLOs that the students actually would benefit from achieving. (For much more on writing and using SLOs, see Chapter 6.)

Achievement

Achievement tests are also linked directly to the SLOs of a particular course, but they are usually administered at the end of a course for purposes of determining the degree to which the students achieved the SLOs of the course. For example, in the China EST program, the achievement tests were designed to be parallel to the diagnostic tests in that they tested the same SLOs. These tests were administered at the end of each course in order to determine how well students had learned or could perform on the course SLOs. For example, if students scored 100 percent on average on SLOs 1, 2, and 3, it was fairly obvious that they had learned those SLOs. If students scored low on-average on certain SLOs, they had not learned them. In addition, comparing their average performances on the achievement test to their diagnostic test scores SLO by SLO was also illuminating. So in the case where they scored 100 percent on average on SLOs 1, 2, an 3 on the achievement tests, but had scored 100 percent, 20 percent, and 60 percent, respectively, on the diagnostic test, it was clear that that the students had learned nothing on SLO 1 because they had started the course at 100 percent on that SLO; it was equally clear that they had improved a great deal on SLO 2 and considerably on SLO 3. Not only was it possible to eliminate some SLOs (and the associated needs), but it was also possible to spot situations where the students scored low at the beginning and made only small gains on a particular SLOs, meaning that the students had not learned them. This might happen on a particular SLO because it was not addressed in the course, because it was poorly presented in the materials, because it was poorly taught, because the students were not motivated to learn the SLO, because the SLO was not appropriate for the students, or because the SLO could not be learned at the students' current level of proficiency. So while it was not possible to determine exactly why learning was not taking place, it was possible to identify where problems lay and to direct our attention to solving those problems. All in all, achievement test information, especially when taken together with diagnostic information (and analyzed from very common-sense viewpoints) can provide very useful information about the degree to which perceived needs are actual needs and the degree to which perceived needs can be met.

Observations

Observations also come in many flavors including at least personal records, participant observations, non-participant observations, and inventories. There is much that the literature has to say about observations for research purposes, but here I will focus on what can be learned from observations that will specifically serve as NA information.

Personal records

Personal records, which may take the form of diaries, journals, logs, or blogs are books, notebooks, and computer files in which stakeholders record their observations, events, experiences, and reflections in their workplace, class-rooms, or laboratories. While the terms tend to be used interchangeably, it seems to me that *diaries* tend to be used for keeping daily records; *journals* for keeping periodic records but with intervals that are more sporadic; *logs* for keeping records of important events (like ships' logs that focus on navigationally important events); and *blogs* for any of the above, but kept online. Consider an example of journals that I used to analyze the needs of my students when I was teaching ELI 83 (advanced writing for scientists) at UHM. I assigned the students to keep journals on a weekly basis where they recorded their thoughts, reactions, and reflections about their academic writing in their major field of study. Some weeks they had specific issues to address like: what the style manual is in their field, what the main journals are in their field, what a professor in their field thinks about writing in their field, and what the benefits and challenges are in writing in their field. Over the 15 weeks of the course, I was able to learn a good deal about what writing in the sciences meant to my students.

Participant observations

Participant observations typically involve an *insider* in a particular situation watching, experiencing, taking notes on, and analyzing the language in use in a particular workplace or ESP classroom. For example, an analyst for an English for restaurant workers course could take a job as a server and make observations on the job. Alternatively, a teacher might keep track of observations of what is going on in her English for restaurant workers classroom. The main point is that observations of some kind are being made (of the language, interactions, turn-taking, activities, attitudes, or other important features) and those observations are being made by someone who can take an *emic perspective* (that is, can view the situation with an insider's understanding).

Non-participant observations

In non-participant observations, an outsider to a particular situation typi-cally watches, makes notes, and analyzes the language in use in a particular workplace or in an ESP classroom. For example, an outsider needs analyst for an English for restaurant workers course might observe waiters doing their jobs for a period of time. Or an outsider might make observations of what is going on in another teacher's English for restaurant workers classroom, without participating at all. The main point is that observations of some kind are being made but those observations are being made by someone who has an *etic perspective* (that is, can view the situation as an outsider).

Inventories

Taking inventories involves counting people, places, and material goods that are likely to be important for the success of an ESP course. How many students will there be? How many teachers? How many rooms? Desks per room? Parking spaces? Tape recorders? Computers? Books? Video cameras? And so on. There are many things that can be counted but not everything that can be counted will turn out to be important. So a certain amount of common sense and judgment must be applied. For example, before leaving for China, I was put in charge of deciding on what we should load up and ship from California to be paid for by limited University of California hard currency funds; what we could buy most economically in Hong Kong (also from hard currency UC funds); and what would be available to us (in Chinese currency and essentially free) from the government in China. Thus, a good deal of inventory thinking went into that project, including finding out first what we could get in China; what we could get most cheaply in Hong Kong; and what we could only get in California. These inventories needed to include not only our academic needs (like textbooks, reference books, typewriters, tape recorders, and copy machines) but also our spoiled-Westerners' personal and family needs (like washing machines and dehumidifiers). Anything that I did not properly think through was probably something that we would have to live without – at least temporarily. This is NA in its most fundamental form. The responsibility was crushing.

Interviews

Generally, interviews involve talking fact-to-face with key stakeholders (or perhaps more accurately, talking person-to-person because nowadays interviews can take place in person, on the telephone, or on the internet by Skype). Interviews may be *unstructured interviews* (without a preordained plan, which is appropriate if you truly do not know at the outset what you need to find out); *structured interviews* (with a prepared list of questions, sometimes called an *interview schedule*, which is more useful if you have a plan and/or want to be able to compare/contrast the results of interviews with different stakeholders); or indeed *semi-structured* (taking a position halfway between unstructured and structured interviews, perhaps with some prepared questions, but also time for unplanned responses).

Individual interviews

Some interviews are question-and-answer sessions with single individuals. If the interviewees are assured that the information exchanged will be kept confidential, this sort of interview is likely to be more revealing and useful.

Individual interviews have the disadvantages of being relatively hard to set up and time consuming. However, especially at the early and late stages of an NA, they can be very informative. At the beginning of an NA, individual interviews can be used to tentatively explore what the issues are in an NA, what questions need to be addressed, and who the key players are. For example, in every NA that I have ever performed, I have found it useful to interview the person in charge, but other stakeholders, such as coordinators, students, and teachers have also proven informative.

At the end of an NA, such interviews may turn out to be useful for *member-checking*, that is, meeting with individuals representing various stakeholder groups to tell them what you think you are finding in the NA in order to find out what they think of your interpretations.

Group interviews

Other interviews may be conducted as question-and-answer sessions with groups of stakeholders. The information gained in these sorts of interviews is not confidential, so it must be taken for what it is: what people are willing to say in front of each other. Nonetheless, such information can turn out to be very useful, particularly if contrasted with and different from what those same people said in individual interviews. Group interviews also have the advantages of being relatively easy to set up and less time-consuming than individual interviews. Group interviews can also be useful at the end of an NA for member-checking as discussed in the previous paragraph. All in all, both individual and group interviews, though time-consuming, can be very useful tools for NA.

Meetings

Meetings are also very important in an NA. Meetings differ from group interviews in that both meetings and group interviews involve multiple people getting together, but group interviews are typically structured around a single person asking questions and the rest of the group answering those questions, while meetings tend to involve more give-and-take with everybody raising issues, asking questions, discussing issues, answering questions, complaining, teasing, and joking. Meeting agendas can be used to push meetings in a number of different directions, including advisory, review, curriculum component, focus group, interest group, or conflict resolution.

Advisory meetings

Advisory meetings are ones where the agenda is to get advice from the group of stakeholders that is meeting. That advice may involve things like enlisting their help in designing interview questions, or items for questionnaires, but may also take the form of getting their suggestions for developing policy, for planning strategy, for doing analyses, for interpreting results, and for member checking. For example, after doing a series of interviews with a few administrators, students, and teachers, I have often found it useful to conduct advisory meetings, especially with the teachers, to brainstorm categories of questions and actual items that will be useful for a student questionnaire.

Review meetings

Review meetings center on an agenda designed to get the group of stake-holders to review, give feedback, critique, or revise something that has been developed for the NA. For example, I might take a draft questionnaire to a meeting of teachers for their review, revisions, and ultimate approval. Once these primary stakeholders have signed off on whatever is being developed, I might then hold further review meetings with other groups of stakeholders. For instance, I might meet with students to get their feedback on the questionnaire, and then with the administrators for their review and consent. Thus review meetings can serve the purpose of soliciting excellent feedback from smart people, but can also serve as a strategy for getting them to buy into the questionnaire (or selection of data-gathering procedures, or list of SLOs, or whatever is being considered).

Curriculum component meetings

Curriculum component meetings are designed to help stakeholders working in a particular area of curriculum work together on common issues. For example, in an NA, those needs analysts working on engineering English within the program might meet separately from those working on the science component. Or based on skills, all those working on the listening component (at Levels A, B, and C) might meet separately from those working on the reading component. Or based on levels, all those working on Level A (including listening, speaking, reading, and writing) might meet separately from those teaching Levels B and C. All in all, component meetings help people focus and only work on what they have in common.

Focus group meetings

Focus group meetings are usually led by a moderator who follows a plan to help stakeholders interact to address a particular issue or set of issues (see for example, Pierce, 2015, pp. 224–230). Thus, focus group meetings are different from advisory or review meetings in that they are considerably more focused, usually to address a particular issue or set of issues. For example, if there is considerable variation in the views among the teachers in the particular institution about what syllabuses ought to be used to organize an NA and the resulting curriculum, focus group meetings might be held to explore what those beliefs are, who believes what, and perhaps how strongly each individual holds their beliefs (that is, how willing they might be to compromise).

Interest group meetings

Interest group meetings are designed to help stakeholders with a particular position on an issue to develop arguments in favor of that position. For example, having found out in a focus group meeting that there is considerable variation in teachers' views about syllabuses, what those beliefs are, who believes what, how strongly those views are held, and how willing teachers are to compromise, it might be useful for the three groups of teachers advocating structural, functional, and task-based syllabuses, respectively, to meet in interest group meetings to come up with their best arguments in favor of their preferred syllabus, and perhaps, arguments against the other two syllabus types.

Conflict resolution meetings

Conflict resolution meetings are designed to help stakeholders with different positions on an issue develop compromises and resolve their disagreements in an NA. For instance, once the different groups of teachers have come up with their best arguments in favor of structural, functional, and task-based syllabuses, the conflict resolution meeting could be steered toward discussion of the positive features of each type of syllabus and then end with discussion of how all three might be used in combination. Reasonable people should see the value of maintaining their own favorite syllabus type, but also the benefits of combining it with the other two, either in layers or alternating (as described in Chapter 2). Notice that in this sort of meeting, information is being gathered, but also that the information is being used to shape compromise as well.

Questionnaires

Questionnaires are "any written instruments that present respondents with a series of questions or statements to which they are to react either by writing out their answers or selecting them from among existing answers" (Brown, 2001, p. 6). Questionnaires are very handy indeed and "amongst the most common research tools that ELT researchers use, mainly because they are useful, versatile, quick to implement, and the data they generate can be analyzed relatively quickly and easily" (Coombe & Davidson, 2015, p. 217). The categories of questionnaires explained next in this section (biodata, opinion, self-ratings, judgmental ratings, and Q-sort items) are listed separately because they serve different purposes and because items for each are often grouped together. Any of these may consist of open-response or closed-response items.

Open-response items allow the respondent to write in their answer or reaction in their own words. For example:

1   *Why do you like or dislike doing pair work activities in class?* _____

Open-response items generally lend themselves to more qualitative analyses. They have the advantages of being exploratory, that is, the results are not restricted to preordained categories, are in the words or the respondents, and may therefore provide surprising results or new ideas. However, open-ended items have the disadvantages of being difficult to answer (especially if the respondent is a learner of English), of often getting low response rates, and tending to draw answers only from respondents who are for some reason unhappy or negative about something.

Closed-response items require the respondents to select from among existing possibilities. For example:

		Strongly agree		No opinion		Strongly disagree
1	*Gender (circle):* Male Female					
2	*Pair work activities in class are useful for learning speaking*	I	2	3	4	5
3	*Group work in class is useful for learning turn-taking*	I	2	3	4	5

Closed-response items generally lend themselves to more quantitative analyses. They have the advantages of being easy to answer and therefore getting relatively high response rates. However, such items only get answers to questions that are asked (that is, there are no surprises) and even those answers tend to be restricted to preordained categories.

I have always used both open- and closed-response items on my questionnaires because I want to benefit from the advantages of each type. Again, the biodata, opinion, self-ratings, and judgmental ratings items described here can be either open-response or closed-response items.

Biodata items

This category of questionnaire items seeks background information about the respondents. Often that information will be important to the NA itself, but additionally this sort of information is often summarized in a report in a section headed *Participants* that describes those people who were studied in the NA (see Chapter 7 for more on this topic). For example, information gathered in this section of a questionnaire might include things like gender, age, educational level, mother tongue, languages learned, time in English-speaking countries, knowledge of the specific purpose English, and experience in the specific purpose content area. All and only the sort of participant background information that is needed in the NA or in the NA report should be included.

Opinion surveys

This category of questionnaire items seeks information from the respondents about their ideas, views, values, or opinions. For example, such items might gather information about their views on: what should be taught; how English should be taught; what they will use English for in the future; what improvements they think need to be made in the buildings, classrooms, and other facilities; and what the priorities should be in the program. Naturally, opinions will vary considerably on these and other issues, and there is no truth to be to be found in such items, but it is important to know what different groups of participants are thinking. In addition, good ideas and solutions to problems sometimes surface in the answers of participants, and it may become obvious that particular issues are very important to participants.

Self-ratings

This category of questionnaire items seeks information from the respondents about how they rate their own abilities, knowledge, or skills. Such self-ratings may be about their abilities in the various English skills, in their study skills, or in their content knowledge. For example, I have often found it useful to find out how students rate their abilities in pronunciation, grammar, reading, writing, listening, and speaking. When each student rates their abilities for each of those skills on a Likert item from 1 (very weak) to 5 (very strong), the averages across all students can indicate how they view their relative strengths and weaknesses as a group, which can be very revealing. In addition, odd ratings (like a student who rates himself 1, 1, 1, 1, 1, and 1 in those categories or one who rates herself 5, 5, 5, 5, 5, and 5) may be worth following up on in terms either of why they think they are so weak or strong across the board, or why they do not take the questionnaire seriously.

Judgmental ratings

This category of questionnaire items seeks information from the respondents about their judgments (feedback) on specific aspects of the NA or program that they can look at. For example, they might be presented with a list of possible reading topics, and asked to check off all those that they judge to be interesting to them. Or, they might be presented with a list of tentative course SLOs and asked to rate each on a Likert item from 1 (not useful) to 5 (very useful) and on a Likert item from 1 (not interesting) to 5 (very interesting). The point of these sorts of questions is to get judgments or feedback on very specific and focused aspects of the potential syllabuses, needs, SLOs, materials, tests, and evaluation procedures.

Q sort

This category of questionnaire items asks the respondents to rank or prioritize aspects of the NA. So in a sense, Q sort is not so much an item type as it is an answer type. I present Q sort here because it appears in all books of this type. However, I do so, not to advocate using such items, but rather to warn against using Q sort. The problem is that if you get respondents to rank something, the results are likely to be unanalyzable. For example, let's say you ask the respondents to rank their reading, writing, listening, and speaking skills from weakest (4) to strongest (1). There are two problems with this strategy. The first is that it assumes that the respondent does not see any two skills as being equal. The second issue is that the numerical results will be unanalyzable by most people. Say four students rank the four skills as follows: 4, 3, 2, and 1; 2, 1, 4, 3; 3, 4, 1, 2; and 4, 3, 2, 1. How will you analyze those results? If you add the ranks for each skill across the four students, they each turn out to be 10, 10, 10, and 10. What does that mean? If you average the rankings for each skill, they will turn out to be 2.5, 2.5, 2.5, and 2.5. What does that mean?

Rather than go on to explain how meaningless the analysis of such rankings will turn out, I would suggest that using Likert items like the following will solve both problems listed above:

Rate your ability in each of the following skill areas:

		Very weak		Just okay		Very strong
1	Reading	1	2	3	4	5
2	Writing	1	2	3	4	5
3	Listening	1	2	3	4	5
4	Speaking	1	2	3	4	5

With such items, a respondent can rate two or more exactly the same (for instance, 2, 2, 3, and 4) so that first problem is solved. In addition, all sorts of analyses make sense: averages for each skill will provide not only a ranking but also some indication of how close each skill is to the others. For example, if the means for the four skills turned out to be 4.23, 3.10, 1.26, and 1.36, it is clear that the order from strong to weak is reading, writing, speaking, and listening, but more precisely, the respondents clearly rated reading as their strongest skill, followed at some distance by writing, and speaking quite a bit lower, but only slightly higher than listening. In short, I strongly recommend that you completely avoid Q sort items or any others that require rankings.

Target language

In this section, I will be discussing three types of language analysis involving written data, spoken data, and the interaction in spoken data. For the sake of consistency and clarity, I will also refer to them as *text analysis*, *discourse analysis*, and *conversation analysis*, respectively. Furthermore, discourse analysis, as I am using it, focuses on the spoken language itself, while conversation analysis focuses on the interactions involved in conversation. Note that people elsewhere in the field sometimes use *discourse analysis* to describe working with both written and spoken language.

Written data analysis

This category of analyses (also known as *text analysis*) seeks to understand the structure and other features of written texts collected as writing samples in the particular ESP involved. Typically, the sample texts are collected from real-life documents common in the contexts where the ESP is used. They are then coded and analyzed for purposes of understanding the structure or other features of the written ESP. For example, business emails in the real world might be collected in an NA for a business English program. Those emails might then be examined for communalities in how they are organized, how abbreviations are used, how people handle the salutations and sign-offs, how transitions between ideas are handled, and what levels of formality are used. Such written data analyses can be very useful if they reveal features in the ESP that the students will need to learn in order to write effectively. Exemplars can also be selected to serve as reading passages in the ESP materials that will be used.

Spoken data analysis

This category of analyses (also known as *discourse analysis*) seeks to understand the structure and other features of spoken English collected as speaking samples from the particular ESP. Gee (2011, p. 8) describes discourse analysis (DA) as a family of research approaches:

> Some of them look only at the 'content' of the language being used, the themes or issues being discussed in a conversation or a newspaper article, for example. Other approaches pay more attention to the structure of language ('grammar') and how this structure functions to make meaning in specific contexts.

In an ESP NA, the focus of a DA will typically be on "language in use" for a specific purpose. For example, in an English for scientific purposes class, a DA of three university lectures (one each in introductory chemistry, physics, and biology) might prove very useful indeed. Such spoken data analyses could be tailored to reveal features in the organization, style, or content of the ESP that the students will need to learn in order to speak effectively. The lectures themselves could also serve as listening passages in the ESP materials development.

Interactional data analysis

This category of analyses (also known as *conversation analysis*) seeks to understand the structure and other features of people participating in real-life *interactions*. Typically recordings of real conversations are recorded, transcribed (into a written form), coded, and analyzed. Features that are interesting for the NA in question will typically be the focus of the analyses. Or the needs analysts may comb through the transcribed data to see what observations or patterns related to the ESP emerge from the analysis. For example, if the NA were for an English for automobile mechanics program, the interactional analysis might focus on four transcriptions of initial-encounter conversations between mechanics and customers, two of which resulted in the customers giving their business to the mechanics, and two of which ended with the customer taking their business elsewhere. In a situation like this, the needs analysts might be looking for interactional features that were different in the successful and unsuccessful (from a commercial point of view) initial conversations. Alternatively, the interactional analysis might simply examine the data to see what features emerged as common across all four conversations in order to better understand the English of auto mechanics. Ultimately, such interactional analyses can reveal features in the ESP that the students will need to learn and can serve as models or listening samples in the ESP materials development.

Computer-aided corpus analysis

Corpora are databases of written, spoken, or interactional data, which nowadays are typically stored in a form that can easily be analyzed by computers. Many such corpora exist but for the most part they are general English corpora. Two such general corpora are: the British National Corpus (see http://www.natcorp.ox.ac.uk/), which contains 100 million words of written and spoken British English from the late twentieth century, and the American English is the Corpus of Contemporary American English (see http://corpus.byu.edu/coca/), which contains 450 million words of written American English gathered between 1990 and 2012.

While such general corpora may not be directly useful in an ESP NA, they may prove useful if needs analysts decide they want to compare something they had found in an analysis of a specific English corpus to a general English corpus.

The first strategy that might serve an ESP NA particularly well would be to look for existing corpora of that specific English type. Four such corpora exist for various types of EAP as follows:

1   The Michigan Corpus of Upper-level Student Papers (MICUSP, see http://micusp.elicorpora.info/), which contains papers written in 16 disciplines by both native and non-native speakers of English. These papers can be sorted and accessed by student levels, nativeness, textual features, paper types, and of course by discipline.
2   The Michigan Corpus of Academic Spoken English (MICASE, see http://quod.lib.umich.edu/m/micase/), which contains 152 transcripts that can be sorted and accessed by speaker attributes (academic position, native speaker status, and L1) and transcript attributes (speech event type, academic division, academic discipline, participant level, and interactivity rating).
3   The British Academic Written English Corpus (BAWE, see (http://www.coventry.ac.uk/research-bank/research-archive/art-design/british-academic-written-english-corpus-bawe/), which contains almost 3,000 assignments written by proficient university students in four general academic areas (Arts and Humanities, Life Sciences, Physical Sciences, and Social Sciences) and at four different academic levels in 30 different fields of study.
4   The British Academic Spoken English Corpus (BASE, see http://www2.warwick.ac.uk/fac/soc/al/research/collect/base/), which includes audio- and video-recordings: 160 lectures and 40 seminars from various university departments in four general academic areas (Arts and Humanities, Life and Medical Sciences, Physical Sciences, and Social Sciences), each of which as 40 lectures and 10 seminars.

Other corpora no doubt exist elsewhere or will be developed as time passes.

A second strategy would be to see what is available online for the specific English that is the focus of a particular NA. For example, just out of curiosity, I searched "corpus of business English" and found a number of resources, including several articles on the topic. I also found a website entitled Mike Nelson's Business English Lexis Site (http://users.utu.fi/micnel/BEC/poskeywords.htm), which provides access to his PhD dissertation, as well as some of the key results of his analysis (based on a corpus of 600,000 words of published materials and a larger corpus of 1 million words of what the website author calls "real" Business English). I suspect that such a search for any specific English would be well worth doing.

A third strategy would be to develop a corpus of the language in use in the ESP at your specific institution. This strategy would clearly be considerably more work, but at the same time, it would provide a corpus of the language most closely related to the particular ESP needed by your students. This could take the form of digitizing the lecture transcriptions, lecture notes, readings, or any other language exemplars that you can collect that would be useful and representative.

Regardless of the strategy you chose to use in collecting the data, analyses of corpora can take a number of forms including useful word lists of the most frequently occurring words or multi-word phrases in the particular ESP in question (see Chapter 5 for additional ideas).

Intuitions

Expert intuitions

The intuitions I am referring to here are insights that stakeholders with expertise in ESP teaching (especially teachers, needs analysts, and administrators) come up with. Around the edges of many of the data-gathering procedures discussed above, there is always the chance that one of the teachers will say something off-the-cuff that perfectly captures an issue, or addresses a question or problem that has been plaguing an NA. Or an administrator may say something that summarizes or characterizes an important issue, problem, or question in a way that none of the teachers would ever have come up with. Such insights can occur when applying one of the above information-gathering procedures, or just while standing in the hall or having lunch, and they may be a surprise to everyone involved. One of the needs analysts may find that she went to sleep one night worrying about some aspect of the NA and woke up with a perfect name for the program, or a way to organize the syllabus, or with a fifth category of things that engineers need to be able to do in English. This sort of thing happens to me often when I am waking up, taking a walk, doing the dishes, or just sitting and thinking.

Several important observations can be made about these sorts of intuitions. First, it is important to notice such insights and intuitions when they arise in conversation or pop to mind. Second, given the expertise level of the people involved here (for example, teachers, administrators, and needs analysts), such intuitions are not based on nothing; they are not coming out of the blue; they are based on experience, knowledge, and expertise. So third, such intuitions are worth paying attention to. I have notepads all over my house and office because I pay attention to these expert intuitions, whether they are coming from me or others around me, by jotting them down before I forget them. Fourth, when I go back and look at such jottings I sometimes end up throwing them away, but other times I put them in a pile with other musings, think more about them, and end up using them one way or another. Regardless of where they lead, expert intuitions should not be ignored out of hand. Indeed, I would go so far as to say that they are a legitimate form of information gathering, analysis, organization, and reorganization.

Non-expert intuitions

The intuitions I am referring to here are insights that stakeholders with no expertise in ESP teaching (especially students, parents, and employers) may come up with. These may pop directly out of their mouths as good ideas as they stand; may trigger a reaction that is a useful thought; or may spark an interchange that leads to an insight. As an example of a student comment that triggered a useful NA insight, consider the day one of my Chinese-speaking B students said, "Teacher, please to speak more slowly." To which I reacted without much thought: "No, you listen more quickly." I suddenly realized that students needed to be able to listen more quickly. After much faculty discussion, we decided to meet this new-found need by teaching the students what is now called connected speech as part of one of our speaking classes in order to help them listen more quickly (that is, more quickly decode the blur of speech that native speakers produce in English). Again, the trick was to notice this exchange, take it seriously, jot it down, discuss it with colleagues, and of course, do something to meet the newly perceived need.

This list is not exhaustive

Table 3.1 may at first seem to be an exhaustive list of the possible NA data-gathering procedures. However, Holme and Chalauisaeng (2006) identified other techniques (see original article for descriptions of each) that they found useful for doing NA in their ESP context: the transect walk (where participants take the facilitator on a walk through their community), mapping and modelling exercises, understanding daily schedules, cause-and-effect diagrams, brainstorming through semi-structured discussion, mapping, well-being ranking, matrix scoring of priorities, and semi-structured interviews. Notice that only a couple of these procedures are shown in Table 3.1, which indicates that the list of procedures will continue to grow as the field becomes increasingly sophisticated at doing NA. Even more interesting to me is the way these authors have combined their procedures so that the total information gathered in their study ends up being greater than the sum of the information gathered from each individual procedure.

Personal reflection – What data-gathering procedures will you use in your ESP NA?

Again, think about a group of ESP students that you teach (or some you would like to teach). What specific data-gathering procedures will you use in an analysis of their needs? Start by listing at least one each from the eight different types of procedures (existing information, tests, observations, interviews, meetings, questionnaires, target language analyses, and intuitions). Then narrow your list down to a much smaller and more realistic list. What are you left with? Why did you choose those procedures? How will you sequence the procedures when you are gathering the data (see the next section)?

Combining multiple procedures

Once the procedures have been selected for an NA based on the criteria at the top of this chapter, it is worth considering how they will be sequenced and how they may naturally be combined in a *case study* (one logical and appealing way of gathering NA information).

Sequencing procedures of various kinds

Common sense can serve you well in planning the sequencing of your data-gathering activities. I have found that these activities tend to move one into the other quite naturally. For example, I have often used the following sequence.

I start by interviewing the head(s) of whatever program is involved in order to get initial information on what the students need to learn, problems they are having, issues that the leadership thinks are important, and who the key players are (that is, coordinators, lead teachers, or other leaders). Such interviews also provide an opportunity to get buy-in from the administrator(s) to the NA process, as well as implicit, if not explicit, permission to work in their program.

Knowing who the key players are is the first step in setting up further interviews with them that can serve many of the same purposes described in the previous paragraph. I also like to meet with these key players on a regular basis to get their advice and feedback along the way. I have even been known to form them into an NA committee with which I meet on a regular schedule.

Observing classes is another activity that I like to include. I prefer to talk with the teacher of a class first, then observe the class, meet with students after the observation, and round out these activities with a meeting with the teacher. It appears that class observations have their own internal sequence of activities.

Back to the meetings with the coordinators or lead teachers, I like to get their advice on directions the NA should go, issues that are important to them, problems they would like to solve, and so forth. I also like to work with coordinators and teachers in developing questionnaires. A good place to begin is brainstorming ideas for what questionnaires there should be and what should be included on each questionnaire. Should there be separate, but parallel questionnaires for different groups of stakeholders (for example, teachers, students, and administrators)? I will also try to get them to suggest actual items for the questionnaires. At some point, I tend to go off by myself and draft tentative questionnaires. I then come back to the coordinators and teachers to get their feedback. I will typically repeat these two steps writing and getting feedback until I am satisfied with the questionnaires.

At various stages of the NA, but especially near the end, I like to talk with participants about what I think I have learned so far and get their feedback about what they think about my interpretations and conclusions. This process, called *member checking* in qualitative research, is very useful. If they *agree* with my interpretations, I have further support for them. If they *disagree* with my interpretations, I may find useful avenues for further investigation, I may decide to reinterpret my results, or I may drop an inter-pretation altogether.

The bottom line here is that, from interviewing the leadership to member checking, the many data sources I use flow one into the other in a natural and orderly manner. The pattern I describe here may be peculiar to me, and that is fine because it works for me. You may find a different pattern that works for you. You also may find yourself doing some case study research as described next.

Using the case study approach

Case studies in ESP NA often take the form of studying a specific well-defined situation in which the special purpose language is actually being used (often drawing on multiple data-gathering procedures). Whether this be case studies of the English used when doctors talk with patients, when bank tellers deal with customers, or when graduate assistants talk with students in a chemistry lab, the focus is on the English in actual use for a specific purpose. For instance, before we left for China, sensing (correctly as it turned out) that large proportions of our students would probably be engineers of one sort or another, two of us decided to do a case study of engineering English. We contacted and *interviewed* three engineering profes-sors, and, among other things we learned two things about engineering that turned out to be important for our NA: (a) engineers specialize very early in their course work – certainly by the third year of their BS degrees and

(b) at least these three engineering professors say they never use multiple-choice tests, favoring instead using short-answer problem formats. That first finding meant that, if we wanted to gather authentic engineering materials that would be common to all engineers, they would probably have to come from 2nd year introductory textbooks and lectures. The second finding affected not only the kinds of items we used in our tests, but also the sorts of exercises we used with students in class.

As a result of our interviews, we did a *literature review*, which involved finding and gathering together second-year engineering textbooks to use as reading materials. We also did *text analysis* of three of those textbooks, especially from the perspective of cohesive devices (that is, identifiable markers in the language that tie it together at an inter-sentential level). In addition, we did *observations* in engineering lectures, and with the professors' permission, we *videotaped several lectures* from sophomore level (that is, introductory) engineering courses at UCLA. We watched those tapes repeatedly, trying to determine what made engineering English different, special, and specific. In the end, we realized that the lectures depended greatly on the formulas and graphs that the professor put on the board and that students could use those visual organizers to help them comprehend what the professor was saying. We also realized that, as in the textbooks, the professors were using cohesive devices (for example, *in addition, however, as a consequence, what I mean is...*, and so forth) to show transitions between different points they were making. Thus, we came to realize that our engineering students (and possibly all of our scientists) needed to learn how to use visual organizers and cohesion markers to help them listen to lectures. These ended up being perceived needs that we incorporated into our listening courses. In the end, portions of the video tapes were incorporated into the materials and used to illustrate and practice those points, among others.

Task 3.1 Abstract from Wozniak (2010, p. 243) – Procedures in an ESP NA

This paper gives a detailed account of an analysis carried out at the French National Skiing and Mountaineering School from August 2008 to June 2009 to assess the language needs of French mountain guides. A targeted literature review highlighted two main points to be taken into account in the design of this language needs analysis: target situations and insiders' expert knowledge. Then, one hypothesis and two research questions were identified. Data gathering methods including unstructured interviews, nonparticipant observation of the foreign language certification process and a questionnaire allowed testing of the questions via triangulation (by sources and methods) to validate the results.

The two questions were: "What are the language needs of French mountain guides? In a context of international mobility, what type of "English" should be taught?" (p. 245).

Read the above abbreviated abstract (also used in Task 1.1) and the research questions added on. Then, working in pairs (if possible), answer the following questions and compare your answers:

1   What four data-gathering procedures did Wozniak use (don't forget to add the literature review)?
2   Wozniak claims to be using triangulation of sources and methods? The sources are probably different groups of stakeholders. What three groups of stakeholders would you have included?
3   The methods are the four procedures you listed in #1. How would you sequence them? What would you do first, second, third? And why?
4   Think for a moment about the *target language* involved. Can you think of other procedures that might have been useful for this study? Why would they have been useful additions?
5   Can you think of other groups of stakeholders (beyond what you listed in #2) that might have been useful additional sources? Why?

Summary and conclusion

To review briefly, this chapter on selecting and sequencing ESP NA data-gathering procedures addressed a number of issues. First, the chapter examined the characteristics of successful NAs; this was followed by a section that considered factors affecting information-gathering choices (characteristics of the information source, situational characteristics, type of information needed, technical measurement criteria, and level of accuracy desired). The chapter then described 32 procedures that ESP needs analysts can choose from in eight categories: existing information, tests, observations, interviews, meetings, questionnaires, target language analyses, and intuitions. These 32 procedures were explained specifically with reference to applying them in ESP NA. The chapter ended with discussion of strategies for combining multiple NA procedures, sequencing those procedures, and using case studies.

The sheer number of procedures described in this chapter may at first be a bit intimidating. However, close examination of the discussions of sequencing and using a case study approach should be reassuring because they illustrate how selecting just a few of the 32 procedures and using them judiciously with different groups of stakeholders can lead to an effective NA. Probably the most common procedures applied in NA are interviews, meetings, and questionnaires – most commonly applied to students, teachers, and administrators in some manner – along with careful analysis of oral and written forms of the special purposes English as it is used in specific contexts. Thinking about NA in those terms may still seem ambitious, but should also be much more realistically within reach of real-life needs analysts.

Note

1 I am not responsible in any way for the acronyms HELP and NICE.

Part II

Doing the ESP needs analysis

Chapter 4

Collecting ESP needs analysis data

In this chapter, you will find answers to the following questions:

- What questions should I ask myself when starting an ESP NA?
- What strategies should I use in collecting NA information?
- What strategies and questions should I use in doing NA interviews and meetings?
- What strategies should I use when observing classes or meeting with learners?
- How can I change my open-ended questions into Likert items on a questionnaire?
- How can I create and administer effective and useful questionnaires?

Before gathering data

Before beginning to collect data from human beings, it is crucial to decide in advance whether the report for the NA will ever be published. Especially if you plan to publish your NA in a journal, or even as a chapter in a book, it is important to realize that many journals and some book publishers require assurances that your NA study was done with the approval of whatever ethics or human subjects committees your institution may have. Many universities and schools, and some companies have such committees. It is important that you find out about this issue in your setting and, if it is required, get approval before gathering any data from human beings. If, on the other hand, the NA will be part of normal curriculum development activities and you have no intention of ever publishing the report, then, in all probability you are exempt from ethics and human subjects requirements. That is not to say that you can act unethically, but rather that you probably do not need approval for your NA.

Knowing where to start collecting data

One of the main issues that I have faced in the early stages of an NA is: what do we need to find out and learn? It may seem odd, but an NA often starts out with a fairly blank sheet. Examining the literature, interviewing people, and holding meetings, as described in the previous chapter, should help. However, during all such activities two main questions ought to be: what are the issues and what are the important questions in this NA?

Ideas for questions to ask yourself

There are a number of questions that you may want to ask yourself to jar things loose and get the data-gathering process going. Some questions you will be able to answer right away, others you may want to tuck away in your mind to answer as time progresses. You may even want to ask these questions of others if you find that you cannot answer them yourself. One source of such questions is Jordan (1997) who poses the following overarching NA questions:

- Why is the analysis being undertaken?
- Whose needs are to be analyzed?
- Who performs the analysis?
- What is to be analyzed?
- How is the analysis to be conducted?
- When is the analysis to be undertaken?
- Where is the ESP course to be held? (pp. 22–23)

Nation and Macalister (2010) also provide a list of questions that can serve as a preliminary way of "focusing on needs":

1 What will the course be used for?
2 How proficient does the user have to be?
3 What communicative activities will the learner take part in?
4 Where will the language be used?
5 What content matter will the learner be working with?
6 How will the learner use the language?
7 Under what conditions will the language be used?
8 Who will the learners use the language with?
9 What will the language be used to do?
10 What language uses is the learner already familiar with? (p. 26)

Lest you think that these are just random questions, Nation and Macalister (2010) categorize the first four as *language* related (including sounds, vocabulary, grammatical structures, functions, set phrases, set sentences, and tasks);

the fifth question as *ideas* related (including topics, themes, and texts); questions 6-8 as *skills* related (including listening, speaking, reading, writing, degree of accuracy, and degree of fluency); and the last two (9–10) as *text* related (including genres, discourse types, and sociolinguistic features).

Both sets of questions listed above deserve attention because they are most probably ones you will want to answer in any report on your NA whether you do so in a presentation (where they may well be asked by your audience) or in an in-house or published written report (where readers and/ or reviewers may also ask about these issues). Notice that Jordan's questions generally address the nature of the project, and the questions from Nation and Macalister cover the overall nature of the learners' needs.

Useful general strategies for collecting NA information

Data collection is always complicated in an NA because you unavoidably find yourself intruding into the territory of people who are busy and often not as interested in your NA as you are. The stakeholders that you need to work with normally include any and all participants in a particular language program. Since they probably do not see your NA as being as important as you do, they may not want to put any effort into it at all. The trick is to cleverly motivate such people to cooperate in your data collection process or at least convince them not to resist the process. Winn (2005, pp. 293–294) listed nine useful strategies that might help you get stakeholders to cooperate in your NA. That is a good starting point, but I have adapted and added to those strategies (based on my own experience) in the dozen strategies that follow:

- Use whatever inside connections you have to gain entrée into the institution you want to study. If you are teaching in that institution, make sure you maintain good relationships with all key players.
- Go through proper channels and seek appropriate permission(s) in early and subsequent stages of the NA.
- If you aren't already working there, consider volunteering to work anywhere you want to collect NA data.
- Be friendly and get to know all key stakeholders.
- If you take the stance that you are trying to learn from your colleagues, rather than trying to be an expert, they are likely to react better.
- You may also find it useful to say that you see your job as facilitating communication between stakeholder groups (for instance, helping to communicate to teachers what students are thinking, and to administrators what teachers' views are).
- In the process, don't forget to have casual conversations before and after all of your NA data collection activities with whoever is around.

- Remember to do three things: listen, listen, and listen. You are not there to give your opinion; you are there to find out what other people are thinking.
- Use a variety of NA information sources so that you can compare and contrast the information results that you get.
- Take your time and talk with a relatively large number of participants from each of the key stakeholder groups. How do you know when to stop? When you find that you are no longer getting new information, or at least, when you are not getting very much new information.
- Make sure that you conduct follow-up interviews after you think your results, interpretations, and conclusions have settled down; the purpose of these follow-up interviews is to see what representatives of your stakeholder groups think of your results, interpretations, and conclusions. You might be surprised how they react. You might even learn something very important.
- Be flexible, patient, understanding, and creative so that you are bending as much as possible to the requirements, wishes, and requests of the stakeholders who are cooperating with you. Remember: they don't have to be cooperative.

Personal reflection – How should you get started in gathering your data?

Think about a group of ESP students that you teach (or some you would like to teach).

Looking back at the two sets of initial questions proposed above, which do you think you should actually address in your NA? (Go ahead and check them off in the book if you like.) Will any of the strategies listed above be impossible in your NA? Why? Are there additional strategies that you think you will need to employ in your NA? Do you think it is important to pause at the beginning of the NA data-gathering process to think through the overarching questions, and strategies that you will need to include? Why or why not?

NA interviews

Strategies for conducting effective NA interviews

Interviews are a common and important method of gathering data for an NA. A number of strategies can be employed that may increase the likelihood of interviews becoming a rich source of information in your NA, whether the interviews are with administrators, teachers, students, parents, future employers, or whoever is appropriate in the particular NA situation.

The strategies I list here are heavily adapted, reorganized, and supplemented for NA purposes from Brown (2001, for more discussion of these and related issues, see pp. 79-85 in that book).

Before any NA interview, it is a good idea to:

- Check your appearance (grooming, clothing, and so forth) to make sure it will not offend people you are interviewing. Keep in mind that sometimes the people you are interviewing come from different cultures where standards are different.
- Make sure ahead of time that you know what you are trying to accomplish in the interview.
- Do the interview by appointment if at all possible, so the interviewee knows you are coming.

During the interview, you should:

- Start with a friendly hello and some small talk (rather than launching directly into Q/A routine).
- Then ask the interviewee for permission to audio-record the interview. If they are not comfortable with that idea, take careful notes. If neither is possible, sit down and write up notes immediately after the interview.
- Maintain a friendly but professional demeanor and manner throughout the interview. This may mean showing empathy where appropriate, and *briefly* sharing similar experiences that you have had.
- However, be efficient by:
  - o Keeping in mind that time you spend talking is time the interviewee is not doing so.
  - o Taking charge and shifting topics when the interviewee is wandering off topic.
  - o Ending the interview when you have all of the information you want/need.

- Listen carefully and learn what things are important for you to listen for in the particular NA setting; this will give you a reason for listening and keep you actively engaged.
- Keep your goals in mind, but be flexible and use follow-up questions when appropriate.
- Control your personal views and cultural attitudes. After all, it is not your views and attitudes that you are investigating in the interview. And you don't want them to prejudice or color how interviewees respond.

On a more negative note, there are also a number of *behaviors to avoid* when doing any sort of NA interview:

- Don't ever disparage the interviewees' background, training, colleagues, institution, and so forth.
- Don't make negative comments about the interviewee's personal appearance, language ability, behavior (for example, don't say things like, "You look nervous"), or answers to your questions (for instance, don't say anything like, "That's a strange answer").
- Don't gossip or share rumors; they may backfire later and, in fact, may make the interviewees wonder if you will later be gossiping about them.
- Don't use stereotypes or make racist, sexist, ageist, or similar comments. Interviewees may shut down completely if they take offence to something you say. Again, it is their views that are important, not yours.
- Don't talk about provocative topics and, if you find that you have wandered into a topic that makes the interviewee uncomfortable, don't insist on continuing on that topic.
- Don't interrupt when the interviewee is talking. Let them finish their ideas so they feel valued.
- Don't disagree with interviewees' views. Once again, it is their views that are important, not yours.
- Don't correct the interviewee's pronunciation, grammar, or vocabulary choices. This is not a language lesson, and you are not a teacher in this situation.
- Don't show any signs of disinterest, boredom, or impatience, even if that is what you are feeling. Be interested, attentive, and patient regardless of what you are feeling.

Specific ideas for interview questions to ask administrators

Fortunately, you do not have to walk into that first interview or meeting with no idea what you are trying to find out. Consider Figure 4.1, which is often called an *interview schedule* that I have used for a first meeting with the Director (or Chairperson) of a unit where I have been commissioned to do an NA. Let's call this hypothetical unit the English Language Institute (or ELI). I would typically introduce myself and explain my authority and reason for being in her unit; I might also ask the questions shown in Figure 4.1.

Note that, when I was coming up with those questions, I had Rossett (1982) in front of me. He suggested using questions that addressed five areas: *abilities, problems, attitudes, priorities*, and *solutions* (see Table 4.1).

Looking back at Figure 4.1, you will notice that I introduced myself right up front and used the authority of the Dean to implicitly get her overall permission to do the NA (in number 1). I also asked to record the conversation (and take notes as well). Such permissions are important of course because I am essentially setting about to nose around this administrator's territory – or at least that is how some people will see it. I then tried to establish a bit of rapport in number 2. Then, while asking factual questions about teachers,

1   Hello, my name is JD Brown. The Dean of the College asked me to help you folks by doing a needs analysis in the ELI. I hope that is okay with you. [*Wait for answer*] Do you mind if I record and take notes during this discussion just so I can remember what we said?
2   How long have you been Director of the ELI? Do you like being director? [*Be sympathetic*]
3   How many teachers work in the ELI? How many are part-time? How many full time? Others (like teaching assistants, and so forth)? Could I talk with some of them? Who might be good to talk to? How would I arrange that?
4   Do you have any other administrators (for example, Assistant Director, Coordinators, Lead Teachers, and so forth)? Would it be okay if I talked them?
5   How many students to you have enrolled at any given time? Are there seasonal or semester by semester changes in these numbers? What are your students' proficiency levels? Do they seem like motivated students to you? Hard working? Would it be possible to observe some classes and meet the students of those classes for a few minutes?
6   What skills and levels does the ELI offer? Do you have a pamphlet or report describing the ELI that I could have a look at?
7   What problems do you see coming up regularly in the ELI? For you? For teachers? For students? What solutions have you come up with or want to try?
8   What attitudes do you encounter among the teachers that you find problematic? Among students? How have you dealt with those attitudes or what do you want to try?
9   Which of these problems in your opinion are the most important for you to resolve?
10 Are there other questions I should be asking you at this point about the needs of teachers and students in the ELI?

Figure 4.1 Interview schedule for a first NA meeting with the directors or chairperson.

Table 4.1 Summary of areas to address and what to ask about

Areas addressed	What to ask about
Abilities	General language aptitudes, proficiencies of students, especially with regard to reading, writing, speaking, listening, pragmatics, but also their abilities in the same aspects of the ESP involved
Problems	Difficulties and problems participants perceive in a particular ESP learning and teaching context
Attitudes	Wants, desires, and attitudes (for example, toward the language being studied, toward existing course objectives, and toward the ESP involved)
Priorities	Topics, activities, functions, skills, grammar points, vocabulary, and so on that stakeholders feel are most important, second most important, third most important, and so on
Solutions	Answers or solutions to whatever problems or issues are uncovered the process of gathering NA data

Source: Originally from Rossett (1982) but adapted here from Brown (2009, p. 280).

other administrators, and students, I again sought permission to talk to or meet with each of the groups of stakeholders in turn (at the ends of numbers 3, 4, and 5). I also asked about the structure of the curriculum and any other general information in number 6. *Abilities* of the students were addressed

Table 4.2 Summary of question types and what to ask about

Areas addressed	What to ask about
Behaviors/ experiences	Encounters or experiences in the ESP settings involved, what students have done in those situations, how students behave in those settings, and so forth
Opinions/values	Opinions, attitudes, ideas, impressions, values, and so forth on various aspects of the ESP and ESP learning processes
Feelings	Emotional reactions and affective responses to particular issues, topics, and components of the ESP and ESP learning processes
Knowledge	Facts, information, and knowledge about the ESP and ESP learning in a particular context
Sensory	Views on visual, auditory, and/or kinesthetic aspects of the ESP and ESP learning processes
Demographic/ background	Descriptive biographical or historical information about the stakeholders that has bearing on the ESP and ESP learning processes

Source: Originally from Patton (1987) but adapted here from Brown (2009, p. 280).

in numbers 5 and 6; *problems* for all stakeholder groups were assessed in number 7; *attitudes* in number 8; *priorities* in number 9; and *solutions* at the ends of numbers 7 and 8. Notice that I end with an open-ended question (number 10) that essentially opens up the floor to things that the Director thinks are important that have not yet covered.

Other questions that you might consider asking would be ones about *demographics* (like numbers 3, 4, & 5), *background* (like the pamphlet or report in number 6), and *opinions* (see number 9) or questions that I did not include here, but might in other contexts, about *behaviors, experiences, values, feelings,* or *knowledge* (as suggested by Patton, 1987, and shown in Table 4.2).

Another very elaborate approach to ESP interviewing that you might want consider is called the Common European Framework (CEF) Professional Profiles. The CEF Professional Profiles are described in Huhta, Vogt, Johnson, and Tulkki (2013). The authors describe a set of *core interview questions* (pp. 29-30), and then add examples of detailed questions and procedures for mechanical engineer English along with a chapter of suggestions for "Creating Your Own CEF Professional Profile" (pp. 180–195).

Meetings in NA

Strategies for conducting effective NA meetings

Meetings are another very common and important method for gathering NA data. A number of strategies can also be used to increase the chances of NA meetings yielding rich and useful information, whether the meetings are with administrators, teachers, students, parents, future employers, or whoever is appropriate in the particular NA situation. The strategies I list here are heavily adapted, reorganized, and supplemented for NA purposes from Brown (2001, for more discussion of these and related issues, see pp. 89–92 in that book).

Before any NA meeting, it is a good idea to:

- Make sure you have clear and/or definite goals for the meeting.
- Arrange for a sufficiently large, comfortable, and quiet place to meet.
- Schedule enough time in that space so that you will not be rushed to leave at the end of the meeting.
- Make sure that all participants have been notified about the meeting including the beginning and ending time, place, and purpose.
- Consider providing respondents ahead of time with any important information they will need to consider before or during the meeting including any handouts. Bring additional copies of that information for those who do not think to bring it along to the meeting.
- If possible, provide some form of appreciation for the participants' cooperation; this need not be elaborate or expensive (for example, coffee, snacks, or handouts to keep), but it will provide a small sign of gratitude for their help.
- Make sure all participants are comfortably seated and ready to begin.
- Distribute any handouts that the participants will need to refer to, making sure everyone has what they will need.

During any NA meeting, you should:

- Start the meeting with a friendly hello and self-introduction (if appropriate).
- Then, ask the participants for permission to audio-record the meeting (if indeed you want to do that). If they are not comfortable with the idea of recording, at least take careful notes. If neither is possible, sit down and write up notes immediately after the meeting.
- Start the meeting by explaining the goals of the meeting and tell participants that you will end the meeting when those goals have been accomplished. That may help keep people focused.
- Maintain a friendly but professional demeanor and manner throughout the meeting. You can briefly join in the discussion when appropriate.
- However, be efficient, by:
  - Keeping in mind that time you spend talking is time the participants are not doing so.
  - Taking charge and shifting topics when the discussion wanders, or gets off topic.
  - Keeping track of time, and not letting the meeting go over the allotted time. Generally, everyone is busy, and many may have places they need to be immediately after the meeting.

- When your purpose or goals for the meeting have been accomplished, do not be afraid to end it early, even if there are still 30 minutes scheduled. Your participants will appreciate it.
- Close the meeting with thanks to all participants for their time and help.

I do not want to repeat them here, but I would also suggest that you look over and heed the *behaviors to avoid* that I provided in the above section on strategies for conducting effective NA interviews.

Specific ideas of questions to ask teachers in meetings

Now consider Figure 4.2 which is a series of questions like those I have used with groups of teachers. Notice that I again introduced myself right up front and used the authority of the Dean to implicitly get her overall permission to do

---

1   Hello, my name is JD Brown. The Dean of the College asked me to help you folks by doing a needs analysis in the ELI. I hope that is okay with you. [*Wait for answer*] Do you mind if I record and take notes during this discussion just so I can remember what we said?

2   Could I find out a little bit about each of you? Could we go around the table and introduce ourselves including at least who you are, where you did your training, and what courses you teach?

3   Who are the *participants* in the ELI? Are there other teachers? Who are the students? Their language backgrounds? Proficiency levels? Do you think they are motivated? Hard working?

4   Why are your students studying English (that is, what is their specific purpose for learning English, their ESP)? What do they need to do with their English when they finish your program? All of them? What percent? What else should I know about their purposes for learning English?

5   Please tell me more about the *settings* in which students will be using their ESP? Where will they use their ESP? What will there work or study place be like?

6   What sort of *interactions* do you expect your students to encounter in their ESP? What will there position be in terms of degree of power? What roles will they be likely to play? Who will they likely talk with or write?

7   What *characteristics* will the ESP input have that your students are likely to encounter, terms of medium (Spoken? Written?), mode (for example, *monologue written to be spoken* like a TV advertisement), and channel (for instance, Face to face? On the phone? In a written note?)

8   What *dialects* do you anticipate they will need to understand and produce in their ESP? British? North American? Regional? Local?

9   What is the *target level* your students need in their ESP to succeed? That is, how good do they need to be in reading? Writing? Listening? Speaking?

10   What anticipated *communicative events* do you foresee for your students? In other words, what tasks do you think they will need to accomplish in their ESP? Be as specific as you can.

11   What *communicative keys* (see definition below) should I know about? In other words, how will they need to perform those tasks? What attitudes will they need to show?

12   Are there other questions I should be asking you at this point about the needs of teachers and students in the ELI?

Figure 4.2 Sample questions for a first NA meeting with teachers.

the NA (in number 1). I also asked to record the conversation (and take notes as well). Such permissions are a courtesy that is important because, again, I am treading on the teachers' territory and I will probably need their cooperation later in the needs analysis (for example, to observe classes and talk with their students). I then tried to establish a bit of rapport in number 2 by having every-one introduce themselves. Of course, this also provides useful information and gives me a chance to observe everybody's reactions to each other.

I then began asking factual questions in this case focused almost entirely on the students and their ESP. Note again that, when I was coming up with the questions in Figure 4.2, I had Munby (1978) in front of me. In his semi-nal book for ESP, Munby suggested covering the following areas of learner needs in what he termed a profile of communicative needs (pp. 34–40):

- Participant (Key background information – number 3);
- Purposive domain (Type of ESP involved – number 4);
- Setting (Physical and psychosocial situation where communication happens – number 5);
- Interaction variables (Roles, role relationships, and social relationships – number 6);
- Instrumentality (Medium, mode, and channel of communicating – number 7);
- Dialects (Dialect variations in the setting – number 8);
- Target level (Level of proficiency needed – number 9);
- Communicative event (Different levels of functions or tasks that will be needed – number 10);
- Communicative key (Particular way communication is accomplished – number 11).

Munby does not present these nine points as specific questions that must be asked in an NA, but rather as ideas for aspects of communication that an NA should cover. What better way to cover them than by asking ques-tions, especially of the teachers? Notice that, like in Figure 4.1, I end with an open-ended question (number 12) that opens up the floor to discussion of issues that the teachers think are important – ones that have not been covered otherwise. This is always a good idea because, as I argued above, you do not always know what all the issues are or what questions to ask when you start an NA.

Collecting NA data on learners

Interviews with administrators and meetings with teachers often serve vital purposes in an NA, but, of course, it is crucial to gather information from the learners as well. Gathering information from learners is not much different (in terms of the strategies you will need to use) from collecting information from administrators and teachers. Hence, if you are meeting with a group of students, it might help to go over the section above on strategies for conducting effective NA meetings. Similarly, if you are interviewing learners, it might pay to read through the section on strategies for conducting effective NA interviews. Beyond that, if learners are younger than you, just remember to treat them with the same respect that you afford the administrators and teachers as colleagues. Students are just young, not dumb. It just happens that they are a few years behind you in the processes that we call life, particularly with regard to learning English. A number of types of data gathering about learners are common in NAs, including classroom observations and meetings.

Specific ideas for observing classes

In my experience, observing classes should only be done by appointment, particularly in an NA, because your goal is to gather information about the needs of teachers and students, not to surprise and *evaluate* the teacher. That said, most teachers will feel put out if you do not give them feedback at the end of the class (or a bit later), by which they typically mean praise of some sort. So, though the goal is not to evaluate their teaching, while you are observing, you should probably jot down some of the positive features of the class, perhaps in some of the following areas so that you will not be left empty handed when they ask for your feedback:

- effective pacing of teaching;
- enthusiastic teaching;
- wide variety of teaching techniques and activities;
- clear objectives or student learning outcomes;
- well-organized teaching;
- relevant and useful demonstrations, examples, and illustrations;
- use of learner-centered activities like pair work or group work;
- ample opportunities for learners to practice the learning points;
- clear and straightforward instructions for all activities;
- efficient use of class time;
- pleasant classroom atmosphere;
- good use of teaching aids like audio-visual, computer, black/white board, and handouts;
- or anything else positive that you may notice.

However, the primary goal of classroom observations in an NA is to gather information. You may want to gather information about the facilities and equipment available, about the resources the teacher can bring into the classroom (for example, software, compact disks, posters). You may also benefit from noticing what approaches, syllabuses, teaching techniques, and exercises are being used during the class because they are probably popular with at least that one teacher. Noticing how the students react to those approaches, syllabuses, teaching techniques, and exercises will give you some idea of how the students feel about them. Also consider what error correction strategies the teacher is using and how the students react to being corrected.

The classroom observations will also give you an opportunity to look at the students' characteristics. Do they come from various language backgrounds, or one? If multiple language backgrounds are represented, do they tend to sit together in language groups? How old are they? What is the mix of genders? Do they seem interested and actively involved in the lesson? Do they all participate in the learner-centered parts? Are there differences in the reactions, motivation levels, and involvement of the students sitting at the front of the room and at the back?

There is no way I can tell you here all of the things you should be looking for with regard to the ESP needs in a particular classroom. So ask yourself what you learned in previous interviews and meetings that you should be looking for in your classroom observations. For example, in one situation, I was told by both administrators and teachers that communicative teaching was going on in all the classes, so I looked for that. In observing ten classes, I realized that only the first, youngest teacher was doing actual communicative teaching the way I would define it, complete with pair work and group work. The other nine teachers were doing very traditional teaching and calling it communicative. For example, putting two students together to work out the answers to a written exercise was called pair work, and choral response was called interactive communication. In short, I learned something from the interviews and meetings with administrators and teachers that led me to investigate further in the classroom observations (and in the interviews with the teachers and meetings with the students that followed those observations).

You may also benefit greatly from keeping track of questions that pop into your head as you are observing, so that you can try to answer them in subsequent data-gathering activities. Indeed, you should probably constantly be asking yourself what the important questions are that you should be addressing. This will afford you the opportunity to ask and address questions that you would never have thought of at the beginning of the NA process. As with the other data-gathering techniques discussed above, jotting down everything as you go along will help you to later recall, summarize, analyze, think about, and report on what you learned in these observations.

After the observation, but before you leave the classroom, simple courtesy dictates that you thank the teacher for letting you visit the class, and either at that point or later in a meeting with the teacher, you should be prepared to give the teacher more detailed positive feedback about the their teaching and their students as suggested at the top of this section.

Specific ideas for meeting with learners

In programs that already have students, I have often found it useful to meet with students individually. Such meetings can be as simple as the following face-to-face interview reported in Orsi and Orsi (2002) for an English for brewers program created for one of Argentina's biggest breweries:

Interviewer:	Can you understand native speakers of English? How well? What if they speak fast?
Learner:	I get lost when they make contraction ... it is difficult to understand Americans.
Interviewer:	Can you take notes from a lecture given by a native speaker of English?
Learner:	It depends on the subject matter.
Interviewer:	Have you ever been in an English-speaking country?
Learner:	Only on vacation.
Interviewer:	What would you like to gain from this program?
Learner:	I want to survive the course and learn about new technology.

(p. 178)

To get a broader perspective, I have also found it useful to observe a whole class and then pre-arrange a more comprehensive meeting with all the students after the class in that same classroom for 30-50 minutes. There have also been times when I have found it useful to meet with all of the students in a program, or with some group of student representatives from across the program, or with students who have already finished the program. In fact, I have never found those sorts of activities to be a waste of time.

In some cases, when the English level of the students has been relatively low, I have used a translator to help me conduct these meetings. In Tunisia one time, I found myself speaking English and French with the students with the translator helping out in Arabic when necessary. Since such young people tend to be very energetic, the whole experience was very exhilarating indeed – and somewhat exhausting.

Since you are not meeting with students to evaluate them or their program, there is usually no need to ask questions about how *good* their teacher is, or how good the objectives, materials, teaching, or tests are, for that matter. Instead, in an ESP NA, while you may want to ask what they think about those aspects of their classroom experiences, as a kind of warm-up or to get a general idea of how things are currently done in their classes, questions focusing on their needs and ESP involved will probably prove more fruitful. For example, you could start by introducing yourself, explaining why you are in their classroom, and telling them that you want to help focus their English studies on the sorts of English they actually need to use. At this point, you may want to ask their permission to record the session. Then open the meeting with some open-ended questions like those shown in Figure 4.3.

1	What experience do you have with learning English?
2	What are your main reasons for learning English?
3	When do you use English for outside the classroom?
4	What do you think you will use it for in the future?
5	How confident are you about using English in these situations?
6	Who do you communicate in English with?
7	What topics do you like to talk about in English? Are they the same topics you talk about in your mother tongue?
8	Do you use English at work? For what?
9	Will you use English at work when you graduate? For what?
10	What do you find most difficult when learning English? (for example, speaking, writing, reading, listening)
11	What experience do you have with learning other languages?

Figure 4.3 Sample questions for meetings with students.

The answers you get from such general questions will probably lead you to asking follow-up questions, or clarification questions, or questions to get more detailed information, and that is as it should be. Among other things when you are taking notes during such a meeting, be sure to keep track of questions that come to your own mind as the meeting moves along. Looking back at those questions may lead you to ask the students additional questions. In addition, near the end of the meeting, be sure to ask if there are any additional questions they think you should have asked, but didn't. And of course, a big *thank you* is always appropriate when you are using other people's time and as a way of ending the meeting.

Task 4.1 Initial data gathering in your ESP NA

So far in this chapter, I have discussed some of the most common data-gathering tools used in NA, including administrator and other interviews, meetings with teachers, class observations, and meetings with students. For each one, I have provided tips that might help you conduct the procedure and sample questions that you might consider using.

1 Which of those four tools do you think you will used in your NA? List them here:

2 Now, go back and look through this section with a pencil in your hand. What tips do you think are particularly important to remember for interviews, teacher meetings, classroom observations, and student meetings? Go ahead and highlight them.

(Continued)

(Continued)

3   Which of the questions that I suggest for interviews, teacher meetings, and student meetings do you think you would like to ask? Go ahead and put a check mark by each useful question in Figures 4.1, 4.2, and 4.3.
4   Are there additional questions that you would like to add to those lists? Go ahead and write them above, below, or in the margins around the existing questions.

Congratulations! You are now at least part way finished planning at least the initial steps in your data-gathering process.

Collecting NA data with questionnaires

When you are gathering open-ended data using interviews, meetings, observations, or other procedures, you may find yourself at a point in any particular procedure where you are not learning much that is new. At that point, you might want to shift gears and try gathering a different type of data. The same thing can happen for all of your qualitative data-gathering methods collectively, at which point you may want to consider shifting to using a questionnaire or set of questionnaires. A questionnaire is easier to use in gathering NA data on a large scale than are any of the qualitative methods discussed so far. As such, it is an ideal tool for gathering broader information about the things you learned in interviews, meetings, and observations. That is why I have waited to this late point in this chapter to discuss questionnaires. Indeed, questionnaires tend to be a late-stage data-gathering tool, used only after many other procedures have been applied to help you learn what the issues, problems, and questions are that you need to survey on a broader scale using questionnaires. Only at that stage should questionnaires be used to find out how widely a particular opinion, idea, complaint, or other issue is held by the participants in a program, to determine how important the issue is, or to get additional details about specific issues.

Changing open-ended questions into narrower more precise Likert items

For example, two students and one teacher may have told you in interviews that they think it is important to learn about *interviewing for a job* in a business English course. However, given that a total of 17 teachers and over 200 students will be affected by any decision you make about teaching interviewing for a job, you would be wise to further investigate: (a) how widely the teachers and students hold the view that job interviewing should be taught; (b) how important job interviewing is in their opinions relative to other things

Learning about job interviewing in English should be included in the business English course	*Strongly disagree* *Strongly agree* 1 2 3 4 5
Please list aspects of job interviewing that you think are especially important to learn:	

Figure 4.4 Questionnaire Likert item.

that could be taught; and (c) what aspects of job interviewing they think are particularly problematic. Of course, you could sit down with all 17 teachers and the hundreds of students in interviews and ask them, among other things, about their views on job interviews, but that method would take enormous amounts of your time, not to mention the time of teachers and students.

Administering one questionnaire to the teachers and another to the students would take much less time (say 15 minutes during a teachers' meeting and 20 minutes of class time for the students) and be much more efficient to administer and analyze. Such a questionnaire could easily contain, along with other items, a Likert item[1] like in Figure 4.4 which would accomplish both (a) and (b) in the previous paragraph and an open-ended question that would help you get at (c) as well.

Additional details (and how important participants feel about those details) can be accomplished in another way. For example, in a meeting with one class of learners, you may have posed the following question: What situations do you use English in? You look at your notes and see that they mentioned *social situations, meetings, emails,* and *on the telephone.* But you want to know more, so you use the seeds planted by the students in your mind and add to them when you formulate the following checklist of questions on the student questionnaire:

Do you ever use English in these situations? (check all that apply)

- ☐ casual conversations
- ☐ discussions with colleagues
- ☐ e-mails
- ☐ meetings with colleagues
- ☐ memo writing
- ☐ negotiations with customers
- ☐ report writing
- ☐ social situations
- ☐ telephone calls
- ☐ other _____

Or perhaps you wish to understand how confident the students are in their abilities to use the language in each of those situations, so you decide to reformulate the item as Figure 4.5.

1 How confident are you using English in these situations?	Not at all confident				Very confident
a casual conversations	1	2	3	4	5
b discussions with colleagues	1	2	3	4	5
c e-mails	1	2	3	4	5
d meetings with colleagues	1	2	3	4	5
e memo writing	1	2	3	4	5
f negotiations with customers	1	2	3	4	5
g report writing	1	2	3	4	5
h social situations	1	2	3	4	5
i telephone calls	1	2	3	4	5
j other	1	2	3	4	5

Figure 4.5 Reformulated Likert item.

An example of actual questions used on a business English NA questionnaire (Figure 4.6 from Huh, 2006) looks a bit different but accomplishes many of the same things. Notice in particular that even with all the detail involved in this questionnaire, Huh uses a number of Likert items and two open-ended questions at the very end.

Section C: Business English Tasks

11. How often do you perform the following tasks in English at work? (Please write down the number on the right column)

FREQUENCY: 0 = NEVER; 1 = RARELY; 2 = SOMETIMES; 3 = OFTEN; 4 = EVERYDAY

						Answer
Example: Writing a resume	0	1	2	3	4	**3**
A Correspondence						
a Email	0	1	2	3	4	
b Phone call	0	1	2	3	4	
c Fax	0	1	2	3	4	
d Writing a business letter	0	1	2	3	4	
e Others:	0	1	2	3	4	
B Writing a document						
a Writing a memorandum	0	1	2	3	4	
b Writing a proposal (e.g., project, plan, etc.)	0	1	2	3	4	

c Writing a report (e.g., sales, meeting, etc.)	0	1	2	3	4	
d Writing a contract/ agreement	0	1	2	3	4	
Others:	0	1	2	3	4	
C Order/Customer satisfaction						
a Placing an order/Purchasing	0	1	2	3	4	
b Receiving an order	0	1	2	3	4	
c Dealing with claims	0	1	2	3	4	
Others:	0	1	2	3	4	
D Business meeting						
a Briefing	0	1	2	3	4	
b Presentation	0	1	2	3	4	
c Negotiation	0	1	2	3	4	
d Conference	0	1	2	3	4	
e Seminar	0	1	2	3	4	
f Social meeting (e.g., party, dining, etc.)	0	1	2	3	4	
Others:	0	1	2	3	4	
E Business trip						
a Business trip to foreign countries	0	1	2	3	4	
b Making a reservation (e.g., hotel, flight, etc.)	0	1	2	3	4	
c Visiting other companies/factories	0	1	2	3	4	
d Sightseeing	0	1	2	3	4	
e Others:	0	1	2	3	4	
	0	1	2	3	4	
F Attending to foreign guests	0	1	2	3	4	
G Interpretation (e.g., meeting, conference, etc.)	0	1	2	3	4	
H Translation (e.g., document, booklet, etc.)	0	1	2	3	4	
I Gathering information on the market or other companies	0	1	2	3	4	
J Reading articles, magazines, and books related to your job	0	1	2	3	4	
K Others (specify):	0	1	2	3	4	
	0	1	2	3	4	
	0	1	2	3	4	

12 How important is it for you to use English in your job?

13 If you can give advice to those who are preparing for a job, what would you recommend them to prepare in terms of English?

Figure 4.6 Questions used on a business English NA questionnaire (from Huh, 2006, pp. 62–64).

Creating an effective and useful questionnaire

The following guidelines are provided to help you create sound question-naires like those described above. These guidelines are heavily adapted from Brown (1997). If you are intrigued by this list, you will find more detailed guidelines with numerous examples in the book length treatment provided in Brown (2001). The following are *potential pitfalls* that you may encoun-ter in designing and using questionnaires – along with ways to avoid those pitfalls:

- *Avoid items that are too long* – Use short items that you can read aloud in one breath; typically that means less than 20 words.
- *Avoid items that are vague, imprecise, or otherwise ambiguous* – Ask colleagues, especially potential respondents to check your items and directions for anything that might be unclear.
- *Avoid items written in unsuitable language* – Proofread the question-naire specifically to make sure that the language will be at the right level and be simple and clear to the respondents; for ESP students in EFL set-tings, consider writing the items in their L1, or providing both English and their mother tongue.
- *Avoid items that use unnecessary words* – Carefully examine each item to ensure that every single word is absolutely necessary, and eliminate any that are non-essential.
- *Avoid items that use negative words* – Rewrite such items in a positive way if at all possible; remember that negative words in English include *no, not, nothing, none, never,* and *nowhere,* but also words that begin with *non-, un-, il-, ir-,* and *im-.*
- *Avoid items that ask two or more things* – Check to make sure that each item addresses one and only one issue, and not two or more at the same time.
- *Avoid items that push respondents toward a particular answer* – Rewrite any items that you think are leading or guiding respondents to respond in a specific way.
- *Avoid items that respondents will answer in a particular way because that is the prestige answer* – Rewrite any items that have a response that respondents might see as the best or right answer (even if it is not true) because it is prestigious.
- *Avoid items that respondents might find embarrassing* – Pilot items and get feedback from a few members of the appropriate stakeholder groups so you can identify and eliminate any words that respondents might find vulgar or otherwise hurtful or offensive.
- *Avoid items that are biased in any way* – Rewrite or eliminate any items that a particular religious, nationality, or ethnic group might find biased, unfair, or insulting.

- *Avoid items that do not apply to a subset of respondents* – Insure that all items are relevant to all respondents, or if some items are not, remove or reword them, or use separate questionnaires for different groups so that all and only relevant items will be presented to each group.

While I am creating an ESP NA questionnaire, I find it useful to also keep in mind that the items on a questionnaire have multiple purposes:

- To help curriculum developers understand the organization involved and how all parts of that organization fit together.
- To give all participants a stake in the curriculum, that is, to make them stakeholders in the true sense of that word.
- To provide teachers and administrators opportunities for constructive reflection not only on the constraints, challenges, and problems in their workplace, but also on available resources, solutions, remedies, and ways forward.
- To foster a sense of trust or at least confidence between and among various stakeholder groups and individuals.
- To promote interest, enthusiasm, and energy for the NA and ESP curriculum development in general.
- To promote acceptance, buy-in, and support for the NA and ESP curriculum development in general.

Hence, you may find that you will need to include items that will promote those six purposes, even though they are not directly related to learner needs or to the NA report that you will ultimately produce.

Tips on administering a questionnaire

Getting a high return rate

A high return rate is crucial for having meaningful questionnaire data. Ask yourself: would you be more prone to believe the results of a questionnaire to which 11 percent of the students responded or one where 97 percent responded? The best way to get a high return rate is to administer the questionnaire at the end of classes where the students must walk past the teacher and give her the questionnaire before they can leave the room. Another way is to call a meeting of the entire organization in an auditorium – one that most people are likely to attend – and then do the questionnaire administration at the end of the meeting (again, with people collecting the questionnaires at the doors). For teacher questionnaires, one useful strategy is to give them the questionnaires and ask them to return them to the office, or an equivalent place, to a box where they must check off their name. That way you can keep giving questionnaires and reminders to teachers whose names are not checked off, while respecting their anonymity, until you have everybody's questionnaire. Unfortunately, I have found that teachers are not above lying (that is, checking off their name without turning in the questionnaire), but fortunately, that is fairly rare.

The worst possible way to administer a questionnaire is to pass it out in classes and tell the students to bring it back in a week. That is guaranteed to fail. Online surveys using something like *Survey Monkey* (https://www.survey monkey.com) may help get a better response rate, but, because many people may look at an online questionnaire and still not respond to it, this approach may simply add the problem of not knowing what the response rate actually was (for more ideas on how to get a high return rate, see Brown, 2001)

General questionnaire administration tips

All of that said, there are a number of things to keep in mind before, during, and at the end of administering a questionnaire in a classroom or larger meeting.

Before:

- Make sure the purpose of the questionnaire is clear to you and anyone else working on creating it with goals that are defined in theoretical and practical terms related directly to the NA.
- Make sure you have carefully evaluated the quality of the questionnaire as described in the previous section.
- Make sure you will have a place to administer the questionnaire that is large enough, well-ventilated, and quiet so that the respondents will be able to concentrate.
- Make sure you will have enough time (or even a little extra time) in that space for respondents to finish the questionnaire.
- Recruit the respondents if necessary.
- Notify respondents ahead of time about the date and place of the administration.
- Make sure that you will have an adequate number of questionnaires on hand (or even a few extras, just in case).

During:

- Make sure all respondents are comfortably seated.
- Distribute the questionnaires in a systematic fashion.
- Read any overall directions clearly and sufficiently loudly.
- Keep track of how long the administration takes so you can adjust the length of time needed for future administrations or so you can describe that in the NA report.
- Note any problems that you had or issues that came up during the administration of the questionnaire so you can discuss them with colleagues or describe them in the NA report if necessary.

At the end:

• Collect the questionnaires quickly, efficiently, and professionally.
• End the administration by thanking the respondents for their time, effort, and cooperation.
• If possible, provide the respondents with some form of reward (it can be as small as a piece of candy that they choose from a basket, or be a gift voucher, movie ticket, or, if you are feeling rich, a $10 Starbucks card) to show that you appreciate their help.

Task 4.2 Designing questionnaires for an ESP NA

Now that you have thought through at least the initial stages of your data gathering with interviews, meetings, and observations, it is time to get yourself ready to design a questionnaire based on what you learn in the initial stage procedures. To that end, please do the following steps as well as you can at this point.

1 Start out by taking out a separate sheet of paper and writing five open-ended questionnaire items like the ones you think you might include on an NA questionnaire for teachers.
2 Now do the same with five 1–5 scale Likert items.
3 Also if you can, convert the open-ended items you wrote in #1 to Likert items.
4 This last step is very important: now, get in pairs and read over each other's items and give each other constructive feedback, and don't forget to revise your questions.

Be sure to follow those steps (especially #4) when you are designing the real questionnaire for your NA.

Collecting NA data on ESP use

Given the specific nature of ESP, many NAs may be breaking new ground and will therefore need to document examples of the sorts of written or spoken language used in that particular ESP.

Gathering data on ESP oral interactions

In this section, I will explore one other general category of data that is very commonly gathered for NAs: exemplars of *oral ESP in use*. As mentioned in Chapter 3, before leaving the US to create the China EST program, we videoed a series of three lectures from three different engineering professors on three different engineering topics. These lectures served as the bases for analyzing how the professors emphasized points in their lectures as well as how they used what we called *connectors* (that is, cohesive devices like conjunctions) in our NA.

Thus, one way to document ESP in use is to observe people using the language in interactions at work or academic sites where it is being used. Other examples include observing bank tellers interacting with customers, or doctors with patients, or an engineering professor during office hours with students. You would probably want to record the interactions with audio or video recording equipment and take notes as well – all of this, of course, with the participants' permission. If you are worried that being recorded will affect the way they communicate, you may want to use some sort of hidden camera technique (and get their permission afterward),[2] or simply audio-record them so often and for so long that they forget about the presence of the recording equipment. You might then consider transcribing a portion of the interaction into a *transcript* (that is, spoken discourse in written form) so that it will be easier to analyze. But then what?

Analysis of such a transcript can take many forms that are described at length and in many different ways in the field of conversation analysis. However, what you are looking for in an NA may not require all the levels of formal analysis that have been developed in conversation analysis (see description in Chapter 3) for research purposes. Perhaps it will be more productive to read through the transcript with a list of questions in front of you that you want to ask.

For example, Basturkmen (2010), who was observing *care workers* communicating in small talk with *clients* analyzed her observations with the following questions:

- When and where does the small talk take place?
- How is it initiated? (Note some samples of language use.)
- What topics are included?
- What kinds of questions do the care workers or clients use? (Note samples of language use.)
- What kinds of responses do the care workers or clients use? (Note samples of language use.)
- Are any difficulties apparent? (If so, what are they?)
- What appears to keep the episodes going or to lead to an abrupt end?
- How are episodes closed? (Note examples of actual language use.) (p. 33)

Basturkmen's questions could clearly be applied equally well to interactions between bank tellers and customers, or doctors and patients, or an engineering professor and students, or any other interactions pertinent to your NA.

Gathering data on written ESP in use

Many resources are available for collecting *written ESP in use* on the Internet. Some of these are in the *public domain*, which by definition means they are not copyrighted and can therefore be used without restrictions in an NA, or even quoted in the report. However, it is sound ethical and professional practice to acknowledgment the source of any material you use including the author (if applicable), title, publication date, the URL for the website where you found it. One good source for public domain resources on a variety of topics in many different disciplines and professions is the *Wikipedia* website (see http://en.wikipedia.org/wiki/Wikipedia:Public_domain_resources).

For example, once in that website, I moved down to the *Contents* box on the left side of that URL and selected *Business and Industry* then clicked on *US Energy Information Agency*, which took me to http://www.eia.gov/, which was displaying December 17, 2014 of *Today in Energy*, with the article shown in Figure 4.7.

Imagine how useful such a document could be as part of an NA for analyzing the ESPs of business or the oil industry. Naturally, the same document could also be used later for materials development in the resulting ESP course, or as part of an assessment procedure.

A number of other collections of written texts (also known as *corpora*) are available online (see the last chapter of McKay and Brown, 2015 for descriptions of many sorts of corpora ranging from written to spoken language corpora and native speaker to learner corpora). However, for ESP NA purposes, two of those corpora stand out as potentially most useful.

I referred to several corpora in Chapter 3. The first corpus, for written English, was the *Michigan Corpus of Upper-level Student Papers* (MICUSP available at http://micusp.elicorpora.info/), which is useful because it provides a large number of papers written by native speakers and second language (SL) learners of English in 16 different disciplines. In addition, as I mentioned in Chapter 3, these papers are classified in the following categories: student levels, nativeness, textual features, paper types, and disciplines. As a result, papers can be selected and/or analyzed in those categories or combinations of those categories.

The second corpus is for spoken English. The *Michigan Corpus of Academic Spoken English* (MICASE available at http://quod.lib.umich.edu/m/micase/) is a valuable compilation of 152 transcripts of the spoken English of native speakers and SL learners. This corpus is classified, as mentioned in Chapter 3, by *speaker attributes* (including academic position, native speaker status, and L1) and *transcript attributes* (including speech event type, academic division, academic discipline, participant level, and interactivity rating). As a result, these transcripts can be selected or analyzed in those categories or combinations of those categories.

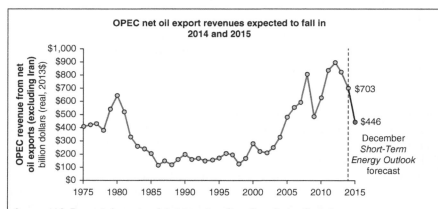

OPEC net oil export revenues expected to fall in 2014 and 2015

Source: U.S. Energy Information Administration, *Short-Term Energy Outlook*.

Note: OPEC is the Organization of the Petroleum Exporting Countries. Iran is excluded because current sanctions make it difficult to estimate revenues. The 2014 revenue estimates are subject to revision as historical production and consumption data are updated.

Based on crude oil market assessments in the *Short-Term Energy Outlook*, EIA estimates that members of the Organization of the Petroleum Exporting Countries (OPEC), excluding Iran, will earn about $700 billion in revenue from net oil exports in 2014, a 14% decrease from 2013 earnings and the lowest earnings for the group since 2010. OPEC earnings declined in 2014 largely for two reasons: decreases in the amount of OPEC oil exports and lower oil prices, with the 2014 average for Brent crude oil projected to be 8% below the average 2013 price.

For similar reasons, revenues for OPEC (excluding Iran) in 2015 are expected to fall further, to $446 billion, 46% below the 2013 level. Brent crude oil is projected to average $68 per barrel in 2015, down from $100 per barrel in 2014 and $109 per barrel in 2013. ...

Prolonged periods of lower oil prices have the largest effect on OPEC countries that are more sensitive to losses in revenue, most notably Venezuela, Iraq, and Ecuador. Governments in these countries were already running fiscal deficits in 2013, and their sovereign wealth funds are smaller compared to other OPEC members. This implies that these countries may not be able to fill budget gaps for as long as other OPEC members.

Further revisions to future budget plans may be required in many OPEC member countries, particularly the countries cited above, because of lower oil prices and large uncertainty over future global economic growth and crude oil production levels. Geopolitical risk may also be elevated because of lower government spending.

Principal contributors: James Preciado, Megan Mercer.

Figure 4.7 Example of ESP in use (retrieved December 20, 2014 from http://www.eia.gov/todayinenergy/detail.cfm?id=19231).

In order to show how useful these texts might be for an NA, I went in search of a text that might serve as part of a written ESP corpus. At the MICUSP site, I selected "Native Speaker" under *Nativeness* and "Mechanical Engineering (Mec)" under *Discipline*. I then chose the first document listed, MEC.G0.03.1. The following is the executive summary provided at the top:

Manufacturing System Design for a Car Assembly Process

EXECUTIVE SUMMARY

We have been assigned the task of designing the manufacturing system for the assembly of a simple vehicle. The manufacturer wishes to anticipate any changes in demand, and also wishes to know the impact of reliability at the system and machine levels (100% system and 95% machine reliability). As a result, three scenarios of demand and reliability were considered: (1) 50,000 units per year with 100% reliability, (2) 50,000 units per year with 95% machine reliability and lastly (3) a 75,000 units per year with 95% machine reliability. This task has been completed.

By performing tasks in parallel at the same station, the total number of stations required for assembly was reduced to 7. In turn, the system reliability was increased in order to meet the yearly demand. Specifically, for scenario 1, the plant can operate a single 8 hour shift for 51 weeks per year. For scenarios 2 and 3, respectively, two and three 6 hours-a-day shifts for 49 weeks per year can be used to meet the yearly demand. Lastly, a future state map is included to implement lean manufacturing methods and reduce the costs of operation. The approach, costs and recommendations regarding the assembly designs are discussed in this report.

The full text is available at http://micusp.elicorpora.info/search/view/?pid= MEC.G0.03.1.

I will show several possible ways of analyzing such a text in the next chapter.

General hints for collecting NA data on ESP use

Use existing data if possible

It may save you time to find and collect existing audio- or video-recordings. For example, as part of our EST NA in preparation for going to China, we found five PBS videotapes of panels of scientists discussing topics (I remember, for example, that one of them was a group of physicists discussing nuclear power). The panel discussions were useful for examining how different scientists in different fields (like physics) talked among themselves when in front of an audience. And the 10-minute question-and-answer portion at the end was useful for examining how scientists spoke differently when directly addressing lay-people and answering their questions.

Get multiple uses out of your data if possible

It is common to gather samples of ESP for an NA, samples that can serve multiple functions in an NA. For example, as mentioned above, before leaving the US to create the China EST program, we videoed a series of three lectures from three different engineering professors on three different engineering topics. Initially, these lectures served as the bases for analyzing how they emphasized points in their lectures as well as how they used what we called *connectors* (that is, cohesive devices like conjunctions) in our NA. Later, we were able to use these same videos to develop listening materials, to gather data for a listening comprehension research study, and for test development. Thinking ahead to multiple ways that NA data may prove useful beyond just gathering data for the NA may turn out to be a very efficient thing to do.

Task 4.3 Using online resources in an NA for samples of ESP use

With a partner, divide up the following so that each of you has committed to visit two of the websites listed earlier in the chapter:

> http://en.wikipedia.org/wiki/Wikipedia:Public_domain_resources
> http://www.eia.gov/ and http://www.eia.gov/about/copyrights_reuse.cfm
> http://micusp.elicorpora.info/
> http://quod.lib.umich.edu/m/micase/

1   On your personal computer or in a computer lab, visit the two websites you agreed to visit and also explore at least one other possible website that might prove useful as a source of data for the way English is used in the ESP that you are most interested in.
2   For each website, take notes on what it contains and how it might be useful in doing an ESP NA.
3   When you next see your partner, share what you learned and decide together which of the website(s) you think would most useful for doing an ESP NA and list at least five ways each website could be useful.

Summary and conclusions

This chapter was designed to help you get started in the information/data-gathering process by suggesting questions that you can ask yourself and strategies you can use in your NA data-gathering activities. More specifically, strategies were offered for conducting NA interviews and meetings including specific questions to ask as well as strategies for observing classes or meeting with learners. Turning to questionnaires, the chapter then explained how open-ended questions at the beginning of an NA can be turned into Likert items on questionnaires, as well as how effective and useful questionnaires can be created and administered. The chapter closed with a discussion of some of the effective ways to gather NA data on actual oral and written ESP in use.

All in all, the data-gathering part of an NA is typically time and energy consuming and quite involved. Nonetheless, the information that is gathered serves as the foundation for everything else in the NA. Indeed, such information will serve as the basis for all analyses, interpretations, results, conclusions, and suggestions for student learning outcomes. So, investing time, energy, and care in the data-gathering part of any NA is well worth all the effort.

Notes

1 *Likert* is pronounced /lɪkərt/. Also, I use the phrase *Likert item* instead of *Likert scale* for reasons that I explain at length in Brown (2011).
2 If you must answer to any sort of ethics review board, you may want to clear this strategy with them before actually using it.

Chapter 5

Analyzing and interpreting ESP needs analysis data

In this chapter, you will find answers to the following questions:

- Why should I use both quantitative and qualitative analyses?
- How can I use simple statistics like frequencies, percentages, means, and standard deviations to analyze my ESP NA numerical data? How should I present and explain my numerical results so that readers can clearly understand what they mean?
- How can I use matrices to analyze and present my ESP NA qualitative data?
- How can I use corpus analysis techniques to analyze and present my qualitative data?
- Why is triangulation important in NAs? What are nine different types of triangulation? What should I keep in mind when using triangulation?
- How can I enhance the quality of my NA results and interpretations?
- What is mixed methods research (MMR)? What are seven MMR techniques for enhancing the quality of an NA? Why should I consider using MMR in my NA?

Quantitative or qualitative analyses?

The first issue most needs analysts will face with regard to analyzing NA data is the question of what type(s) of data to analyze. As shown in earlier chapters, both quantitative and qualitative information can certainly be gathered in an NA, and most people doing NA naturally want to analyze their data in the best possible ways. The differences between quantitative and qualitative data are many. However, in the simplest terms, quantitative research tends to analyze data that are expressed as numbers, while qualitative research tends to analyze data that is expressed in words. The two research approaches clearly vary in many other possible ways, but that is beyond the scope of this chapter (see Brown, 2004, 2009, 2014 for much more discussion of these differences). I need to add that ESP NA in particular may require additional linguistic analyses, which are a different category altogether that includes some of both quantitative and qualitative thinking, as I will explain below.

Personal reflection – Should I use quantitative or qualitative analyses in my ESP NA?

Think about a group of ESP students that you teach (or some you would like to teach). What types of data will you be gathering? Will they be quantitative or qualitative, or both?

Based on the introduction above, what are the advantages of each? How have those advantages informed your choice?

Analyzing quantitative ESP NA data

In this book, the quantitative analyses will include frequencies, percentages, averages, and standard deviations. Nothing more technical will be covered here. These forms of analysis are usually sufficient for purposes of conducting NAs because they are sufficient for revealing a great deal in an NA, and they are:

- easy to calculate;
- easy to interpret;
- easy to present;
- intuitive in meaning;
- easy to explain to any educated audience;
- easy for any educated audience to understand.

In addition, numbers carry weight with many audiences (especially certain kinds of administrators) where qualitative results explained in words will not.

Frequencies and percentages

Among the easiest quantitative data, analyses, and results to use are frequencies and percentages. *Frequencies* are simply the number of something in a particular category. If you have 225 students responding to an NA survey and 97 of them are male and 128 female, the frequencies you are dealing with are 225, 97, and 128, respectively. Percentages are those same numbers expressed differently. As you probably already know, you calculate percentages by dividing each frequency in subcategories by the total of those frequencies in all categories and then multiplying by 100 (or you may have learned to move the decimal place two places to the right). So in the above example, 97 of the 225 respondents were male, or about 43 percent (97/225 = 0.4311111 or about 0.43; 0.43 × 100 = 43 percent) and 128 of the 225 respondents were female, or about 57 percent (128/225 = 0.5688888 or about 0.57; 0.57 × 100 = 57 percent). Clearly, frequencies and percentages are particularly useful for describing participants in an NA in terms of numbers and percentages of people in different categories.

For example, in their NA for second language EAP writing, Matsuda, Saenkhum, and Accardi (2013) surveyed 74 writing teachers. In describing the educational background of these teachers (see Table 5.1), the authors presented the frequencies (#) of their major fields in terms of degrees earned and major fields of studies in each. I have added the percentages (%) to the right.

Notice in the note at the bottom of Table 5.1 that Matsuda et al. (2013) felt the need to explain that the frequencies in the table added up to more than 74, which was the number of participants. Naturally, it would have been better if they could have avoided this problem, for instance by wording the question such that they respondents were asked provide only their *highest degree*. That might have avoided this confusion, and then the figures might well have added up to 74. But, it is easy to be critical of such problems after the fact. In reality, the authors found that their data and response pattern were confusing. Things do go wrong in studies. It is not the end of the world. The best strategy in such situations is to openly and honestly explain what happened in the NA report just like Matsuda et al. (2013) did.

Frequencies and percentages are also useful for showing the numbers and percentages of persons or answers in different categories. For example, Spence and Liu (2013) reported on an ESP NA study for process integration engineers

Table 5.1 Degrees and major fields of study (adapted from Matsuda, Saenkhum, & Accardi, 2013, p. 72)

Degree (n)		
Major	#	%
Doctoral degree (n = 19)		
Literature	10	52.63
Rhetoric/composition	6	31.58
Linguistics	2	10.53
Applied linguistics	1	5.26
Master's degree (n = 56)		
Literature	19	33.93
Rhetoric/composition	11	19.64
Creative writing	9	16.07
TESOL	6	10.71
Applied linguistics	2	3.57
Linguistics	1	1.79
Other	8	14.29
Bachelor's degree (n = 47)		
Literature	22	46.81
Linguistics	3	6.38
Creative writing	2	4.26
English education	1	2.13
Rhetoric/composition	1	2.13
TESOL	1	2.13
Other	17	36.17

Note: The total number of responses is greater than the number of respondents because they were asked to identify all degrees they held (rather than just the highest degree). However, some respondents only provided information about their graduate degrees.

Table 5.2 Tasks requiring English writing skills (adapted from Spence & Liu, 2013, p. 103)

Type of writing	% Daily (#)	% 2–3 times/ week (#)	% 1 time/ week (#)	% 1–3 times/ month (#)	% Never (#)
Writing emails	92.16 (47)	5.88 (3)	0.0 (0)	1.96 (1)	0.0 (0)
Writing minutes of meetings	23.5 (12)	33.3 (17)	17.6 (9)	17.6 (9)	7.8 (4)
Writing reports	49.0 (25)	31.4 (16)	15.7 (8)	2.0 (1)	2.0 (1)
Writing proposals for projects	19.6 (10)	31.4 (16)	25.5 (13)	13.7 (7)	9.8 (5)
Writing business letters	19.6 (10)	29.4 (15)	11.8 (6)	13.7 (7)	25.5 (13)
Writing memos	51.0 (26)	19.6 (10)	15.7 (8)	9.8 (5)	3.9 (2)
Writing presentation slides	21.6 (11)	29.4 (15)	29.4 (15)	15.7 (8)	3.9 (2)

Note: Bracketed number indicates number (#) of participants who selected this response.

at a company in Taiwan. Table 5.2 shows the responses for tasks that respondents reported they needed in writing English. Notice that the tasks are listed down the left side and then the percentages (%) and frequencies (#) are given in separate columns to indicate how many respondents reported needing to do each task: daily, 2–3 times per week, 1 time per week, 1–3 times per month, and never. It is easy to see that almost everyone reported writing emails in English daily (92.16 percent) and that writing memos (51 percent) and reports (49 percent) were also daily activities for many respondents. Basically, all the tasks were fairly common, but the table makes it possible to see which tasks were relatively more or less important to these respondents.

Means and standard deviations

The arithmetical average that we were all taught in school is also a useful statistic for describing all sorts of data in an NA from the average age of the participants to their average answers on Likert 1–5 sorts of items. The average that most of us are familiar with is known in most research circles as the *mean*. I will refer to it that way from now on. The mean (often symbolized simply as M) is the same in most cases as the *average*. This value is calculated, as you know, by adding up the numbers involved and dividing by the total number of values. For example, for a group of nine respondents who are 13, 14, 14, 15, 15, 15, 16, 16, and 17 years old, the mean age would be 15 (13+14+14+15+15+15+16+16+17 = 135; 135/9 = 15).

The *standard deviation* (often symbolized simply as S or SD) is another commonly reported statistic, which indicates a sort of average of the differences of each of the numbers involved from the mean. The SD is calculated by dividing the sum of the squared differences by the number of values and taking the square root of the result (see top of next page). So in this case, the SD would be 12/9 = 1.3334; then the square root is 1.1547 or about 1.15. Thus the ages in this case can be reported as having a mean of 15 and SD of 1.15.

Values −	Mean =	Difference	Squared =
13 −	15 =	−2	4
14 −	15 =	−1	1
14 −	15 =	−1	1
15 −	15 =	0	0
15 −	15 =	0	0
15 −	15 =	0	0
16 −	15 =	+1	1
16 −	15 =	+1	1
17 −	15 =	+2	4
			Sum = 12

If all of that seems a bit hard to follow, just remember that the *SD* was defined above as "a sort of average of the differences of the values from the mean" and use the *Excel* spreadsheet that you probably already have available to calculate the mean and *SD*. A spreadsheet is a program designed to help you manipulate numbers and calculate various sorts of things, like means and standard deviations. A spreadsheet is made up of columns (with letter labels like A, B, and C) and rows (with number labels like 1, 2, and 3). For example, consider Figure 5.1, which shows the upper left corner of my Excel spreadsheet. The squares inside the spreadsheet are called cells, and they each have a unique address corresponding to their column and row labels (for example, the cell in the upper left corner of the spreadsheet is cell A1 and the one to the right of it is B1).

I will next show you the process of calculating means and standard deviations. To begin with, look at Figure 5.1 and notice that I labeled two columns as Ages (in cell B1) and Grade (in cell C1). I then put some numbers below those headings (Ages: 13, 14, 14, 15, 15, 15, 16, 16, and 17 in cells B2 to B10; and Grade: 8, 8, 8, 9, 9, 9, 10, 10, and 11 in cells C2 to C10) to simulate data in an NA.

To calculate the mean, I started in cell B11 just below the Ages data, where I typed =average(b2:b10) and hit the <enter> key, which told the computer that I wanted to do something (=) in cell b11; what I wanted to do was to calculate the mean (average) for the numbers in the range () from cell b2 to b10 (b2:b10), and the computer did exactly what I told it to do with the result being 15.00.

To calculate the *SD*, I began in cell B12 two cells below the Ages data, by typing =stdevp(b2:b10) and hit the <enter> key, which told the computer that I wanted to do something (=) in cell b12; what I wanted to do was to calculate the *SD* for the numbers in the range () from cell b2 to b10 (b2:b10), and the computer did exactly what I told it to do with the result being 1.15.

Next, I copied cells B11 and B12 and pasted them into cells C11 and C12 (see Figure 5.2) and the result was a mean of 9.11 and standard deviation of 0.99 for Grade. This brief demonstration just gives you a taste for how a spreadsheet program can help you analyze your quantitative data. For more help with using Excel to do quantitative analyses with examples from our field, see Brown (2001, 2005a, 2014) or Carr (2008, 2011).

Figure 5.1 Initial spreadsheet layout.

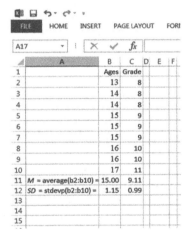

Figure 5.2 Calculating means and standard deviations in a spreadsheet.

Task 5.1 Analyzing quantitative ESP NA data

I find the best way to enter data into my Excel spreadsheet program is with a partner. One person can read each number while the other enters it into the spreadsheet, and then both can look up to check that the number was entered correctly. Then the whole process is repeated over and over and over. If the data set is large, switching roles occasionally may help avoid fatigue and inaccuracy.

(Continued)

(Continued)

On your personal computer or in a computer lab, work with a partner (if possible). Start by opening the Excel spreadsheet program that is found on many if not most computers nowadays. Together follow these steps:

1   Look at Figure 5.2 and copy the labels at the top of columns B and C and the data shown in rows 2 to 10 in those two columns.
2   Then label the mean in cell A11 as *Mean* and calculate the mean in cell B11 using the *=average* function shown in Figure 5.2. Did you get the same answer I did (15.00)?
3   Next, label the standard deviation in cell A12 as *SD* and calculate the standard deviation in cell B12 using the *=stdevp* function shown in Figure 5.2. Did you get the same answer I did (1.15)?
4   Now, block copy cells B11 and B12 to cells C11 and C12. Did you get the same answers I did (9.11 and 0.99)?
5   Now change one of the data points in either column to a different number. Did the *mean* and *SD* for that column change?
6   Try calculating these statistics for a data set of your own. Also try using Excel's help screens to figure out how to calculate other statistics. Play as much as you like, you will not break Excel.

Now for a real-life example, consider a table describing some of the answers from Litticharoenporn's (2014) NA for oral English as a foreign language at an international school in Thailand. Notice that she is describing the answers to questions about the relative importance of six aspects of oral English. She also shows the frequency of respondents who selected each option 1, 2, 3, or 4 and the *M* and *SD*.

Table 5.3 Teachers' views on relative importance of six aspects of oral English

Item	1	2	3	4	M	SD
1 Pronunciation/intonation/stress patterns of American English	0	5	22	9	3.11	0.62
2 Lecture note taking	2	8	25	1	2.69	0.62
3 General listening comprehension (besides formal lectures)	0	0	13	23	3.64	0.49
4 Ability to give formal speeches/presentations; ability to participate effectively in class discussions	0	2	24	10	3.22	0.54
5 Ability to communicate effectively with peers in small-group discussions, collaborative projects, or out-of-class study groups	0	0	10	26	3.72	0.45
6 Ability to communicate effectively with teacher in or out of class	0	1	13	22	3.58	0.55

Note: 1 = very unimportant, 2 = unimportant, 3 = important, 4 = very important.

Task 5.2 Interpreting the quantitative ESP NA analyses of colleagues

Look at Table 5.3 and answer the following questions:

1   For the means, which of the six oral English skills do the teachers in this study feel is the most important? (That would be #5 with the highest mean of 3.72, right?)
2   How many teachers thought that oral skill (item #5) was *very important* and how many thought it was *important*? (26 & 10, right?)
3   And which do the teachers think is the least important? (That would be #2 with the lowest mean of 2.69, right?)
4   Looking now at the *SD*s, which of the skills were the teachers most in agreement about? (That would be #5 with the lowest *SD* of 0.45, right?)
5   What do you think determines how big the *SD* is? (Notice that for both #3 and #5, which have the lowest *SD*s, all of the teachers selected either 4 or 5 for *important* or *very important*. Where the *SD*s are higher, you can see that the responses are spread over more options, like #2 where all four options were selected by someone.

Did you notice that answering my questions about the means and *SD*s in Table 5.3 in Task 5.2 was very straightforward and simply relied on common sense? Your interpretations of such descriptive statistics should do just the same.

Analyzing qualitative ESP NA data

In this section, I will explore some of the basic techniques for analyzing qualitative data including various sorts of matrices (for example, effects matrices and site dynamics matrices) and different general computer tools and software available for analyzing qualitative data.

Using matrixes for analyzing ESP NA qualitative data

Based on the work of Lynch (1997) and Miles and Huberman (1984, 1994),[1] I have become an inveterate believer in and user of matrices to help in the process of analyzing qualitative data. They can help in discovering patterns, analyzing and thinking about those patterns, revising such patterns, and ultimately in reporting the patterns in research papers and reports, including those for NAs. A *matrix* in this context "is a table, grid, or array used to display data in two dimensions. Typically, one set of categories will be labeled across the top of the matrix and another set labeled down the left side of the matrix" (Brown, 2014, p. 94).

Types of matrices

One type of matrix is an effects matrix. Table 5.4 presents an example of an effects matrix, which displays the issues brought up with regard to three curriculum issues labeled across the top (objectives, tests, and materials) by three groups of teachers (in the schools labeled down the left side). Their views are described/summarized inside the matrix. Notice how clearly the data are displayed and sorted so that they can be analyzed, understood, and reported.

Miles and Huberman (1984, pp. 95–121) discuss six types of matrices in depth: checklist, time-ordered, conceptually clustered, role-ordered, effects, and site-dynamics matrices. All six are shown in Table 5.5 with the type of matrix in the first column, a description of the two dimensions typically involved in the second, and an example of what the matrix is useful for in the third. Notice that Table 5.5 is itself a matrix – one that compares six different types of matrices in terms of the dimensions they show and how they can be useful in qualitative analyses (for more on these six types of matrices, see Brown, 2014, pp. 94–102).

Table 5.4 An example of an effects matrix for groups by issues

Groups	Curriculum issues		
	Objectives	Tests	Materials
ESL Teachers at McNamara Adult Ed School	Think objectives should be can-do lists	Want tests of what they learn	Want fun and colorful materials that teach grammar and vocabulary
ESL Teachers at KPIS Center for Adult Ed	Want objectives that are statements describing what students will be able to do at end of course	Want tests of the objectives with separate scores reported for each objective	Need lesson plans that will help them set up communicative activities
ESL Teachers at McKinley High night school	Want to see formal student learning outcomes (also known as SLOs)	Want tests based on SLOs that can be used for pass–fail decisions	Want materials that are durable and not too expensive

Table 5.5 Six types of matrices

Type of matrix	Dimensions: Example	Useful for
Effects matrix	Groups of people or institutions by outcomes or effects: groups (students, teachers, and administrators) by curriculum issues (objectives, tests, materials), as in Table 5.4	Useful for uncovering or displaying various outcomes or effects from the different perspectives of groups
Site-dynamic matrix	Outcomes or effects by processes or dynamics: objectives/tests/materials by how groups differed, problems that arose, and how they changed	Useful for uncovering or displaying the processes or dynamics of change that underlie various outcomes or effects
Checklist matrix	Presence of conditions or components by groups of people or institutions: components (numbers of ESL students, ESL teachers, & ESL classes) by school (Kennedy, Lincoln, and Taft schools)	Useful for revealing or displaying presence of components or conditions in different institutions or groups of people
Time-ordered matrix	Phenomena or processes by when they occurred: school phenomena (% attendance, class size, and teacher absenteeism) by month (Jan, Feb, Mar, Apr, May, June)	Useful for revealing and displaying when particular processes or phenomena have occurred
Conceptually clustered matrix	Groups or institutions by conceptual categories that cohere: groups (7th-, 8th-, and 9th-grade students) by mental characteristics (attitudes, motivation, and anxiety)	Useful for revealing and displaying how groups or institutions differ in conceptual categories that go together
Role-ordered matrix	Role-based groups by issues: role groups (students, teachers, and administrators) by issues (tests, materials, and teaching)	Useful for revealing and displaying the different views of role groups on various issues of interest

Looking for patterns in matrices

Lynch (1997, pp. 84–87) analyzed his effects matrix by looking at the data for three distinct types of patterns: general patterns, specific difference patterns, and specific similarity patterns.

Seeing *general patterns* involves reading through the data set a few times, considering the entire data set as a whole, and summarizing it in your mind. For example, in Table 5.4 above, after I read it through several times, I noticed two general patterns: (a) that the three groups of teachers are more or less in agreement about objectives and tests, but diverge considerably in their views about materials; and (b) that some form of objectives is important to all three groups, even in testing.

In the process of seeing general patterns, you may also want to think about the data from the perspective of *specific difference patterns*. For instance, in Table 5.4, I noticed that the three groups of teachers diverged considerably in their views about materials. They also diverged in the labels that they gave to course objectives with two groups calling them objectives and one labeling them student learning outcomes (SLOs).

In addition, to searching for general and specific difference patterns, you may benefit from thinking about the data in terms of *specific similarity patterns*. For example, looking again at Table 5.4, you may have noticed that, though the three groups of teachers used different labels for objectives, they agreed that objectives were important in their own right and as a basis for testing. You may not always find that all three perspectives (general patterns, differences, and similarities) yield insights in every data set, but it is worth looking for them just the same.

Personal reflection – Should I use matrices to analyze the qualitative in my ESP NA?

Think about a group of ESP students that you teach (or some you would like to teach). What types of matrices might you want to use in analyzing their qualitative data (effects matrix, site-dynamic matrix, checklist matrix, time-ordered matrix, conceptually clustered matrix, or role-ordered matrix)? Why did you choose the ones you did? How will you set out to look for general patterns, specific difference patterns, and specific similarity patterns?

Using general computer tools for analyzing ESP NA qualitative data

Any discussion of analyzing qualitative data needs to at least mention some of the computer tools available for coding, sorting, and analyzing qualitative data. Fortunately, there is a central website that not only reviews a number of these computer tools, but also supplies information that should help you choose which, if any, you might want to pursue. It is called the *Computer Assisted Qualitative Data Analysis* (CAQDAS) website, and it can be found at http://www.surrey.ac.uk/sociology/research/researchcentres/ caqdas/support/. At the current time, CAQDAS reviews the following:

- ATLAS.ti (http://www.atlasti.com/)
- Dedoose (http://www.dedoose.com/)
- Digital Replay System (DRS) (http://thedrs.sourceforge.net/)
- HyperRESEARCH (http://www.researchware.com/)
- MAXQDA (http://www.maxqda.com/)
- Mixed Media Grid (MiMeG) (http://sourceforge.net/projects/mimeg/)
- QSRNvivo (http://www.qsrinternational.com/)
- Transana (http://www.transana.org/)
- QDA Miner (http://provalisresearch.com/)
- Qualrus (http://www.qualrus.com/)

If you are looking for software that is specifically designed for *language* research, you might like *TalkBank* (http://talkbank.org/), which has software designed for conversational analysis of data like that found in *CLAN* (http://childes.psy.cmu.edu/clan/). There are also a number of concordancing programs, but I will cover those in the next main section.

Naturally, new computer-based analytical tools are surfacing on a regular basis. A quick search of the Internet will lead you to the latest available software and the latest versions of the programs listed above. However, my advice on such software in Brown (2014) is probably germane here as well:

> [M]y experience with such tools is that they generally have a fairly steep initial learning curve and must be relearned each time they are used if they are only used occasionally. They are therefore often not worth the required effort for researchers who are doing one-off, small-scale projects, or who only do research occasionally. If, on the other hand, you are planning to do research for the rest of your life and want to use such software regularly, the time and effort you will need to put into learning how to use the software may ultimately save you enormous amounts of time and effort in the future.
>
> (p. 50)

Using specific computer software tools for analyzing ESP NA corpora

In the previous chapter, I showed how easy it is to find corpora of ESP written texts and spoken discourse. And, of course, those texts can be used for developing reading and listening materials or for models of how a particular ESP is commonly written or spoken. However, analytical tools can be applied to those corpora that may prove very useful for ESP NA, for ESP teachers, or even for ESP students. Some of the cheapest (because they are free) and easiest to use are these four:

- *The Compleat Lexical Tutor* – a free website that contains a variety of relatively easy to use vocabulary and corpus tools (see http://www. lextutor.ca/); includes the *Corpus Concordance English* at http:// lextutor.ca/conc/eng/); and the *User Text Concordance* that lets you copy any text you like into it at http://www.lextutor.ca/conc/text/.
- *WebCorp: Concordance the web in realtime* – a free website that lets you generate word lists for any website as long as you know the website's address (URL); found at http://www.webcorp.org.uk/live/wdlist.jsp.
- *Wordle – Beautiful Word Clouds!* – a free website that lets you generate word clouds from vocabulary lists or other text; found at http://www. wordle.net/.
- *AntConc* – a free software program that is fairly easy to use; downloadable from http://www.laurenceanthony.net/software.html; useful help can also be found at http://research.ncl.ac.uk/decte/ toon/assets/docs/AntConc_Guide.pdf, or http://www.youtube.com/ watch?v=O3ukHC3fyuc.

Each of these computer tools has great potential for analyzing spoken and written corpora in an ESP NA, as I will demonstrate next.

The Compleat Lexical Tutor

I will first show how the *The Compleat Lexical Tutor* (http://www.lextutor. ca/conc/text/) can be used to analyze ESP texts. In the previous chapter, I showed how to find and download a public domain article from *Today in Energy* (retrieved later on December 20, 2014 at http://www.eia.gov/ todayinenergy/detail.cfm?id=19231) entitled *Using the public domain article OPEC net oil export revenues expected to fall in 2014 and 2015*. Using *The Compleat Lexical Tutor*, I block copied the text from the article and pasted it into the space provided (see Figure 5.3). After pressing the *submit* button (at the bottom of the screen shown in Figure 5.3), the analysis looked (after a bit of exploration) like Figure 5.4. Notice that the analysis provides a list of the vocabulary items in the text to the left along with the frequency of each item. Such a list can be very useful in an NA (especially if done across a large number of texts in the ESP) for determining what specialized vocabulary the students are likely to need to know because it is very common (that is, high frequency).

However, ESP is far more than specialized vocabulary. Among other things, ESP must consider grammar. The analysis to the right in Figure 5.4 is called a concordance. Concordances allow you to line up vocabulary items (or phrases) so that you or your students can examine what sorts of words precede and follow those vocabulary items. This can be useful in many ways. For example, I noticed in Figure 5.4, that the word *average*, which

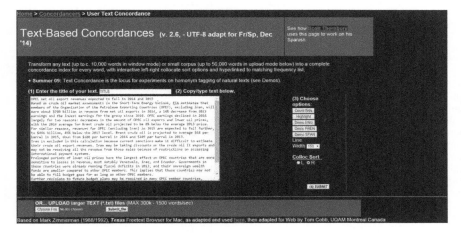

Figure 5.3 Copying text into *The Compleat Lexical Tutor.*

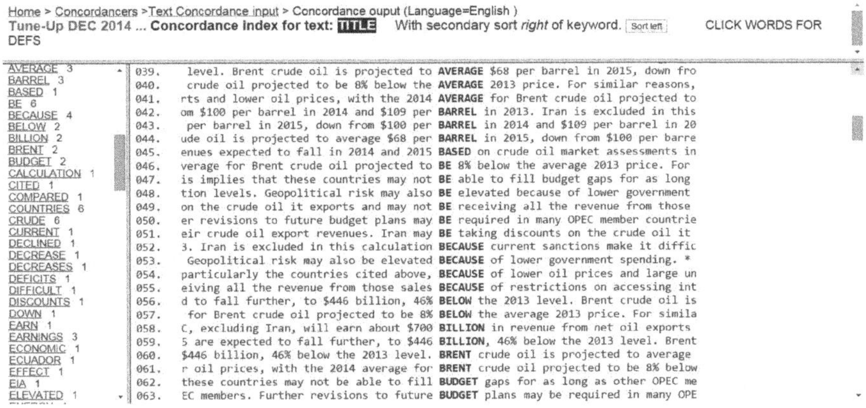

Figure 5.4 Analysis that resulted from *The Compleat Lexical Tutor.*

had a frequency of 3, was used as a noun and as a verb. And so perhaps the students need to learn that fact in this ESP, that is, that *average* is not only a noun, but like many nouns, it can also function as a verb.

However, the word *barrel*, which appears three times, is only used in the phrase frame *$xxx per barrel*, so perhaps the students will need to learn that phrase as a chunk. Notice that *Brent* appears twice, but only as *Brent crude oil*. That is some specialized vocabulary that might need to be looked up and perhaps taught as a phrase. And so forth. Do you see how useful this sort of analysis might be for an ESP NA?

Word	#	Word	#	Word	#	Word	#	Word	#
design	30	scheme	8	graph	5	time	4	recommendations	3
task	25	tasks	8	hour	5	work	4	reduce	3
table	24	approach	7	implementation	5	years	4	reduced	3
year	24	hours	7	meet	5	considered	3	regarding	3
figure	23	labor	7	michigan	5	copyright	3	regents	3
production	23	manufacturer	7	shift	5	create	3	required	3
reliability	23	operators	7	sold	5	day	3	results	3
system	19	process	7	state	5	determined	3	rpw	3
manufacturing	18	seen	7	added	4	flow	3	simple	3
designs	16	throughput	7	analysis	4	given	3	statement	3
assembly	14	two	7	breakdown	4	goal	3	student	3
station	14	units	7	buf	4	impact	3	university	3
machine	12	weeks	7	cars	4	implemented	3	uses	3
pams	12	costs	6	corpus	4	lastly	3		
demand	10	precedence	6	daily	4	lean	3		
line	10	profit	6	decreased	4	made	3		
number	10	same	6	discussed	4	micusp	3		
order	10	section	6	first	4	million	3		
stations	10	three	6	following	4	mtbf	3		
car	9	used	6	map	4	mttr	3		
information	9	using	6	page	4	operation	3		
shown	9	assumptions	5	parallel	4	paper	3		
buffers	8	buffer	5	shifts	4	plant	3		
cost	8	components	5	simulation	4	possible	3		
scenarios	8	future	5	size	4	rate	3		

Figure 5.5 Word frequency list produced using *WebCorp* for the mechanical engineering text.

WebCorp

WebCorp (http://www.webcorp.org.uk/live/wdlist.jsp) can also be used to produce word counts, but what makes it particularly useful is that it can do so for websites, any websites. As a result, you need not even copy the text, but can simply refer to the URL of any websites containing the ESP you need to analyze. For example, I entered the URL (that is, http://micusp.elicorpora. info/search/view/?pid=MEC.G0.03.1) for the mechanical engineering text that I collected in the previous chapter entitled *Manufacturing system design for a car assembly process*. After I pressed the *submit* button, *WebCorp* provided me with a word list (one which usefully eliminated all the function words like *the*, *and*, *of*, and so forth). I then trimmed out numbers and all words with frequencies (#) of 2 or less and produced the list shown in Figure 5.5.

Wordle – Beautiful Word Clouds!

Wordle – Beautiful Word Clouds! (http://www.wordle.net/.)[2] can transform word counts or text into attractive word clouds. Again, using the mechanical engineering text described above and in the previous chapter, I was able to easily create one for the many word cloud possibilities available at that website (see Figure 5.6). This word cloud not only shows the vocabulary in

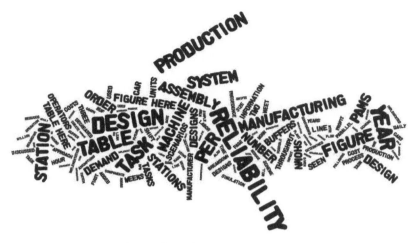

Figure 5.6 Word cloud for mechanical engineering text.

the passage, but does so in such a way that the size of the words is related to their relative frequencies, that is, the larger the words are the more frequent they are. Thus, *reliability*, *design*, *table*, *task*, *per*, and *year* appear to be very frequent and probably important to consider, while *station*, *assembly*, *production*, *system*, *manufacturing*, and *figure* are a bit less frequent, and so on.

AntConc

AntConc (http://www.laurenceanthony.net/software.html) is a software package that is also fairly easy to use. Once again using the mechanical engineering passage, I used *AntConc* to create a word list. Again, I trimmed numbers out and any words with frequencies of two or less to create the word list shown in Figure 5.7.

Notice that, unlike the word list created with *WebCorp*, the function words are included when *AntConc* counts. Notice also that the counts here are slightly different from those given by *WebCorp*. For example, here *design* has a frequency of 29, while in *WebCorp* it was 30. I am hard pressed to explain such differences, except to say that the various programs use different algorithms with different criteria for counting. Nonetheless, the relative standing of the various vocabulary items is very similar.

While word lists are fine in their way, I also wanted to see how particular vocabulary items were used in context. For example, I wanted to see how the most common content word, *design*, was used in this text, so I used *AntConc* to create a concordance for the same mechanical engineering file on the word *design*. The result of this analysis is shown in Figure 5.8. Notice that the word *design* is mostly used as a noun and indeed as a capitalized

Freq	Word	Freq	Word	Freq	Word	Freq	Word	Freq	Word	Freq	Word
131	the	16	with	8	on	5	assumptions	4	map	3	lastly
71	of	15	as	8	scenarios	5	been	4	one	3	lean
69	and	14	assembly	8	scheme	5	buffer	4	page	3	made
60	to	14	station	8	tasks	5	future	4	parallel	3	million
56	in	13	below	8	that	5	graph	4	shifts	3	mtbf
42	for	13	can	8	two	5	have	4	simulation	3	mttr
41	a	13	were	7	approach	5	hour	4	size	3	only
29	design	12	machine	7	labor	5	implementation	4	sub	3	operation
25	table	12	pams	7	manufacturer	5	meet	4	which	3	or
25	task	11	this	7	operators	5	section	4	while	3	plant
25	we	11	will	7	our	5	shift	4	work	3	possible
25	xa	10	demand	7	seen	5	sold	4	would	3	rate
23	figure	10	line	7	throughput	5	state	4	years	3	recommendations
23	production	10	number	7	units	5	time	3	all	3	reduce
23	reliability	10	order	7	weeks	5	used	3	also	3	reduced
23	year	10	stations	6	components	4	added	3	any	3	regarding
21	each	9	shown	6	costs	4	analysis	3	considered	3	results
19	be	8	after	6	first	4	breakdown	3	create	3	rpw
19	system	8	are	6	it	4	buf	3	determined	3	should
17	here	8	at	6	precedence	4	by	3	flow	3	simple
17	is	8	buffers	6	process	4	cars	3	following	3	under
17	manufacturing	8	car	6	profit	4	daily	3	given	3	uses
17	was	8	cost	6	same	4	day	3	goal	3	well
16	designs	8	hours	6	three	4	decreased	3	impact		
16	per	8	information	6	using	4	discussed	3	implemented		

Figure 5.7 Wordlist created with *AntConc* for the mechanical engineering text.

proper noun in many cases to label various specific designs (for example, Design #1, Design #2, and so forth). However, it is used as a verb in one instance (see the second row of Figure 5.8) showing the need to teach the fact that nouns can function in several ways, and even transform sometimes into verbs. Notice also the phrases *design scenarios* and *design Table* in the first and last rows, respectively, where design is functioning as an adjective or compound of some sort. ESP students may need to understand these varying uses of the word *design* in their ESP. I hope you can see how these forms of analysis are well worth considering in an ESP NA.

For more on using computers in specific purposes language teaching, see Bloch (2013), and various chapters in the Marcia, Cervera, and Ramos (2006) edited collection. Also for information about using corpus studies in ESP, see Flowerdew (2011).

Task 5.3 Analyzing ESO NA samples of ESP use online

With a partner, divide up the following so that, using different data sets, each of you has committed to using different websites and software as follows:

1   On your personal computer or in a computer lab, visit one of the following websites and find a sample of language use in the ESP that interests you.
2   Copy that text into a Word file. Recall from the previous chapter that the following websites may prove useful:

http://en.wikipedia.org/wiki/Wikipedia:Public_domain_resources
http://www.eia.gov/ and http://www.eia.gov/about/copyrights_reuse.cfm
http://micusp.elicorpora.info/
http://quod.lib.umich.edu/m/micase/

3   Using *The Compleat Lexical Tutor, WebCorp: Concordance the web in realtime*, or *AntConc* described above, create a word list for your ESP language use file.
4   Now create a concordance for that same file.
5   Look at your word list and concordance results and jot down anything you notice about them. For example, what words are most frequent (in the word list)? Are those frequent words always the same part of speech (in the concordance)? Are any of the words used repeatedly in the same phrases?
6   With your partner, share what you learned from creating and analyzing the word list and concordance. Also discuss and jot down the ways you think such analyses might be useful for doing an ESP NA and later for creating the materials and teaching the resulting course.

#		
1	FigurexA0here Manufacturing System	Design for a Car Assembly Process EXECUTIVE
2	STATEMENT We have been tasked to	design the manufacturing system for the assembly
3	/week, 49 to 51* weeks/year * Varies with	design scenarios Manufacturing Operations 2. Inspe
4	machine 5. Each station used has 95% efficiency	(Design #2 & Design #3) 6. Failure of one machine d
5	Each station used has 95% efficiency	(Design #2 & Design #3) 6. Failure of one machine does not
6	section. 4 TASK ANALYSIS In order to	design the manufacturing system for this applicati
7	line schematic was generated for each	design and is shown in Figures 3 and 4,
8	the manufacturer. The space occupied for	Design 1 is 972 m2, while Designs 2 and 3 occupy 1
9	0here Figure 3: Production Line Scheme for	Design #1 FigurexA0here Figure 4: Production Line
10	0here Figure 4: Production Line Scheme for	Design #2 & #3 5 DESIGNS This section outlines the
11	were performed for the manufacturing process	design. The results of RPW can be
12	year and fulfill the requirements of	Design 2, without implementing a second assembly l
13	the production goal of 75,000 units for	Design 3, a third shift can be added
14	work with the same reliability of	Design 2. The production outcome and labor hours
15	outcome and labor hours of each	design can be seen in Table 5, below.
16	be seen in Table 6, below. Each	design requires 7 stations to be constructed, whil
17	to exceed the initial investment cost.	Design 3 will be profitable from the first
18	is $14,800 for Designs 1 and 2, and $14,480 for	Design 3.\xA04. The cost of marketing the
19	that were produced were sold. Table 7:	Design 3 because of the quantity needed to
20	first two Designs, but greater for	Design 3 will be profitable after 1 year, Designs
21	* This price is decreased to $14,480 to	Design 3, because of the quantity sold 6 CONCLUSIO
22	were asked to create a process	design for the assembly of a car
23	50,000 unit demand per year for scenario 1,	Design 1 can be implemented. This entails operatin
24	the same task assignment order. Specifically,	Design 2 uses two 6 hour daily shifts for 49
25	shown in Figure 4, on page 9. Lastly,	Design 3 uses three 6 hour daily shifts for 49
26	calculations. Iterative Approach in PAMS System	Design We initially created a 7 station system
27	shown in Table 4, on page 10. For	Design 1 with 100% efficiency, we achieved our exp
28	in Figure 7 below. Throughput for each	design can be seen in Table 8, below.
29	8: Throughputs using PAMS simulation for each	design TablexA0here

Figure 5.8 Concordance created with AntConc for the mechanical engineering text.

Triangulation

One important tool for analyzing data in an NA is *triangulation*. As Long (2005a) put it, *triangulation* "involves the researchers comparing different sets and sources of data with one another ... to increase the credibility of their data and thereby, eventually, to increase the credibility of their interpretations of those data" (p. 28). Triangulation is a research strategy that has been applied in a number of NAs over the years (for examples see Bosher & Smalkoski, 2002; Cowling, 2007; Gilabert, 2005; Holme & Chalauisaeng, 2006; Jasso-Aguilar, 1999, 2005; Kikuchi, 2001, 2004; Wozniak, 2010; or Zhu & Flaitz, 2005). Using triangulation can substantially increase the quality and dependability of an NA, or as Long (2005a) put it, "It is difficult to overemphasize the likelihood that use of *multiple measures,* as well as multiple sources, will increase the quality of information gathered, whether or not the findings are used for triangulation by methods" (p. 32).

In Brown (2014, pp. 20–21), I found that many different authors writing about triangulation had listed 3, 4, or 5 types different types of triangulation. Looking at those lists side by side and reflecting on my own experience, I managed to come up with a list of nine types of triangulation (that is, stakeholder, method, location, time, perspective, investigator, theory, interdisciplinary, and participant-role). I am sure at least some of them will prove useful in your NA. In more detail, those nine (with considerable adaptation for ESP NA purposes) are as follows:

- *Stakeholder triangulation* – Including multiple stakeholders as sources of information (for example, EAP students, teachers, and administrators).
- *Method triangulation* (also called *overlapping methods*) – Analyzing multiple data gathering procedures (for instance, interviews, meetings, and questionnaires in an EOP setting).
- *Location triangulation* – Examining data from multiple sites (such as business English NA data at a bank, a retail store, and a business office).
- *Time triangulation* (also called *stepwise replications*) – Scrutinizing data from different points of time (for example, data gathered at the beginning, middle, and end of a semester or school year in an EAP setting).
- *Perspective triangulation* (especially *negative case analysis*) – Using multiple perspectives to analyze data (for instance, a positive and negative viewpoints).
- *Investigator triangulation* (also called *inquiry audits* or *peer debriefing*) – Having three needs analysts examine the same data independently.
- *Theory triangulation* – Examining the data from three theoretical perspectives (such as error analysis theory, task-based theory, and learning theory).

- *Interdisciplinary triangulation* – Examining the data from the perspective of three academic fields (for example, linguistics, language pedagogy, and the ESP content area)
- *Participant-role triangulation* (especially with *member checking*) – Needs analysts switching roles with other stakeholders at a certain point (for instance, the students or teachers become the needs analysts).

I have most often used and seen others use *stakeholder* and *method* triangulation in ESP NAs, followed by occasional location, time, perspective, and investigator triangulation. I don't recall ever finding theory, interdisciplinary, or participant-role triangulation in an actual ESP NA study. However, that does not mean that those three could never be useful in an NA.

Whatever combinations of different perspectives, sources, or data types you choose to triangulate in your NA, they will work better together if you use the following strategies:

- Judiciously limit the number of types of triangulation you will use so you do not end up with too much data to analyze properly. At the same time, make sure that you have enough types of triangulation so that you can benefit substantially from having multiple data sources. Clearly, using all nine types of triangulation would bury any needs analysts in data for the rest of their lives (after all, $3 \times 3 \times 3 \times 3 \times 3 \times 3 \times 3 \times 3 \times 3 = 59,049$), but using only one type of triangulation may not be enough to be of much value. This first choice of how many types of triangulation to use and how much data to gather will depend on the size of the organization involved, the resources available, the number of people who can help, and the importance of the NA.
- Carefully select the types of triangulation you will use so you include key stakeholder groups, data-gathering techniques, and so forth. For example, it is important to insure that the strengths of some groups or techniques can compensate for weaknesses in other groups or techniques, or as Huberman and Miles (1994) suggested, "pick triangulation sources that have different biases, different strengths, so they can complement one another" (p. 438).
- Prudently sequence the procedures and triangulation in such a way that each step builds on what you have learned in the previous steps because "carefully sequenced use of two or more procedures can be expected to produce better quality information" (Long, 2005a, p. 33). For instance, using interviews–meetings–questionnaires in that sequence may make much more sense than using the sequence questionnaires–meetings–interviews, especially if the needs analysts can use the initial interviews to figure out what questions to ask in the meetings and then what they

learn in the meetings to decide what questions they need to address more broadly in the questionnaires.

- Carefully check to make sure your triangulation is based in well-grounded theory. Such theory need not be any more complicated or fancy than the ideas considered in this book. In fact, your triangulation should be both feasible and sensible. But to a considerable degree, having a well-grounded and clearly explained theoretical perspective can help overcome criticisms of bias on the part of the needs analysts. For example, in a sort of circular way, grounding an ESP NA in say communicative and task-based theory up front could head off criticisms that everything is biased in favor of communicative and task-based language teaching.

- Nonetheless, thoroughly scrutinize the degree to which your own preconceptions or biases may have affected what data and triangulation types you have chosen and your interpretations of the resulting data. For example, three needs analysts may have different viewpoints on what communicative language teaching is and those individual preconceptions might affect or bias the parts of the NA they are in charge of. Such differences should be recognized and discussed as early as possible in the NA process.

- Finally, carefully consider the degree to which you may have been influenced by interesting, salient, or even exotic data. For example, in the qualitative data from a questionnaire, if only 8 percent of the student respondents wrote something in the open-ended questions, you would be wise to ask yourself if you are relying too much on those responses because, as a language teacher, you tend to be more attracted to the words (produced by only 8 percent) rather than to the numbers (produced in the Likert items by 98 percent of the students). It is also important to ask if the 8 percent who answered the open-ended questions might not tend to be complainers and negative, while the other 92 percent are more-or-less satisfied.

Personal reflection – What are the characteristics of your ESP NA?

Think about a group of ESP students that you teach (or some you would like to teach). What three types of triangulation do you think might make the most sense for your NA? Why did you choose those three? What issues did I warn about that you should keep in mind about triangulation while using it? How might the strengths in one of those three forms of triangulation help to counteract weaknesses in another form?

Enhancing and corroborating the quality of NA results and interpretations

Long (2005a) contended that *"all* approaches to NA, new or old, could benefit from some serious work on issues of reliability and validity" (p. 22). I agree, but I would frame the issues differently. I have argued elsewhere (Brown, 2004, 2009) that quantitative researchers should try to enhance and corroborate the reliability, validity, replicability, and generalizability of their research methods, data, results, and interpretations, and that similarly, qualitative researchers should try to enhance and corroborate the dependability, credibility, confirmability, and transferability of their research methods, data, results, and interpretations.

In actually performing NAs, I have come to realize that NAs generally lend themselves more to using qualitative research methods than to quantitative methods. Indeed, a number of other needs analysts have consciously favored and applied qualitative methods (Courtney, 1988; Holliday, 1995; Jasso-Aguilar, 1999, 2005; Sawyer 2001), while others may have done so without even thinking about it because qualitative methods are so important in curriculum work generally. I would even venture to say that most needs analysts rely on qualitative data and results more than they would realize (or admit). Certainly, questionnaires with Likert items are often used in NAs, but careful analysis of many NA studies will reveal that only simple descriptive statistics (for example, frequencies, percentages, means, and standard deviations) have been used in most cases. Moreover, those simple statistics are very often interpreted in relationship to qualitative data like interviews, meetings, classroom observations, and open-ended items on questionnaires.

In short, I have come to believe that NAs are typically and perhaps appropriately qualitative in terms of the methodology applied. Hence, framing NAs in qualitative terms rather than quantitative ones might be most beneficial in most cases. It follows then that enhancing and corroborating the quality of an NA might best be generally framed in qualitative terms of dependability, confirmability, credibility, and transferability as shown in Table 5.6.

Table 5.6 (a) lists each of these four terms in the first column, then (b) defines them in the second column, (c) suggests types of triangulation or other techniques that can be used to enhance an NA with regard to each of the techniques, and (d) provides a definition or explanatory example for each technique. Thus Table 5.6 is meant to stand alone, and I will not explain it further.

At this point, I should clarify what I mean by *enhance* and *corroborate* in that table. What I am saying here is that you can use this table to help you enhance the quality of your project by planning in advance how you will use some of the techniques in the last column to enhance the dependability,

Table 5.6 Key concepts for enhancing or corroborating the quality of needs analyses (combined and adapted from Brown 2009, p. 283; Brown, 2014, pp. 120–121)

Concept	Definition	Enhanced or corroborated by
Dependability	Consistency of observations, effects of changes over time in a study, and so forth. that help better comprehend and describe the NA context being studied	Method triangulation (for example, looking for ways that information from methods overlaps or diverges) Time triangulation (for instance, exploring ways that information stays constant or changes over time. Investigator triangulation type one (for example, examining how interpretations converge or diverge across researchers in an NA)
Credibility	Fidelity of identifying and describing important aspects of a NA context especially as represented by various viewpoints within that context	Prolonged engagement (doing an NA over a relatively long period of time) Persistent observations (gathering NA data repeatedly and often) Stakeholder triangulation (for instance, gathering data from students, teachers, and administrators) Investigator triangulation type two (for example, presenting result to peers outside the NA for feedback and evaluation) Perspective triangulation (for example, including negative and positive case analysis) Participant-role triangulation (switching stakeholder and needs analyst roles, especially asking stakeholders for feedback and evaluation of interpretations as they surface)
Confirmability	Verifiability of the data that serve as the basis of interpretations in the NA	Keeping records and data from the NA so they can be audited Making those records and data available to NA readers/consumers
Transferability	Meaningfulness of the NA results and their applicability to all appropriate contexts	Provide a clear and detailed description of the context, the data collection, the analyses, the results, and the interpretations to NA readers/consumers

credibility, confirmability, and transferability of your NA. For example, if an NA is designed to gather three types of information like interviews, observations, and questionnaires (that is, method triangulation), from students, teachers, and administrators (that is, stakeholder triangulation), perhaps without knowing it, the needs analysts may have enhanced the *dependability* and *credibility* of their NA, respectively. If they also take the simple steps of keeping and storing their NA records and data and making them available to NA report readers/consumers, the *confirmability* of the NA will have been enhanced. If, in addition, the needs analysts provide a clear and detailed description in their NA report of the context, the data collection, the analyses, the results, and the interpretations to NA readers/consumers, they have enhanced the *transferability* of their NA. Adding other strategies from the last column in Table 5.6 would not be necessary, but may in fact further enhance the dependability and credibility of the NA.

Consider how effective it would be if a group of needs analysts overtly examined and corroborated whether and to what degree using their specific techniques had enhanced and strengthened the dependability, credibility, confirmability, and transferability of their NA. Also contemplate how the entire NA would be strengthened if the needs analysts were to include an explanation of all of this in their NA report.

Applying mixed-methods research techniques

A natural extension in NA of the notion of triangulation discussed above is mixed-methods research (MMR). I am not the first author to point this out; as far back as 1996, Berkowitz was suggesting the use of qualitative and mixed-methods approaches in NA. Given that the most common types of triangulation in NAs are stakeholder and method triangulation, an NA can fairly easily be turned into an actual MMR study by insuring that the methods include both quantitative and qualitative data and analyses. There are a number of advantages to taking this additional step.

First, qualitative and quantitative data, analyses, and results have different strengths and weaknesses. Thus the strengths in one can be used to compensate for the weaknesses in another. For example, qualitative methods are effective for discovering new ideas, raising new questions, and formulating new hypotheses about the needs in a particular setting, while quantitative methods are more effective for examining how widely stakeholders agree with those new ideas, answering the new questions, and of course, testing the hypotheses (for much more on the relative strengths and weaknesses of qualitative and quantitative methods, see Brown 2014, pp. 15–18, 63–64, 91–94).

Second, people respond differently to qualitative and quantitative methods. Some people are more likely to understand and be convinced by quantitative data, analyses, and results, while other people will find qualitative results explained in words easier to understand and accept.

There are probably also people who respond equally well to both two types of information. In any case, why not use both quantitative and qualitative methods and reach all possible audiences?

Third, additional insights can come from the very fact of combining quantitative and qualitative methods. Most people in the field today accept that qualitative and quantitative data have value in their own ways, but MMR provides extra value. To get this bonus, it is also necessary to interpret how the qualitative and quantitative data combine or interact in what is called a *meta-interpretation*. Put another way, meta-interpretation makes it possible to learn much by simply examining how the qualitative and quantitative data work together.

MMR techniques that can help increase the value of an NA

MMR does not occur simply because the researcher combines qualitative and quantitative data and analyses in one study. Indeed, seven conscious techniques can be used to help needs analysts benefit from the added value of MMR: convergence, divergence, elaboration, clarification, exemplification, inspiration, and interaction. As such, you might want to seriously consider systematically applying some of the seven MMR techniques to enhance the quality of your NA study (all but *inspiration* are briefly summarized from Brown, 2014, pp. 133–137 with ESP NA provided). In a bit more detail, the seven MMR techniques are:

- *Convergence* – Discovering and showing how multiple data sources provide evidence that supports the same conclusions (for example, interviews students, meetings with teachers, and questionnaires for both teachers and students all indicate that students need significant work specifically in their ESP *speaking ability*).
- *Divergence* – Inspecting and showing how multiple data sources contradict each other with the goal of understanding how those contradictions may lead to their own conclusions or to additional investigations (for instance, one open-ended item on an NA questionnaire indicates that most of the 4 percent of students who answered it are very unhappy with the role-play activities in class, while the Likert-scale questions show that 74 percent think that role-play activities are useful or very useful; a finding that leads to further investigation of the beliefs underlying both points of view).
- *Elaboration* – Analyzing and showing how information from one data source may amplify or increase understanding of information from another data source (for example, post-questionnaire interviews with students in an NA indicate that most students in a sample of the 74 percent who thought role-play activities were useful or very useful also thought that group work, class presentations were useful).

- *Clarification* – Investigating and showing how information from one data source may help illuminate or explain information from another data source (for instance, an end-of-study NA meeting with teachers reveals that the role-plays students were thinking of were probably the fun task-based activities that teachers used last semester).
- *Exemplification* – Searching for information in one data source that can serve as an instance or case of some conclusion drawn from another data source (for example, one teacher in the NA meeting with teachers says that, "students really seemed to like the fact that they could actually accomplish something with the language" – a quote that might usefully be put in the NA report to illustrate how the students felt about the task-based activities and might also serve as justification for further NA research into what other reasons students might have for finding such activities useful).
- *Inspiration* – Being open to the possibility that information from one data source and information from another data source may stimulate an idea in an entirely different direction (for instance, two results – the post-questionnaire-interview result indicating that students found role-plays, group work, and class presentations useful and the teachers meeting result that the students were probably referring to role-plays like the fun task-based activities teachers used last semester – inspire the collection of sample descriptions of the tasks, group work, and presentations that teachers used last semester as part of the NA).
- *Interaction* – Shifting cyclically back and forth between qualitative and quantitative data sources looking for ways that conclusions from applying some or all of the above six techniques connect or interrelate with each other (for example, a next step in the NA might be to take what has been learned about the students positive attitudes toward task-based, group work, and presentation activity activities, and add Likert items to the questionnaire in the next semester to determine what percentage of students still feel that way about those three types of activities; answers to those questions might then in turn lead to interviews to determine why students feel the way they do, and so forth).

It is important to recognize that needs analysts do *not* have to use all of the MMR techniques listed above in order to produce a decent mixed-methods NA. In fact, these techniques might better be viewed as a list of options that needs analysts can choose from to enhance their analyses and explanations. The choices they make among the options will probably be determined by the various constraints in the context of the particular NA involved. In most situations, however, it may be wise to select those options that will help create NA results and interpretations that the important stakeholder groups will believe, buy into, trust, and use in building the ESP program. No NA will ever be 100 percent persuasive to everyone involved, but applying more of these MMR techniques will usually be more persuasive than fewer. Thus, you should seriously consider using MMR and the associated techniques of convergence, divergence, elaboration, clarification, exemplification, inspiration, and interaction so that you and your NA can benefit from the meta-interpretations that are likely to result.

On a side note, I must point out that a number of NAs have claimed that they are mixed-methods studies without really being MMR. Such NAs often include a number of different data-gathering techniques, some quantitative and others qualitative, but the authors have not taken the time and care to examine how the various data sources converge, diverge, elaborate, clarify, exemplify, inspire, and interact with each other to provide additional meta-interpretations. Thus, such NAs are not truly MMR. Those who care about and understand MMR will refer rather snidely to such NAs that haphazardly throw together multiple data sources as *multiple-methods* research in stark contrast in their minds to *mixed-methods* research.

Why use MMR techniques?

The purposes of using MMR techniques are two: to enhance the interpretations in an NA and to corroborate the quality of the study. Using one or more of the seven MMR techniques described in the previous subsection will most certainly *enhance the quality* of the meta-interpretations and any meta-inferences that are draw from NA data, and that should help make an NA effective, but also should be satisfying to the needs analysts themselves.

Using one or more of the seven to corroborate the quality of an NA study will not only involve examining how different data sources and combining those data sources is important, but simply using MMR may not be enough. You should probably also consider explaining any MMR techniques you use in your NA report. Writing a convincing explanation about your use of MMR will probably involve briefly explaining what MMR is, how you used MMR techniques to enhance the NA, and why that is important to the conclusions and suggestions that arose from the NA. Such an explanation is not difficult to write, nor need it be overly technical in nature. However, doing so may help convince the readers/consumers of the NA report that it is trustworthy and believable.

Pierce (2012) provided just such an explanation. She was studying the extent to which undergraduate students in a new Second Language Studies (SLS) Bachelor of Arts (BA) degree program needed or wanted to be provided with teaching experience as part of their degree, and if they did so, how that need might best be met. She collected data from 35 SLS BA students and 13 faculty members, using an iterative process that included four instruments: focus groups, group interviews, Internet-based surveys, and the Delphi technique.[3] She analyzed her quantitative data by calculating descriptive statistics and her qualitative data by coding the themes that she found. Generally, her results revealed that most students felt a need for getting teaching experience during their BA programs. The findings also indicated that the SLS degree program might benefit from the addition of a professional internship or practicum course open to students who had both teaching and non-teaching orientations.

One unexpected result she found was that the various stakeholders held quite different perceptions of the professional identities of these BA students. My reason for selecting this particular paper as an example is that, in a section headed "Strength of the Study" (Pierce, 2012, p. 80), she openly defined and discussed the issues involved in using MMR as follows:

> MMR can be defined as the use of qualitative and quantitative research approaches, including methods, analysis, etc. for the purpose of greater depth of understanding and corroboration of findings (Johnson, Onwuegbuzie & Turner, 2007, p. 124). Though the use of different data collection instruments arose in order to address ambiguity and questions at different stages of the project, the added benefit of employing mixed methods allowed for triangulation of findings across data and a deeper understanding of what the findings meant. A prime example of this was in the exploration of teaching experience for BA students. Initially, survey findings indicated that BA instructors had different conceptions of teaching experience. The Delphi technique then helped to generate consensus around teaching experience and defined key elements of a meaningful teaching experience which were later corroborated in focus groups. Focus group findings also expanded the results of the Delphi technique to include how components of a meaningful teaching experience could fit together.

In discussing her synthesis of data types, Pierce added (pp. 80–81):

> The synthesis of quantitative data from surveys and qualitative data from focus groups was crucial to gaining a genuine understanding of student needs and how the Department could best support students. For example, providing information to students in order for them to gain teaching experience through self-directed teaching was the highest ranked option for Departmental support on the surveys. However, this finding was not corroborated in focus groups and self-directed teaching was found to be selected due to concerns about student choice and Department resources rather than an actual preference for the option. Moreover, focus group findings suggested that students needed, and the Department should provide, a higher degree of support. Had findings been restricted to those in the surveys and not further explored in focus groups, an incomplete and less accurate picture of students' needs would have driven program development.

Task 5.4 Interpreting ESP NA analyses using MMR techniques

With a partner, re-read the information in this subsection about the Pierce (2012) NA. Then separately jot down answers to the following questions:

1   Does Pierce use technical vocabulary and jargon to explain how she used MMR techniques to enhance and corroborate the quality of her study?
2   What did she do to enhance the dependability, credibility, confirmability, transferability of her study?
3   What different types of triangulation did Pierce use?
4   Did Pierce use convergence, divergence, elaboration, clarification, exemplification, inspiration, or interaction? How so?
5   Do you feel that she successfully enhanced and corroborated the quality of the interpretations and meta-interpretations in her NA?

When you are finished answering the five questions, compare your answers with your partner's answers, especially for how they converge and diverge. Discuss what you find. Why do you think you agree and/ or disagree on these issue?

Summary and conclusion

This chapter opened with an examination of the importance of using both quantitative and qualitative analyses in most NAs. On the quantitative side of the analyses, the chapter showed how to use simple statistics like frequencies and percentages to analyze ESP NA numerical data and included examples. The chapter also explored ways to use somewhat more advanced statistical analyses like the means and standard deviations to further understand numerical data. Importantly, the chapter also looked at strategies for presenting and explaining numerical results so that readers can clearly understand what the numbers mean. On the qualitative side of the analyses, the chapter focused particularly on ways to use matrices for analyzing, understanding, and presenting ESP NA qualitative data. In addition, the chapter explored some ways to use corpus analysis techniques for analyzing and presenting actual oral and written ESP language use.

In terms of more global interpretations, the chapter explained the concept of triangulation, why you should consider using it in your NA study, what your nine options are for triangulation, and what you should keep in mind when using triangulation. The chapter continued by explaining strategies that you can use to enhance and corroborate the quality of your NA results and interpretations. The chapter then turned to the concepts underlying mixed methods research (MMR), including seven MMR techniques (that is, convergence, divergence, elaboration, clarification, exemplification, inspiration, and interaction) that you can use not only to enhance the quality of your NA, but also to help you better understand your results and interpretations. The chapter ended with a discussion of why you should seriously consider applying at least some MMR techniques to your NA.

The forms of analysis laid out in this chapter were meant to be fairly straightforward, and they should be sufficient for doing most ESP NAs. However, if you find that you want to do more with your statistical analyses, matrix analyses, and language use analyses, you might consider exploring further in the manuals, help screens, and published sources that I have provided. Perhaps you will find it encouraging that I had no help in learning how to use Excel, how to use matrices, and how to use all the computer-based language-use tools that I demonstrated in this chapter. I learned them all on my own, long after finishing my graduate studies (in 1982).

I should also point out that, in much of my previous work, I have shown great concern (some would say too much concern) with the reliability, validity, replicability, and generalizability of quantitative results, and the more or less analogous concepts of dependability, credibility, confirmability, and transferability of qualitative results, respectively. Truly those issues are important in the high-stakes formal research that is published in refereed journals and many other reports. However, if triangulation is judiciously applied, and if mixed-methods techniques are used to strengthen the meta-interpretations across various data types and analyses, I am confident that NA results and interpretations can be sufficiently sound for local curriculum purposes and local consumption. Since it is not difficult to apply the notions of triangulation and mixed methods techniques, you should seriously consider using them. I assure you that the benefits will be many.

Notes

1 Also see Miles, Huberman, and Saldaña (2014).
2 Note that I was unable to run the *Wordle* web program in my Google browser. However, it ran well in Internet Explorer after I updated my Java program.
3 For those interested, "The Delphi technique is well suited as a method for consensus-building by using a series of questionnaires delivered using multiple iterations to collect data from a panel of selected subjects" (Hsu & Sandford, 2007, p. 1). See the cited article for more information.

Part III

Using the needs analysis results

Chapter 6

Using the NA results in the rest of the ESP curriculum

In this chapter, you will find answers to the following questions:

- What are student learning outcomes (SLOs)?
- What different types of SLOs are there?
- What do I need to know to write effective and efficient SLOs?
- What strategies should I use in revising and organizing my SLOs?
- What strategies can I use to get teachers to accept and use the SLOs?

Student learning outcomes defined

In general terms, *student learning outcomes* (SLOs) are statements of what the needs analysis shows the students should be able to do by the end of their training (that is, by the end of the course or program). Or as Cheng (2011) put it, "a teacher needs to identify appropriate learning objectives. In other words, what will the students learn in a course, and what will they gain when they exit the class?" (p. 51). Over the years, SLOs have had many different names: *learning objectives, behavioral objectives, performance objectives, instructional objectives*, or just plain *objectives*. More recently, it is fashionable to call them *student learning outcomes* – so fashionable I will be. However, what they are called really does not matter. If you want to call them *slithy toves*,[1] that is fine with me. What is important is that they be put on paper and used. Indeed, when SLOs are put on paper, a tentative description is created of what the NA says the students need to be able to do by the end of their training. Then and only then, do the teachers and program have some idea of what the expected outcomes will be. That knowledge in turn can be used to inform the organization and creation of materials, teaching, learning, assessment, and ultimately course or program evaluation. When a program has SLOs, it has something to build on. Otherwise, there is no basis for organizing or creating anything.

Different types of SLOs

SLOs can be described as falling on a continuum that ranges from very precisely defined SLOs to what I call embedded SLOs to what are known as experiential SLOs, as shown in Figure 6.1. Let's consider these three main categories in more detail.

Precisely defined	Embedded	Experiential
SLOs	SLOs	SLOs

├---------------------------------------┼---------------------------------------┤

Figure 6.1 Continuum of SLO types.

Precisely defined SLOs

Precisely defined SLOs are the ones often described as the ideal SLOs because they are very detailed and clear in that they describe who will be able to do what and when, but also under what conditions they will be able to do it and how the teachers will know that they can do it. For example, the SLOs in Table 6.1, which are from the China EST program B-level reading course, are precisely defined with all the *who, what, when,* and *how* parts that I listed in the previous sentence. Note how many of the conditions (under which the students will be required to perform) were pulled out of the list of SLOs (because they were becoming highly redundant) and asterisked to a single statement below the list. Note also that the SLOs repeatedly refer to a 600-word passage. Passages of about 600 words were systematically used in the B-level reading courses, and shorter passages were used in the A-level course and longer passages in the C-level. The readability levels of passages were also systematically varied across the levels with about eleventh-grade readability (that is, determined to be at a suitable level for reading by an average student in the eleventh grade in the US system, which is the second to last year of high school) for the B level and lower and higher readability levels for levels A and C. Note also that, on our tests, there was not a separate passage for each SLO. We only used a few 600-word passages on our tests for this level and applied multiple SLOs to each passage such that one passage might include items for SLOs 1, 2, 3, and 15, and another passage might also have items for those four SLOs.

Embedded SLOs

I call these *embedded SLOs* because they provide structure and organization to the materials, assessment, and teaching, but do not have very precise

Table 6.1 Example SLOs adapted from China EST B-level reading course*

The students should be able to do the following:

1   Skim a 600-word passage for six minutes, then answer multiple choice factual questions (without the passage) with 60 percent accuracy.
2   Answer multiple factual questions on a 600-word passage in six minutes with 70 percent accuracy.
3   Answer multiple factual questions about a graph, chart, or diagram in three minutes with 70 percent accuracy.
4   Take notes in outline format on a 600-word passage including main ideas and sub-ideas (i.e., at least two levels) with 70 percent accuracy.
     ...
14   Fill in meanings of unknown words based on sentence level context with 70 percent accuracy.
15   Identify sentences which function as examples in a 600-word passage with 70 percent accuracy.
16   Identify sentences which function as analogies in a 600-word passage with 70 percent accuracy.

Note: * "All reading passages will be on general science topics and will be at grade 11 reading level, which is equal to junior year (next to last) ability in U.S. high school, or approximately the red cards in your 4a SRA reading cards. [Note that the students understood that the cards in the SRA kits were color coded to reflect different readability levels, in this case eleventh grade, which meant that the red cards were suitable for an average student in the eleventh grade in the US system.] The multiple-choice questions will each give you three choices."

meaning until they are embedded in that curriculum. That is to say, the conditions and even the very nature of the performances required of the students by the end of the course are not clear and precise until everything is in place.

Examples of embedded SLOs, in this case for health-related English, are presented in Table 6.2. Notice that there is a beginning ("Learners should be able to ..." at the top) and then the SLOs are organized more or less hierarchically into categories with the easier *part of the body* topic at the top and the more complex *emergency services* tasks at the bottom. In each case, the verbs that are used are reasonably observable, and some conditions are specified. However, there are no specifics about how the SLOs will be observed or what criterion level students would need to reach to pass the course. Given the nature of this particular publication, which was meant to be general, the information supplied here was sufficient, and it is useful. However, these SLOs would really only take on any level of precision after they were developed into materials and activities to teach them and assessment activities to assess them. A certain level of precision would necessarily arise because of the need to define what should be observed or assessed at the end of the course and how.

Table 6.2 Extract of SLO format for health-related English (adapted from van Ek & Alexander, 1980)

7. Health and welfare – Learners should be able to deal with various aspects of health and welfare:

7.1 parts of the body	refer to some parts of the body where simple gesture does not suffice to locate the source of pain, disorders, etc.
7.2 positions of the body	refer to and inquire about positions and movements of the body, sitting, standing, lying down, etc.
7.3 ailments/accidents	report illness, injury, accident; say whether they have been ill before and whether they have been operated upon; say whether they have to take medicine regularly, if so, what medicine.
...	
7.9 emergency services	ask for police or the fire department, ask for an ambulance, a doctor, ask for the consul.

Nonetheless, these embedded SLOs might be sufficient as a summary for an NA. Once embedded into a particular context, teachers would need to decide how they will observe the students at the end of the course to determine if or how much the students had learned of each SLO, which would naturally lead to thinking about the conditions under which each SLO would be performed and criterion levels necessary for passing the course. In one sense, I think it could be argued that, only at that point, would the embedded SLOs be complete. My point is that embedded SLOs are what they are: a useful starting point, which can, of course, always be improved by adding precision that will help in understanding the conditions involved and the criterion levels expected of students.

Experiential SLOs

Experiential SLOs are like embedded SLOs in that they do not take on much meaning until they are placed in a particular context. However, experiential SLOs are even more loosely defined in that they simply describe an experience that the teachers want students to have by the end of the course, rather than a particular knowledge or behavior. For example, in addition to the precisely defined SLOs described in Table 6.1, that course had one additional experiential SLO: "By the end of the course, the students will have read five articles of their choosing in *Scientific American* as verified by a 100–200 word summary written in English that any educated native speaker can understand." How the quality of the summaries would be judged and the criterion level for passing were never made clear. While this SLO was not precisely defined, it did serve our purpose which was to get the students to do more extensive reading of scientific English (on any topics that interested the students) than what we were able to provide in class. Our students had a genuine interest in learning English because of who they were and because they were likely to find themselves in an English-speaking country doing postgraduate work in the sciences within a few months. Hence there was no reason to worry that they would cheat, write fake summaries, or copy from other students. In any case, we simply wanted them to experience such reading, and we felt this was a perfectly legitimate experiential SLO.

And everything in between

Naturally, SLOs may not fall exactly into one of the three categories described above. Indeed they can fall at other points on the continuum shown in Figure 6.1. For example, consider the SLOs for an NA that reveals that an EAP program should be based on project-work with students selecting three projects from a list of 50 possibilities to do during the course. Such SLOs would probably best fit somewhere between embedded and experiential SLOs because they are likely to have elements of both experiential and embedded SLOs. The students need to experience doing the projects (*experiential*) as one purpose of the course. At the same time, teachers will naturally want to give feedback on the projects and might be required to grade them, so conditions (perhaps in the form of a rubric; see Table 6.12) and ultimately criteria for grading and for passing the course might need to be set. Since these conditions and criteria might not be revealed until the materials, teaching, and assessment were developed, the SLOs would also be *embedded*. Thus these SLOs might be best described as experiential and embedded – though somewhat closer to the embedded part of the continuum.

Personal reflection – What are the characteristics of your ESP NA?

Think about a group of ESP students that you teach (or some you would like to teach). Do you think that using some form of objectives or SLOs will be important to your NA? If not, be sure to read on in this chapter. If so, is it important what they are called? And, what are at least two reasons that SLOs are important to use in an ESP NA? Also, what are the three types of SLOs explained above? How are the three types different from each other, and why should you consider using all three types?

Writing SLOs

So clearly, I believe that it is important to remember that SLOs can come in many forms – especially when you first start writing and working with them. From my point of view, the form of the SLO is not as important as getting something on paper. After all, SLOs can only serve a useful purpose if they have been written down somewhere. Only then, can they be arranged, revised, deleted, added to, revised again, rearranged, refined, and on. What I am saying is that it is more important to just get them written down than it is to make sure they are perfect in terms of form at the outset.

Given that they come in many forms, you may legitimately ask why they are always described as though they should be written in a certain way – the precisely defined way. I suppose that is because precisely defined SLOs are the clearest most complete SLOs. However, precisely defined SLOs are not necessarily appropriate for all sorts of situations, syllabuses, or indeed, learning outcomes. Nonetheless, precisely defined SLOs do provide an ideal for writing clear and precise statements of what the students should be able to do by the end of the course, and if real-world SLOs fall short of the precisely defined SLO model, they will at least have been written as clearly and completely as possible under the circumstances.

Precisely defined SLOs are typically described as containing a beginning, an observable behavior, a set of conditions, and a criterion level as follows:

- *Beginning* – indicates *when* and *who*, usually something like: *By the end of the course, the students...* . So an SLO is something that will happen by the end of the course (*when*) and students (*who*) will be doing it.
- *Observable behavior* – describes *what*, that is, the behavior that will be observed by the end of the course. The *what* is usually framed as a verb describing what the students will be able *to do*. But it is not just any verb because it must be an observable verb (more about this below).
- *Conditions* – describes *what in more detail*, that is, the observable behavior is made clearer or more precise by describing the conditions under which the behavior will be performed and observed.
- *Criterion level* – explains *how well*, that is, it sets the criterion level that students must reach to have demonstrated their learning, to pass, or to be considered successful.

An example of a clear and precisely defined SLO for an EAP course might look something like this:

By the end of the course, the students will identify the topic sentences in each of three paragraphs of a business letter (written at 9th grade readability level)[2] by correctly underlining them with 67% accuracy.

The parts in that SLO are:

- *Beginning* – when and who: *By the end of the course, the students.*
- *Observable behavior* – what: *identify the topic sentences ... by correctly underlining them.*
- *Conditions* – more details about what: *in each of three paragraphs of a business letter (written at 9th grade readability level).*
- *Criterion level* – how well (criterion): *with 67% accuracy.*

Let's consider each of the four parts of an SLO separately and in more detail.

Beginning

The beginning is usually a phrase that explains when the SLO will be accomplished and who will do so. Most SLOs begin with some variation of the following:

- *By the end of the course, the students in ESP 201 will be able to:*
- *At the end of the training program, the workers will demonstrate their abilities to:*
- *By the end of the program, the trainees at Company X will be capable of:*
- *As of December 15th, the learners in EAP 11 will have mastered 70% of the following skills:*

Clearly, that opening phrase can be worded many ways, as long as it is clear when the SLOs will be achieved and who will be achieving them. That phrase is then followed by a list of the behaviors that will be observed.

Observable behavior

The *observable behaviors* are typically described using verb infinitives or gerunds. An example of a *verb infinitive format* might be something like:

By the end of the course, the students in ESP 101 will be able to:

1   *Identify ...*
2   *Write ...*
3   *Solve ...*

An example of a *gerund format* might be something like:

By the end of the program, the trainees at Company X will be capable of:

1   *Describing ...*
2   *Comparing ...*
3   *Listing ...*

It is important to note that verbs vary considerably in terms of the degree to which they can be observed. For example, verbs like *understand, know, enjoy, appreciate,* and *believe* are important verbs, and I often want to know about them with regard to my students. I want to know if they *understand* X, if they *know* Y, if they *enjoy* Z, and so forth. But alas, I cannot open their heads and look inside to see if they *understand, know,* or *enjoy.* Instead, I have to infer these things from behaviors I can observe. For example, I can give students a problem to solve using a certain concept. If they *solve* the problem by getting the right answer (or at least a reasonable answer), I can infer that they *understood* the concept. Thus *solve* is a verb that can be observed, and observing it tells me the degree to which students *understood.* Other readily observable verbs (from Gronlund & Brookhart, 2009) that might prove particularly useful in writing EAP SLOs are shown in Table 6.3 for language behaviors and study behaviors. Gronlund and Brookhart (2009, pp. 143–146) supplied lists of useful verbs in a number of categories, but two additional categories that might prove particularly useful for writing SLOs for any mathematics- or science-related ESPs are shown in Table 6.4.

For additional ideas for verbs to use in writing SLOs for other specific ESP purposes, I would suggest going online and searching something like "writing business course objectives" or "writing engineering course objectives." For example, I searched "writing nursing objectives" and within seconds I had found I-Tech (2010), which is a guide for writing good learning objectives for nursing. Naturally, what is good for *nursing courses* might be good for *nursing English courses,* especially if the nurses will probably have to learn to do those things *in English.*

I-Tech (2010) presents a particularly useful series of verbs for nursing that are organized into the cognitive domain categories used in the original Bloom (1956) taxonomy of the cognitive domain: knowledge, comprehension, application, analysis, synthesis, and evaluation. I have adapted that information in Table 6.5. Notice that Table 6.5 includes the six categories in the original 1956 cognitive domain taxonomy, but also adapts those notions to the nursing world, including training nurses. Thus, each category is labeled (for instance, "Knowledge"), a series of observable verbs is supplied (for example, "Describe, define, ... state"); and a nursing example is provided (for instance, "Identify the three primary modes of HIV transmission").

I-Tech (2010) also presents analogous information for the five categories of the Krathwohl, Bloom, and Masia (1956) taxonomy of the affective domain: receiving, responding, valuing, organization, and internalizing. Again, I have adapted that information in Table 6.6. Notice that Table 6.6 includes the five categories in the original 1956 affective domain taxonomy, but also modifies those notions to fit the nursing world. Thus, each category is labeled (for example, "Receiving"); a macro-behavior in the nursingcontext is provided (for instance, "willing to listen") in parentheses; observable

Table 6.3 Verbs for use in writing EAP SLOs (adapted from Gronlund & Brookhart, 2009, p. 144)

Language behaviors		Study behaviors	
abbreviate	recite	arrange	look
accent	say	categorize	map
alphabetize	sign	chart	mark
articulate	speak	circle	name
call	spell	cite	note
capitalize	state	compile	organize
edit	summarize	copy	quote
hyphenate	syllabify	diagram	record
indent	tell	find	reproduce
outline	translate	follow	search
print	verbalize	itemize	sort
pronounce	whisper	label	underline
punctuate	write	locate	
read			

Table 6.4 Useful verbs for writing math and science ESP SLOs (Gronlund & Brookhart, 2009, p. 145)

Math behaviors		Lab science behaviors	
add	interpolate	apply	manipulate
bisect	measure	calibrate	operate
calculate	multiply	conduct	plant
check	number	connect	prepare
compute	plot	convert	remove
count	prove	decrease	replace
derive	reduce	demonstrate	report
divide	solve	dissect	reset
estimate	square	feed	set
extract	subtract	grow	specify
extrapolate	tabulate	increase	straighten
graph	tally	insert	time
group	verify	keep	transfer
integrate		lengthen	weigh
		limit	

verbs are listed (for example, "Ask, choose, ... select"); and an example is provided (for instance, "Ask open-ended questions to elicit information during a counseling session").

My guess is that Tables 6.5 and 6.6 would be very useful to anyone doing an NA for nursing English. I would also suggest that similar information is

Table 6.5 Cognitive domain categories and observable verbs for nursing SLOs (adapted from I-Tech, 2010, p. 4)

Cognitive domain categories	Observable verbs	Example
Knowledge	Describe, define, identify, list, name, recognize, reproduce, state	Identify the three primary modes of HIV transmission
Comprehension	Articulate, distinguish, estimate, explain, generalize, infer, interpret, paraphrase, rewrite, summarize, translate	Explain the difference between HIV and AIDS
Application	Apply, change, construct, demonstrate, modify, operate, predict, prepare, produce, show, solve, use	Use WHO clinical staging definitions to assist in clinical decision making
Analysis	Analyze, categorize, compare, contrast, differentiate, identify, illustrate, infer, outline, relate, select, separate	Outline effective strategies for managing nutrition complications in HIV-infected patients
Synthesis	Compile, create, design, diagnose, diagram, discriminate, explain, generate, modify, organize, plan, relate, reorganize, separate, summarize, write	Design an HIV-prevention counseling program based on the Ministry of Health's counseling standards and guidelines
Evaluation	Appraise, assess, compare, conclude, contrast, criticize, critique, describe, evaluate, explain, interpret, justify, summarize, support	Evaluate the risk faced by health care workers of contracting HIV on the job

probably available online for any field for which you might find yourself doing an ESP NA.

Conditions

The *conditions* in an SLO are any circumstances or characteristics that might affect the performance of whatever behavior is expected for the students by the end of instruction. If you ask yourself how you would know if the student understands or can do the SLO, you will probably find yourself thinking about how you will observe or test it, and under what conditions. So you might find yourself describing as conditions any observation procedures, the types of test items or rubric that will be used to rate the performance, the difficulty of the listening passage, the readability of the reading passage, the topic of the material, and so on. Any such information that is crucial to the performance described in an SLO should probably be included in the conditions.

Table 6.6 Affective domain categories and observable verbs for nursing SLOs (adapted from I-Tech 2010, p. 5)

Affective domain categories (macro-behavior in nursing context)	Observable verbs	Examples
Receiving (willing to listen)	Ask, choose, describe, give, identify, locate, select	Ask open-ended questions to elicit information during a counseling session
Responding (willing to participate)	Answer, assist, discuss, greet, help, participate, present, read, report, select, tell	Present clients with risk-reduction strategies appropriate to their needs
Valuing (willing to be involved)	Complete, demonstrate, differentiate, explain, follow, initiate, join, justify, propose, read, share	Demonstrate ability to provide a client with an HIV-positive test result in a compassionate and supportive manner
Organization (willing to be an advocate)	Adhere, alter, arrange, combine, compare, defend, explain, integrate, modify	Integrate professional standards of patient confidentiality into personal life
Internalizing values (willing to change one's behavior)	Act, display, influence, listen, modify, perform, propose, question, serve, solve, verify	Act objectively when solving problems

Criterion level

Some teachers think that setting a criterion level of say 70 percent is just *arbitrary*, so it shouldn't be done. Yes, any such criterion level is arbitrary, but when teachers in the US system are asked to grade their students, they have no trouble deciding that an A is 90 percent or above, a B is 80–89 percent, a C is 70–79 percent, a D is 60–69 percent, and an F is 59 percent or below,[3] which is not only arbitrary, but arbitrary at five levels. Teachers do such things to send students signals that such-and-such a performance will be graded in these ways. But then, if the teacher finds that too many students are getting low grades, suddenly *grading on a curve* is invoked as a way of adjusting the grades upward. What I am saying is that criterion levels are arbitrary in SLOs as well, but sometimes these criteria are useful and necessary because they send signals to the students about what is expected of them (for example, a 90 percent criterion would clearly indicate that the SLO is considered very important, while 60 percent would not), and in any case, criterion levels can always be adjusted up or down later when experience indicates the need. At very least, using criterion levels will force the needs analysts and teachers to think about these issues and what it means to pass an SLO, a course, or a program.

Task 6.1 Writing precisely defined SLOs for ESP students

Individually, think of a specific group of ESP students that you are or will be teaching. Now, decide on a particular ESP course that you would like to teach with them. Then:

1   Write at least five precisely defined SLOs for those students in that course. Don't forget to include in each the following components: a beginning, an observable behavior, a set of conditions, and a criterion level. Also write one experiential SLO.

2   If possible, work with a partner and give each other feedback on your five precisely defined SLOs. In the process, answer the following questions about your SLOs:

    a   Are all five components present in each SLO?
    b   Are all five components clear and sensible?
    c   Is it possible that some of your SLOs will improve over time as embedded SLOs?

3   For your experiential SLO, how will you know that students have experienced it?

4   Revise your SLOs based on the feedback you get. Are they improved by the revisions?

Refining, revising, and organizing SLOs

I mentioned above that a good way to conclude an NA is to create a set of SLOs that reflect the needs revealed in the NA in terms of what the students should be able to do at the end of their training. Thus it makes sense to think of the SLOs as part of the NA. In many cases, I have found this to be true in a very real sense, because, while writing SLOs, I have found that I tend to (a) fill gaps in my original concepts of students' needs that were not revealed in the initial NA, (b) flesh out perceived needs to make them clearer and more achievable, and (c) organize the SLOs in some way that will make sense to teachers and students.

Filling gaps in SLOs

Gaps in the SLOs occur because some needs or aspects of needs were overlooked in the NA process. Thus needs analysts will often find themselves fleshing out the needs when specifying them as SLOs. For example, an NA may have revealed that a group of business English students will need to write emails, but in the process of including email writing as an SLO, the needs analysts realize that these students may also need to use messaging as part of their work as well. The needs analysts realize that the conventions of email and message writing – especially in terms of length, conciseness, and abbreviations – are very different. So they go back and confirm with their informants that messaging is a growing part of what business people are having to do in English and then fill the gap that they found by adding an SLO for messaging.

Fleshing out SLOs

Needs analysts may also find themselves fleshing out perceived needs in the process of writing SLOs because the needs perceived and listed during the NA process were too broadly or not clearly defined. Fortunately, fleshing out the SLOs can increase the degree to which a specific purpose need is clear, complete, and achievable. Take the example in the previous paragraph of a need to write business emails. While trying to state that as an SLO, the needs analysts might realize that writing emails will require students to know how emails are typically organized, how emails need to be relatively short, why they should never write emails in all caps, what sorts of salutations are appropriate, and what sorts of sign-offs are appropriate. These could become five separate SLOs, but since doing that might lead to a total list of hundreds of SLOs, the needs analysts might alternatively decide to include those five as components of a single fleshed out SLO as follows:

> By the end of the course, our business English students will be able to write business emails that are appropriately organized, have appropriate salutations and sign-offs, and are not too long or written in all-capital letters as judged by using an email writing rubric covering those five points with 60% accuracy.

Once the email writing rubric is developed, it clearly becomes part of the fleshing out process and, in the end, part of this SLO.

One approach that I have often found useful for filling in gaps in SLOs for an ESP curriculum is to refer to one or more taxonomies. More formally, a *taxonomy* is a systematic and hierarchical outline of classifications, categories, and groupings. There are many such taxonomies, but in educational circles generally, Bloom's taxonomy (referred to above) is the grandparent of them all. For instance, looking at the six main categories in the original Bloom's (1956) taxonomy of the cognitive domain in Table 6.7, needs analysts might realize that they have ample aspects of *knowledge, comprehension, application, synthesis,* and *evaluation* built into their SLOs, but

Table 6.7 Outline of Bloom's (1956) taxonomy of the cognitive domain six main categories with revision by Krathwohl (2002)

Bloom (1956) original	Krathwohl (2002) revised
1.0 Knowledge	1.0 Remember
2.0 Comprehension	2.0 Understand
3.0 Application	3.0 Apply
4.0 Analysis	4.0 Analyze
5.0 Synthesis	5.0 Evaluate
6.0 Evaluation	6.0 Create

that they skipped *analysis* altogether. Thus they are setting out to teach their students how to synthesize (or put pieces together) without first teaching them to analyze (or break things into their constituent pieces). They might therefore decide that they want to add analysis to their thinking about the students' needs.

Notice on the right side of Table 6.7 that Krathwohl (2002) provided an updated and revised taxonomy of the cognitive domain that usefully separates the knowledge dimension (things we know) from the cognitive process dimension (things we do mentally). Krathwohl's cognitive process dimension, outlined in Table 6.8 opposite, focuses on doing things mentally in a way that can be very helpful in fleshing out a set of SLOs. For example, an NA might reveal that students of tourism English need to learn how to create promotional projects, and the needs analysts had already included SLOs for planning and producing such projects in English, but a quick glance at the three subcategories under 6.0 in Table 6.8 would remind them that *generating* such a promotional project is also a step that students probably need to learn. Thus they decide to flesh out the promotional project SLOs to include generating projects, and then have the students generate their own promotional projects as a final part of the course. Similarly, an NA for science English reading might have indicated that students need to do four of the subcategories listed under 2.0, but the needs analysts might also want to consider the other three categories under 2.0 in order to more completely flesh out their reading SLOs.

Organizing SLOs

Organizing or sequencing SLOs is necessary so that teachers and students can make sense of them. Indeed, I have found that situations where teachers and students do not understand how the SLOs and subsequent materials and teaching are organized will be completely untenable. So it is crucial that the SLOs be clearly organized. How a set of SLOs should be organized will depend to a large extent on which of the 12 syllabuses or combinations of

Table 6.8 The cognitive process dimension of the revised taxonomy (Krathwohl, 2002, p. 215)

1.0 Remember – Retrieving relevant knowledge from long-term memory.
   1.1 Recognizing
   1.2 Recalling
2.0 Understand – Determining the meaning of instructional messages, including oral, written, and graphic communication.
   2.1 Interpreting
   2.2 Exemplifying
   2.3 Classifying
   2.4 Summarizing
   2.5 Inferring
   2.6 Comparing
   2.7 Explaining
3.0 Apply – Carrying out or using a procedure in a given situation.
   3.1 Executing
   3.2 Implementing
4.0 Analyze – Breaking material into its constituent parts and detecting how the parts relate to one another and to an overall structure or purpose.
   4.1 Differentiating
   4.2 Organizing
   4.3 Attributing
5.0 Evaluate – Making judgments based on criteria and standards.
   5.1 Checking
   5.2 Critiquing
6.0 Create – Putting elements together to form a novel, coherent whole or make an original product.
   6.1 Generating
   6.2 Planning
   6.3 Producing

syllabuses (discussed at length in Chapter 2) are being used. Generally, however, SLOs will be organized chronologically, organized in the sequence of the final product, hierarchically organized, or hierarchically layered.

Chronologically organized SLOs would be arranged in terms of when they would be expected to occur first, second, third, and so on. For example, a set of civil engineering English SLOs might be organized in terms of arriving at the worksite, determining the problem, listing options, taking measurements, calculating alternative solutions, deciding on the problem solution most likely to succeed, reporting that solution to the client, carrying out the solution, and evaluating the job effectiveness. Thus the SLOs would be organized more or less in terms of the order of events in which they would be likely to occur in real life.

Organizing in sequence of the final product involves arranging the SLOs in the same order that they would normally be arranged in the final project. For example, SLOs for writing a business memo (the final product) could be arranged in terms of formatting and salutation, introducing the topic, creating the explanation or argument in the body of the memo with paragraphs that have topic sentences and supporting details, and writing an effective conclusion. Thus the order of the SLOs would reflect the order in which the various elements of a memo appear in such a document (even though real people may proceed to do the task in a different order, for example, starting by creating the explanation and then doing the formatting and salutation, and writing the introduction).

Hierarchically organized SLOs need to be organized too. The rationale for organizing structural SLOs is typically to arrange them from the easiest to most difficult grammar items, or the most frequent to least frequent. Skills-based SLOs are more likely to be organized from the lowest-level skills to the highest. In addition, all the taxonomies discussed above are meant to be more or less hierarchical. That is, the main categories 1.0 Knowledge to 6.0 Evaluation in the original Bloom's (1956) taxonomy are arranged more or less in order from lowest ability or skill to highest. Thus organizing SLOs in the same order as one of these taxonomies will tend to create a hierarchy.

Hierarchical layers of macro- and micro-SLOs or main topics and sub-topics can also be created. For instance, Table 2.3 in Chapter 2 for medical English is arranged hierarchically with the macro-functions organized chronologically (that is, taking a history 1, taking a history 2, examining a patient, …) and the subparts of each unit organized into two functions, reading skills, and a case history. Similarly, the outline in Task 2.1 is organized around main topics and subtopics. Clearly then, SLOs can also be sequenced with a combination of some sense of chronological and hierarchical principles in whatever way(s) that the needs analysts think will best represent the needs in a particular institution and be clearly understood by the key stakeholders (usually the teachers and students). Note, however, that the SLOs themselves will generally most resemble whatever units are at the lowest or bottom level of the hierarchy.

So far, most the taxonomies I have presented have been for the general cognitive domain. However, other taxonomies exist that might help in fleshing out and hierarchically organizing SLOs. For example, two such taxonomies jump immediately to mind. One is a taxonomy for native speaker *reading* from Barrett (1972) and the other is a taxonomy for ESL/EFL *listening* by Lund (1990). Additional taxonomies for the content skills related to specific ESPs may be easily accessible online. For example, I went online and searched for "science course taxonomy" and soon found a science specific alternative to Bloom's taxonomy at http://www.learningsolutionsmag.com/articles/1116/a-learning-science-alternative-to-blooms-taxonomy (Sugrue, 2013). Searching "business course taxonomy" led me to a business taxonomy webpage at http://www.logicmanager.com/erm-software/2014/10/06/risk-management-technology-projects-succeed/, and a much more detailed business function taxonomy webpage at https://wiqime.files.wordpress.com/2010/10/bft_01.jpg. My point is not that these particular websites are the end-all in taxonomies for helping to fill in gaps or organize science or business English courses, but rather that this strategy of searching online for ideas will take a few moments and can reap a great many ideas and resources.

Personal reflection – How will you refine, revise, and organize your SLOs

Think about a group of ESP students that you teach (or some you would like to teach). Once you have a tentative set of NA-based SLOs for your students, what steps will you take to fill in gaps in and flesh out your SLOs. Will your SLOs be organized chronologically, sequentially, hierarchically, or hierarchically layered? Why?

Getting teachers to accept and use the SLOs

For a variety of reasons some teachers simply do not like objectives, SLOs, or whatever you want to call them. I have found that following simple guidelines (and telling the teachers about these guidelines) will help teachers to accept the whole idea of creating and using SLOs. These guidelines are synthesized from Brown (1995, p. 96) which discusses 10 benefits of using SLOs, from Brown (1995, pp. 96–97) which discusses how to implement SLOs, and from experiences I have had since writing that earlier book.

Teachers are more likely to accept and use SLOs if they are told that the SLOs are designed to help:

1   Convert the perceived needs of the students into teaching points, that is, they should help in deciding what the students should be able to do at the end of instruction.
2   Clarify the teaching points, that is, they should help in thinking through the skills and subskills that underlying different needs and instructional points.
3   Organize needs and teaching points in a sensible way that can be understood by all stakeholders.
4   Decide on the appropriate level of specificity for the teaching activities that will be used.
5   Provide a blueprint for the development of assessment instruments, materials, teaching strategies, and course or program evaluation procedures that match the needs of students and teachers.
6   Continue the professional development of all teachers and administrators by encouraging them to draw on the collective energies and strengths of all participants in developing curriculum that supports classroom teaching and learning by actually *lessening the load* on all concerned.

7   Evaluate overall course and program effectiveness by serving as the basis for systematic examination, change, modification, development, and improvement of the curriculum (including perceptions of students' needs, course SLOs, assessment procedures, materials, teaching, and program level evaluation).

Naturally, once teachers are told these seven things, it is crucial that these guidelines actually be implemented.

SLOs will actually function better (and teachers will be more likely to accept them) if the SLOs are:

1   Allowed to range in type; precisely defined SLOs may work well in many situations, but a range of possible types of objectives should be allowed so they can be tailored to the needs found in the particular setting.
2   Allowed to vary in level of specificity, but in general are just right; SLOs that are too specific may begin to trivialize and restrict the teachers' options; SLOs that are too broad will be vague and provide little guidance to teachers as to what students should be able to do by the end of the course.
3   Connected directly to the needs of the students and teachers involved; not only will such SLOs be ultimately more useful to ESP students, but also, if students perceive a direct connection to their needs, they are likely to be more highly engaged in the learning.
4   Well-written, following the guidelines provided in this chapter so they are much more likely to be observable, useful, and accepted.
5   Viewed as flexible so they can be modified in response to changes in the types of students, changes in teaching staff, changes in language teaching theory and practice, and changes in perceptions of students' needs; conversely, they should never be seen or treated as though they are permanent; SLOs that are set in cement are by definition dying.
6   Developed by consensus, especially among all teachers so that each teacher has had a voice in the creation of the SLOs and a stake in their success.
7   Used as a core curriculum that accounts for 60–70 percent of the time that teachers spend with their students; this will provide commonality across courses when there are multiple sections, but also leave 30–40 percent of the time to the discretion of the teachers to spend reinforcing learning of the objectives in novel ways, teaching other points that they have observed that the students need to learn, or just doing things they like to do in class. (For example, the last ten minutes of the week in every ESL/EFL/ESP class I ever taught was devoted to singing songs with me playing the guitar. What was the pedagogical value of this activity? Who cares?)

8   Designed to help the teachers teach, that is, not hindering them in any way in their already difficult job. Conversely, SLOs should never restrict what teachers do in the classrooms that they feel will enable students to perform well by the end of the course.

I think that guidelines 1 and 4–8 are self-explanatory; however, guidelines 2 and 3 probably need some elaboration, which I will provide in the next two subsections.

Guideline 2: Recognize that SLOs can range in level of specificity

Needs analysts must keep in mind that sometimes it is necessary to differentiate several levels of specificity in writing SLOs. For instance, sometimes, it is best to write SLOs in *hierarchical layers* with goals as the upper level and SLOs as the details, or with main SLOs and subsidiary SLOs (Seedhouse, 1995), while in other instances it may be better to express SLOs as macro-skills and micro-skills (Kimzin and Proctor, 1986), or as various combinations of the above like the goals, microskills, and SLOs in Asahina and Okuda (1987). Sometimes, it is also useful to write SLOs that are *sequentially arranged* as in terminal SLOs (those that will be achieved at the end of the course) and *enabling SLOs* (those SLOs along the way that will help get the students to the final SLOs). In still other cases, straightforward *single-level* sets of SLOs may suffice (as in all the examples shown in Brown, 1995, pp. 99–101).

In my experience, one important aim of writing SLOs is to find just the right level of specificity. Useful SLOs will not be so broad that they fail to express what the course is about, nor will they be so specific that they trivialize instruction. Useful SLOs will be at just the right level of specificity to be maximally useful and helpful to teachers.

Deciding which SLOs best match what the needs analysts learned in the NA process is an important part of creating a defensible curriculum. Indeed, finding the right level of specificity for those SLOs is how needs analysts can best make what they learned in the NA useful in the classroom. In short, if the SLOs are not properly specified in terms of types of SLOs and levels of specificity, an NA may still fail even after much dedicated struggle and work in the NA information gathering, analyses, and reporting stages.

Guideline 3: Be sure to connect the SLOs directly to the NA

In addition to recognizing that SLOs need to be stated at the appropriate level of specificity, one other caveat that I need to explain is that the SLOs should be directly connected with the NA results. A great place for an NA to end is with the specification of SLOs based on the NA results:

> Put another way, objectives [or SLOs] are the link that connects the NA to the rest of the curriculum (i.e., to the materials, testing, teaching, and program evaluation). Indeed, specifying objectives [or SLOs] is a way of fitting what was learned in the NA to the actual instruction that will be delivered.
>
> (Brown, 2009, p. 284)

Some NAs fail to connect the SLOs directly to the NA and thus the NA need not have been conducted at all. What I mean is that it is important to openly and explicitly link the SLOs that come out of an NA directly to the sources of information that revealed the need for those specific SLOs. Consider the following example that does not make the connection very well: Chaudron et al. (2005, pp. 232–233) bounced from an excellent description of how their Korean Language NA information was gathered directly to their two task-based objectives without revealing how the information in their analysis actually led them to select those particular tasks. The authors did in fact state that they identified a number of possible tasks and that they "gradually narrowed to two distinct tasks...": "making automobile rental reservations" and "following street directions." However, they failed to describe how the larger number of target tasks were identified, or how they "gradually narrowed" their choice to two tasks. Oddly, the needs analysts then dropped the *car rental* task, when they found out that in reality few foreigners rent cars in Korean. A new *shopping for clothing* task was then used instead, but with no explanation of how their NA information showed that *shopping for clothing* was important. In fact, the link may have been obvious to the researchers, but they never explained it to their readers.

In contrast, Kimzin and Proctor (1986) clearly linked their objectives to the information upon which it was based. Table 6.9 shows how they explicitly listed which information sources led them to include each objective in a column labeled *Justification Sources*. Under A. Lecture Organization the first objective for their microskill is **Identify the major topic** for which they list four Justification Sources: (a) they found it in their Case study for a student in the Art 474 course on p. 20; (b) it was ranked eighth out of 11 on the student questionnaire; (c) it was the second item listed in Richards (1983) in their literature review; and (d) it was the first item listed in Harper et al. (1983), which was an earlier NA done in the same institution. My point is that it is crucial to openly and explicitly understand and explain how the SLOs are based on the NA, why an obvious outcome of a specific NA is a particular set of objectives, and just how the NA information

Table 6.9 Very abridged goals, SLOs, and microskills for ELI 70

Goal #1 Students will be able to follow the basic ideas of a lecture.

Microskills	Justification Sources
A. Lecture Organization	
70/1 **Identify the major topic.**	Case studies Art 474 p. 20
	Student questionnaire Ranked 8th out of 11
	Richards (1983) Item 2
	Harper et al. (1983) Item 1.0

SLO: Identify 2 out of 3 major topics within a 30-minute academic lecture by writing a 1 to 3-sentence explanation for each topic with 80% accuracy.

...

led to the selection of the particular SLOs involved. (For more on how they presented their microskills, see Kimzin & Proctor, 1986, or Brown, 1995, pp. 64–66.)

Personal reflection – How will you get the teachers to accept and use the SLOs?

Think about a group of ESP teachers you might have to work with in a particular ESP program. Now go back through the section above on getting teachers to accept and use SLOs, and highlight those strategies that you think will work best.

Using SLOs as a bridge from the NA to all the other curriculum elements

One reason SLOs serve as such an excellent ending point for an NA is that they can then serve as a bridge between the NA and the other curriculum elements (for much more on these curriculum elements, see Brown, 1995, 2005b). For example, for the B-level speaking course in the EST program in China, our overall goal was "To develop speaking ability in free conversation in pairs, small groups, large groups, and with professional colleagues, and in general to develop conversational strategies leading to formal discussion." In the course plan shown in Table 6.10, for each *week*, we listed the main SLOs as *type of interaction* (or macro-function) that would be presented and practiced as well as *subject* or topic that would be used to contextualize each macro-function. We also had specific micro-functions embedded within each macro-function, but we did not want to overwhelm the students when we distributed this plan as a handout on the first day of class and explained it to them.

Thus the SLOs served as a framework for organizing the entire course around the needs we perceived for our students. However, these SLOs also served as a bridge from the NA to all of the other curriculum elements in considerably more detail, that is, from the NA to the materials, NA to the assessment, NA to the teaching, and NA to course or program evaluation.

From SLOs to materials

"Once learning objectives have been determined, ESP teachers face another basic consideration: What input materials and output tasks are suitable for achieving the chosen learning objectives?" (Cheng, 2011, p. 54). For example, based on the SLOs described in Table 6.10 and the associated text, the three teachers assigned to the class produced four or five daily modules for the particular type of interaction associated with each week. Situation 3.5 shown in Table 6.11 is an example of these modules, in this case for the fifth day of the third week, which addressed the SLO and macro-function for *addressing a problem*.

The module shown in Table 6.11 is for an in-class physics problem group work activity. Since it was developed modularly, the description in Table 6.11 should stand on its own. Thus readers should be able to read through the description and visualize what the *input materials* would look like (to use Cheng's 2011 terminology) and how a teacher would organize and get the students to do the output task (again to use Cheng's terminology) in their classes. Of course, it would help if the readers had the *Activities Book* referenced in the **Materials** part of Table 6.11. The *Activities Book* was created just to help the teachers organize all of the disposable materials that

Table 6.10 Weeks, SLOs, and topics for EST B-level speaking course (abridged from Hilferty & Brown, 1982)

Week	Type of interaction	Subject
1	Exchanging personal information	Personal relationships
2	Exchanging opinions	Social problems
3	Addressing a problem	Environmental problems
4	Agreeing and disagreeing	Consumerism
5	Giving advice	Problems in modern life I
6	Social planning	Problems in modern life II
7	Informing	Science and the occult
8	Argument	Presentation and discussion
9	Suasion	Presentation and discussion

Table 6.11 Module from EST B-level speaking course (adapted from Hilferty & Brown, 1982)

Situation 3.5 Physics Problem Group Work	
Description:	In this activity, students seek and provide explanations for everyday scientific phenomena.
Materials:	A copy of a different everyday physics problem for each group (cut the *Activities Book* pages into strips) and the problem solutions for the teachers' reference in later discussion.
Procedures:	1 Divide the class into 4 groups of 5 or 6 with discussion leaders appointed. The leaders should start the discussion, take notes, and report back to the class. Make sure that there is at least one physics student in each group.
	2 Explain that the assignment is to provide a simple though scientific answer that can be explained in 5 minutes or less. If the group is not sure of the answer, they should propose a possible solution.
	3 Give each group one of the physics problems and have them plan a five-minute explanation.
	4 Have the discussion leader from each group present the problem and solution. Help students keep within the 5-minute time limit.
	5 Encourage students to address questions to the presenter if they disagree with, or do not understand, an explanation.

would be needed; these were meant to be cut up, used, and then thrown away each time the course was taught (so that teachers would not have to keep track of all the little bits and pieces involved in the materials). This *Activities Book* contained three pages for Module 3.5 that listed 15 physics problems (from Walker, 1977), the answers to those physics problems, and a list of the gambits (see Keller & Warner, 1979a–c) that the students might find especially helpful for accomplishing this task.

The three teachers involved in this course taught the modules and then met to compare notes and revise each module. Ultimately, the entire collection of modules was rewritten and assembled by two of the teachers in Hilferty and Brown (1982). Thus the NA for speaking level B was clearly linked to the materials and teaching materials designed to address the needs of our EST students.

For more information on evaluating and developing ESP materials from SLOs, I highly recommend Chapters 9 and 10 of Hutchinson and Waters (1987, pp. 96–127). Readers may also find three edited-collection books on general materials development of interest, one by Byrd (1995) and two by Tomlinson (1998, 2003). Two other books discuss materials development for academic English (Charles and Pecorari, 2016) and business English (Nickerson and Planken, 2016).

From SLOs to assessments

As Cheng (2011, p. 59) put it, "ESP practitioners need to gauge how much their students have learned. Indeed, evaluation of student learning in ESP classes is a topic of persisting interest and is, thus, another basic consideration in ESP teaching."

For example, in a very real sense, the embedded SLOs described in Table 6.10 were not complete until the assessment procedures were developed, used, and revised. As discussed earlier in the book, we had learned in our needs analysis that the students in this program had enormous reservoirs of knowledge about English vocabulary and grammar, but they needed to develop their abilities to use that knowledge to actually read, write, listen, and speak the language, especially in light of the fact that they were all ultimately headed to English speaking countries for postgraduate work or studies. In our infinite naïveté, we called what we felt they needed *fluency*. At that point, there was very little written in the literature on what fluency was, but we wanted our students to develop it, so we needed to figure out what we meant by that. It turned out that we were able to do that by developing assessments for our students in the EST B-level speaking course.

We decided that we would use three oral interview tests during each term – all three of which were to be very similar. In a sense, the first two were meant to serve as practice (with feedback from us) for the third, which was the final examination. These interviews were conducted in the first, fifth, and ninth weeks of the 10-week term. We decided to keep the interviews short at about five minutes for each student. When students walked into the interviews, they already knew that we were going to ask them to select three cards from a stack of face-down cards (there was one card for each SLO with three possible prompts on the other side). While recording each interview, we used one prompt from each card to get students talking (and using the functions taught in the course). After five minutes, we thanked them and asked them to send in the next student. We made no attempt to score them while the interviews were going on, but instead took the tapes home and listened to them for scoring later.

In order to do scoring that would encourage students to practice and develop their fluency, we decided to score the interviews primarily for fluency. We developed a rubric for doing just that. Our rubric (see Table 6.12)[4] had categories labeled across the top and scores down the left side. Our first category was *fluency* because that was our ultimate goal with regard to the students' abilities to perform the functions we were teaching. We also included columns for *meaning, exponents,*[5] *register/style,* and *intonation/stress,* and we labeled the scores of 1–3 down the left side of the rubric.[6] We included *meaning* as our second category because we felt that focusing on getting their meaning across would help them stop thinking about accuracy and instead learn fluency. *Gambits* (see Keller & Warner, 1979a–c) were useful chunks or language formulas that we taught them (at different levels of formality) to help them perform the functions in the course. We included gambits in the rubric because we wanted students to use the chunked language they had practiced in class (and at home), which we felt would contribute to their fluency. We included *register/style* in the rubric because we wanted them to learn to choose the right level of formality from among the gambits and generally use the correct level like fluent Chinese speakers of English. We included *intonation/stress* (as opposed to something too vague like *pronunciation*, or something too specific like *phonemes*) because we wanted our Chinese speakers of a syllable-timed language to focus on using *stress on content words* and *stress timing* (both of which are important characteristics of English) to help them get their meaning across and make them more fluent, and what we would describe today as *intelligible*.

Once we had our rubric labeled, we started filling in the squares by writing a prose description of the language behaviors that would describe an examinee with a score of 3 for the first category. We started by describing

Table 6.12 Rubric from EST B-level speaking course evaluation (Brown, 2012b)

Score	Fluency	Meaning	Gambits	Register/style	Intonation/stress
3	Almost completely appropriate flow, pauses, hesitations, fillers, speed, connectedness, and back-channeling	Successfully got meanings across most of the time	Used many of the exponents taught in the course	Used correct register/style most of the time	Used correct intonation and stress most of the time
2	Not a 3 and not a 1; that is, not *almost completely appropriate* nor *mostly inappropriate*	Got meanings across some of the time (not a 3 and not a 1)	Used some of the exponents taught in the course (not a 3 and not a 1)	Used correct register/style some of the time (not a 3 and not a 1)	Used correct intonation and stress some of the time (not a 3 and not a 1)
1	Mostly inappropriate flow, pauses, hesitations, fillers, speed, connectedness, and back-channeling	Did not succeed in getting meanings across	Used very few of the exponents taught in the course	Seldom used correct register/style	Seldom used correct intonation and stress

a performance of 3 in fluency: "Almost completely appropriate flow, pauses, hesitations, fillers, speed, connectedness, and back-channeling." We next filled in the square for a performance of 1 which was just the opposite of what we wrote for a three: "Mostly inappropriate flow, pauses, hesitations, fillers, speed, connectedness, and back-channeling" in this case. A score of 2 quite naturally became "Not a 3 and not a 1; that is, not *almost completely appropriate* nor *mostly inappropriate*" as shown in Table 6.12. (For much more on developing, using, and analyzing rubrics, see Brown, 2012b.)

For additional information on assessment in ESP, see Anthony (2017); Douglas (2000, 2013); Dudley-Evans and St. John, (1998, pp. 210–229); and Hutchinson and Waters (1987, pp. 144–156).

From SLOs to teaching

Naturally, because SLOs are closely related to materials and assessment, they figure in teaching as well. For example, at first glance, the development of our rubric may seem to have been easy. That process was anything but easy because it involved our having to understand what we meant by *fluency* as well as change and add to what we were teaching the students. In order to prepare the students to achieve our SLO functions as measured by our assessment procedures and rubric, we had to teach and set up activities for students to understand and practice *flow* in their speech, appropriate *pauses* and *hesitations*, suitable *fillers* to fill pauses that were becoming too long, appropriate *speed* (which often meant they needed to slow down) and *connectedness*, and appropriate *back-channeling*. In addition, we needed to explain and have them practice getting their meaning across, using the gambits we wanted them to know, finding the appropriate register and style, and using English intonation and stress. We developed the rubric for assessment purposes, but it also helped us to understand what we meant by fluency and what we should teach the students in order to help them develop the fluency that our NA had revealed they needed. Clearly, the SLOs in this case were not finished when we laid out the macro-functions we wanted to teach and the topics we would cover. Indeed, until we had the rubric we did not truly understand what the conditions were under which we wanted students to be able to perform the functions, nor did we know what we should do with the students to help them perform those functions fluently.

Once we had taught the course straight through once and used the rubric a few times, we revised the rubric and started regularly using it to give direct feedback to the students during the next term. In fact, we started going to the dormitories and meeting with all the students, playing the tape for them and explaining why we gave them the scores we did on the rubric.

Thus the rubrics became not only in integral part of how we defined the SLOs, but also an essential part of the teaching and materials in the form of a feedback tool.

From SLOs to course or program evaluation

In addition to linking the ESP NA to the materials, teaching, and assessment, the SLOs can also provide a sound basis for course or program evaluation. Once the materials, teaching, and assessment are at least tentatively in place, it is wise to keep curriculum activities moving along by constantly updating and improving the SLOs, materials, teaching, and assessment, which is a classic definition of *formative evaluation*. In fact, over the years, I have come to think of formative evaluation as just another form of needs analysis, but a form that is on-going with much more and better information to base it on.

To maximize the flexibility, effectiveness, and efficiency of any program (as explained in Brown, 1995, pp. 232–239), it may be wise to set up such formative evaluation as a regularly scheduled part of the curriculum activities on cyclical basis. For example, when I was director of the EAP program in the ELI at UHM, we had certain activities that we performed regularly each Fall Semester and others that took place on a regular basis in Spring Semester. In Fall Semester, we conducted an orientation meeting for teachers; reviewed and updated our NAs documentation; revised the SLOs as necessary; and revised our materials and assessments if needed or developed new ones as necessary (all to be ready for Spring Semester). In Spring Semester, we implemented all of the above; then we reviewed and revised the ways we supported teachers; we analyzed, revised, and reported to the full faculty on the norms, reliability, and validity of our placement tests (to be ready for Fall Semester); and we improved the teacher-orientation materials (also to be ready for Fall Semester). These cyclical activities provided our curriculum development activities with shifting and useful foci throughout the year and kept the different components of our EAP curriculum in reasonably good shape. Equally important, because our program was keeping up with formative evaluation in this ongoing way we were ready at a moment's notice when we were required to do *summative evaluation* (that is, evaluation that sums up how well the course or program is meeting the needs of the students, usually imposed by an outside agency, like the university's evaluation committee, or the regional accreditation association, or other agency). (For much more on course and program evaluation, see the chapters on this topic in Brown, 1995, pp. 217–246; Nation & Macalister, 2010, pp. 123–135; Richards, 2001, pp. 286–309; or books like Alderson & Beretta, 1992; Lynch, 1997; Norris, Davis, Sinicrope, & Watanabe, 2009.)

Task 6.2 Using SLOs as a bridge from NA to other curriculum components

Noden (2002) describes an English for home-cleaning purposes program for employees of a company in the Virginia suburbs of Washington, DC. The author lists a dozen things that employees need to do with English in their work. Half of those are:

- Understanding spoken and written directions (especially with regard to finding particular locations)
- Explaining feedback cards to customers
- Responding to feedback (i.e., practicing good customer service)
- Ordering and refilling supplies
- Asking for assistance and responding to requests for assistance
- Discussing paycheck issues (e.g., late payments, incorrect amount, lost checks)

(pp. 192, 194)

A   Based on this chapter, jot down one or two ways you would use these embedded SLOs to bridge the following (if you were in charge of using these observed needs in a training curricululm):

1   the NA and materials;
2   the NA and assessments;
3   the NA and teaching;
4   the NA and course or program evaluation.

B   If possible compare your answers to those of a partner. Feel free to steal your partner's ideas (and share your own), if they seem useful, and add those ideas to your lists in A above.
C   After reading this chapter and doing A above, have your convictions become stronger or weaker that SLOs are important to use in any ESP program? Why? Does your partner agree?

Summary and conclusions

In summary, this chapter explored some of the key issues involved in effectively using the results in an NA. The first issue was interpreting the NA results in terms of what they mean for SLOs. The chapter defined SLOs and differentiated between three types: precisely defined, embedded, and experiential SLOs. The chapter then explained in detail some of the tricks involved in writing effective and efficient SLOs. A number of strategies were also explained for revising and organizing SLOs. The chapter also explained a number of approaches for getting teachers to accept and use SLOs. Once in place, however, it is still necessary to use those SLOs as a bridge from the NA to all the other curriculum elements including connecting NA to materials, NA to assessments, NA to teaching, and NA to course or program evaluation.

Clearly then, the central issues involved in using NA results all have to do with applying what was learned in the NA to creating an entire curriculum based on it. Or as I put it in Brown (2009):

> Naturally, in educational programs, needs analyses focus on the learning needs of students, and then, once they are identified, needs are translated into learning objectives [that is, what I am calling here *SLOs*], which in turn serve as the basis for further development of teaching materials, learning activities, tests, program evaluation strategies, etc. Thus needs analysis is the first step in curriculum development.
>
> (p. 269)

Notes

1 For those curious about my choice of words here, *slithy toves* is from a poem called the "Jabberwocky" in the first chapter of Lewis Carroll's (1871) book *Through the Looking Glass, and What Alice Found There* (available free on the Project Gutenberg website at http://www.gutenberg.org/ebooks/12). The first couplet in that poem is: "'Twas brillig, and the slithy toves / Did gyre and gimble in the wabe; …". He illustrated in this poem what happens when all the content words are replaced with nonsense words.

2 That is, at a suitable level for reading by an average student in the ninth grade in the US system.

3 For those unfamiliar with the US system, a grade of A is considered *excellent*; B is *above average*; C is *average*; D is *below average*; and F is *failing*. Inexplicably, there is no E in this system.

4 Note that the original rubric has been lost in the mists of time, so the one you are looking at in Table 6.12 is one that I reconstructed from memory in Brown (2012b). I am fairly sure that it is a reasonable approximation of the rubric we developed.

5 We used the term *exponents* to mean either (a) chunks of language that are typically unanalyzed grammatically like *'Scuse me* or (b) widely applicable formulas like *Can you tell me if there is an X near here?* into which students learn to substitute applicable vocabulary items (for example, in this case, X could be *market*, *hospital*, *restroom*, and so forth).

6 Note also that we started with a 1–5 scale but soon abandoned it because it was too difficult to write descriptors for such fine-grained judgments with students whose abilities did not vary all that much with regard to these advanced skills, and in any case, we did not need a 1–5 scale for giving students feedback on these issues.

Chapter 7

Reporting on the ESP needs analysis project

In this chapter, you will find answers to the following questions:

- How can I organize and write my NA report?
- Who should I write the NA report for?
- How can I describe the NA itself?
- How can I report the findings and the SLOs in an NA report?
- Should I publish my NA report?
- How can I account for the various views expressed in any NA?

Reporting on the NA project

Organizing an NA report

Any full-scale report that results from an NA should probably contain an *introduction* that describes the context in which the NA project was conducted, including the situation and any theoretical assumptions or framework (usually drawn from the literature) involved, as well as a description of the purpose of the NA including a list of the goals of the project and its research questions. Such a report should probably also contain a clear account of the NA *methods* that were used with separate subsections for: *participants*, including at least a description of the people who cooperated in the study (for instance, administrators, teachers, students, future employers) and how they were selected; *materials*, including any materials that were used (for example, observation forms, interview schedules, questionnaires, tests) with detailed descriptions (maybe even with the materials themselves included in appendices) and explaining where the materials came from or how they were developed; and *procedures*, providing a step-by-step listing and explanation of exactly what was done in the NA at each stage (for example, planning, data gathering, analyzing data, interpreting the results, developing SLOs, reporting the results, and using the NA). Naturally, an NA report should also probably contain *results* and *discussion* sections that directly report and address the initial NA goals and answer the initial research questions and also list the tentative SLOs that are suggested by the NA results. A final *conclusion* section is also common where you can: consider the limitations or constraints that arose in conducting the NA; describe the strengths of the NA (for example, how the dependability, credibility, confirmability, and transferability were enhanced or confirmed and/or how the mixed-methods techniques described in the previous chapter were used to increase the value of combining quantitative and qualitative data and analyses together); evaluate the quality of the NA and the its results; and discuss how the NA results have been, are being, or will be used. Thus, a handy outline for many NA reports might be something like the following:

I   Introduction

    A   Description of the ESP context.
    B   Discussion of the theoretical assumptions and framework.
    C   Purpose of the NA and goals or research questions (RQs) that guided the research.

II   Methods

    A   Participants – describe the people who cooperated in the study and how they were selected; if you needed, applied for, and got approval from your institution's ethics or human subjects committee, describe that process as well.
    B   Materials – discuss any materials that were used in detail and explain where they came from or how they were developed (consider appending the actual materials).
    C   Procedures – a step-by-step listing and account of exactly what was done in the NA.
    D   Analyses – a step-by-step listing and description of the quantitative and qualitative analyses that were conducted (note that this section is most often included in NAs that are theses or dissertations; in other NA documents, such descriptions should probably be integrated into the results section along with the results that are directly related to each form of analysis).

III   Results – a technical reporting of the quantitative and qualitative results of the study, often in tables and charts with prose explaining how to read each table and chart and pointing out what the important aspects are of each; typically these are ordered roughly in the same order as the RQs.

IV   Discussion

    A   Discuss the NA results – directly address the NA goals and answer the initial research questions in clear non-technical language.

B   List SLOs – list and discuss the tentative SLOs that are suggested by the NA results.

V   Conclusion

A   Limitations of the NA – critically consider any limitations or constraints that were encountered.
B   Strengths of the NA – describe how the dependability, credibility, confirmability, and transferability were confirmed and/or how mixed-methods techniques were used to increase the value of the NA by blending quantitative and qualitative data and analyses.
C   Evaluation – evaluate the quality of the NA and the NA results.
D   Discuss how the NA results have been, are being, or will be used.

VI   References
VII   Appendices – often serve very important purposes in NAs for showing the questionnaires or other instruments used in the NA, listing the SLOs, and providing additional statistics that would interrupt the flow of the narrative if included in the body of the report.

Examples of how actual ESP NAs have been organized

In this section, I will provide examples of how published ESP NAs have been organized from Huh's (2006) business English NA, Noda's (2011) EAP NA, and the Dibakanaka and Hiranburana (2012) English for chief flight attendants NA. These three examples illustrate how the organization of such reports can vary away from the idealized model outline given above, while by-and-large still providing the same sorts of information.

Table 7.1 shows a two-level outline of the headings used in the Huh (2006) report on a business English NA. Notice that Huh followed the idealized outline shown above almost to the letter with some quite appropriate elaboration in the Introduction and Results sections. This is not surprising given that I was her advisor on this research.

Table 7.2 outlines the two-level section headings from the NA for an academic listening and speaking course reported in Noda (2011). Noda appears to vary away from the idealized outline discussed above, until you realize that each subsection (Interviews, Questionnaire Survey, and Class Observations) in the Methods section describes the appropriate participants, materials, procedures, and analyses involved in that particular form of data gathering. Notice also how useful it is to readers that the Discussion section headings are the research questions for the study.

Table 7.3 outlines the three-level section headings from the NA for an e-learning competency-based English course module for chief flight attendants reported in Dibakanaka and Hiranburana (2012). The headings in Dibakanaka and Hiranburana vary considerably from the idealized outline

Table 7.1 Outline of the section headings in Huh (2006)

(Abstract with no heading)
Introduction
    Hawai'i English Language Program and the Business English Course
    Task-based Needs Analysis
    Literature Review of Business English Needs Analysis
    Research Questions
Method
    Participants
    Instruments
    Procedures
    Analyses
Results
    Business English Tasks Performed by the Korean Business Professionals
    Frequency of Business English Tasks
    The Importance of English Perceived by the Korean Business Professionals
    Recommendations for Potential Job Applicants
    Korean Business Professionals' Previous Experiences of Business English Courses
    Korean Business Professionals' Attitudes Toward and Wants for Business English
    Courses
Discussion
Conclusion
Acknowledgements
References
Appendix A: Questions for Semi-Structured Interviews
Appendix B: Questionnaire for Korean Business Professionals
Appendix C: Business English Tasks

discussed above. Nonetheless, the general shape of the outline is familiar (Abstract, Introduction, Research Elaborations, Findings, Conclusions, References, Appendices) and most of the same types of information are provided by Dibakanaka and Hiranburana that were provided by Huh and by Noda.

Who should an NA report be written for?

From the very beginning of the report writing process, you should be considering the *audiences* for the report. Even with full-scale published reports like those described in the previous subsection, the audiences may differ. Most of the NA and other curriculum related reports I have written have been aimed at the audience of the teachers and teacher coordinators directly involved in the project. Since those two groups are pretty much the same audience, the writing style I have used was meant to be useful for them. However, since those two groups have usually served as separate sources of information and have generally different sets of concerns, I have had to keep them in mind when deciding what sorts of content I should include that would be useful and interesting to each of the groups and both.

Table 7.2 Outline of the section headings in Noda (2011)

Abstract
Introduction
    ELI 80 Advanced Listening and Speaking Course
    Needs Analysis
    Research Questions
Methods
    Interviews
    Questionnaire Survey
    Class Observations
Results
    Interviews
    Questionnaire Survey
    Class Observations
Discussion
    What Skills Do the ELI 80 Students Prefer to Learn in ELI 80?
    Does the Course Meet the Students' Perception of Language Needs? If not, What
    Suggestions Could Be Provided About the Course?
Conclusion
Acknowledgements
References
Appendix A: Survey Questionnaire: ELI 80 Students' Views of Academic Listening and
Speaking
Appendix B: Descriptive Statistics

Table 7.3 Outline of the section headings in Dibakanaka and Hiranburana (2012)

Abstract
Introduction
Research Elaborations
    Literature Review
        English for Specific Purposes (ESP)
        Needs Analysis
        Competency and Competency-Based Approach
        e-Learning and Instructional Design
    Materials and Methods
        Scope of the Study
        Assumptions of the Study
        Data Collection
    Data Analysis
Findings
    Phase I
    Phase II
        Course Design
        Objectives of the Course (listed in this section)
    Phase III
Conclusions
References
Authors (academic ranks, affiliations, & email addresses)

Occasionally, I have found myself also having to cater to people (like ministers of education) who consider themselves very important, and who by definition, do not have time to waste on my report. For those sorts of people, I usually provide an *executive summary* of two to five pages that touches on the high points of the larger report. Naturally, in such cases, I also attached the full report, which they no doubt ignored. Clearly, an executive report must be written using language that even a "very important" person can understand.

Other times, I have found it useful to write short articles/reports for newsletters and other shorter-form publications to let the profession know about curriculum development projects that I have been involved in. Naturally, I tried to write these articles at the appropriate length for the publications involved and tailored the vocabulary and style for the appropriate audiences.

There are a number of other possible avenues for *dissemination* of information about an NA that needs analysts should consider, each with its own style and length requirements. In addition to full-scale reports and newsletter articles, you might want to consider disseminating your NA results through written reports published as institutional curriculum monographs, journal articles, and even books,[1] or oral presentations at faculty meetings, public meetings, and professional conferences. Certainly, you will want to inform those groups of people who are most likely to benefit from your work so that they can actually use the results to create materials, assessment procedures, and teaching strategies for whatever course or program is involved. However, you have gone to a lot of trouble to do your NA, and your colleagues have done a lot of work in using the NA for curriculum development, so perhaps you owe it to everybody involved to also spread the word about the project at your institution, in your local area, or more broadly in the profession.

Personal reflection – How will you organize your ESP NA?

Think about doing an NA for a group of ESP students that you teach (or some you would like to teach). Do you think that your report on the NA will best be organized following the pattern that I provided? Or are you more likely to follow the outlines that I took from Huh (2006), Noda (2011), or Dibakanaka and Hiranburana (2012)? Or will you organize you report in some completely different way? Why did you choose the organizational pattern you did? How would you like to let the world know about your NA project?

What types of information should be included in an NA report?

Describing the participants in an NA report

Typically, the people who contributed information to the NA are described in the Participants section of the report. Naturally, information about those people like their educational levels, gender, ages, nationalities, languages they speak, majors, academic status, years in English-speaking countries, English proficiency levels, or anything else that might be appropriate and pertinent to the NA report should be included. I generally do this in prose or in a table like Table 7.4, or both. Note that separate descriptions may be necessary for different key groups (for instance, teachers, students, and administrators). Other information like an accounting of how the participants were selected, or what percentage of the total cooperated in each group, or what the return rate was for any questionnaires may prove useful to readers. The point is that readers will need to know about the people involved in the NA with as much detail as possible. For an additional example of a table used to describe the participants in an NA, see Table 5.1.

Describing the materials used in an NA

The procedures used to gather information in the NA are typically described in a section of the report labeled as Materials. Materials might include things like interview schedules, questionnaires, tests, or classroom observation sheets. They can be described in prose or tables or both, and the information provided might include descriptions of where the materials were originally developed, how they have been adapted, or how they were developed from scratch. Other information that might be useful includes example items, rubrics, or questions for each procedure, or how they were organized. For example, Janssen, Nausa, and Rico (2012) used a questionnaire "designed following one developed by Gravatt, Richards, and Lewis (1997, as cited in Richards, 2001, pp. 80–86) because of the perceived similarities between these authors' university EAP setting for non-English background and the IPD setting" (p. 55). Table 7.5 shows how they described that questionnaire. Notice how the authors number the sections, then describe the construct being measured in each section, and tell readers how many items (questions) the section had, including what types of items and the number of each. Thus the organization and characteristics of the items on the questionnaire are very clear. The point is that readers will need to know what the materials were like that were used for gathering the information in the NA, again, with as much detail as possible.

Wise authors will also append the actual instruments they used to the end of their NA report so that readers can see the actual format and

Table 7.4 ELI 70 and ELI 80 student biodata (adapted from Kimzin & Proctor, 1986)

N = 28				
Native language:	10 Chinese	(36%)	1 Samoan	(4%)
	5 Vietnamese	(18%)	1 Tamil	(4%)
	3 Indonesian	(11%)	1 Lingala/French	(4%)
	3 Korean	(11%)	1 Kikngo	(4%)
	1 Japanese	(4%)	1 Man`de	(4%)
	1 Thai	(4%)		
Age:	18 to 57 years; Mode = 24 years; Mean = 26.3 years			
Sex:	25 Males (86%); 3 Females (11%)			
Time in US:	6 months to 7 years; Mode = 6 months; Mean = 3.2 years			
...				
Academic major:	8 Engineering	(29%)		
	5 Social sciences	(18%)		
	4 Science	(14%)		
	3 Humanities	(11%)		
	8 Liberal arts/ undeclared	(29%)		
Current student status:	18 Undergraduate	(64%)		
	10 Graduate	(36%)		

content for themselves. From my point of view, this is a very admirable practice indeed.

Reporting the findings of an NA

The findings of an NA are usually described in the Results section of an NA report. Different strategies are used to describe quantitative, qualitative, or mixed-methods results, and naturally, the form that these accounts take will differ depending on the type of data and analysis involved, but a few examples of each may prove helpful.

Quantitative results, because of their numerical nature, are well suited to presentation in tables. I generally organize quantitative tables with clearly labeled columns and rows like those shown in Table 7.6 where the column labels are Item, *N*, Mean, *SD*, and the numbers that respondents had to choose from for each Likert item. The Likert statements that respondents were addressing in each case are provided down the left side of the table. This format makes the table relatively easy to read because a clear picture of what happened numerically on each item is displayed. For example, for item 1 "oral presentation," you can see that 72 (*N*) people answered the item, the mean was 3.46, the standard deviation (*SD*)

Table 7.5 Organization of an ESP questionnaire for a Colombian English for PhD students program (from Janssen, Nausa, & Rico, 2012)

§	Questionnaire section construct	Question number, types
§1	Project description, authorization of data use for research purposes	1 yes/ no
§2	Personal biodata	11 items: 5 pull-down menu multiple-choice items; 6 open-ended items
§3	Academic biodata	31 items: 7 pull-down menu multiple-choice items; 24 open-ended items
§4	Time uses	19 items: 9 pull-down menu multiple-choice items; 10 open-ended items soliciting further commentary
§5.1	Historical English language use in different domains	18 items: 17 5-point Likert-scale items, 1 open-ended item soliciting further commentary
§5.2	Time investment in English language study during schooling	5 items: 4 5-point Likert-scale items, 1 open-ended item soliciting further commentary
§5.3	Reported skill level, different general English language abilities	8 items: 7 5-point Likert-scale items, 1 open-ended item soliciting further commentary
§5.4	Difficulty, different general English language abilities	8 items: 7 5-point Likert-scale items, 1 open-ended item soliciting further commentary
§6.1	Relevance of different general English language abilities for success during PhD	10 items: 9 5-point Likert-scale items, 1 open-ended item soliciting additional commentary
§6.2	Relevance of different general English language abilities for success after PhD	10 items: 9 5-point Likert-scale items, 1 open-ended item soliciting additional commentary
§6.3	Dis/agreement with statements about Programa IPD	6 items: 5 5-point Likert-scale items, 1 open-ended item soliciting additional commentary
§7	Programa IPD speaking sub-skills	25 items: 24 5-point Likert-scale items; 1 open-ended item soliciting additional commentary
§8	Programa IPD listening sub-skills	17 items: 16 5-point Likert-scale items; 1 open-ended item, soliciting additional commentary
§9	Programa IPD writing sub-skills	27 items: 26 5-point Likert-scale items; 1 open-ended item, soliciting additional commentary
§10	Programa IPD reading sub-skills	17 items: 16 5-point Likert-scale items; 1 open-ended item, soliciting additional commentary
§11	Programa IPD vocabulary and grammar sub-skills	6 items: 5 5-point Likert-scale items; 1 open-ended item, soliciting additional commentary.
§12	Thank you and final comments	1 open-ended item, soliciting additional commentary

Table 7.6 Students' responses on the requirements in non-ELI courses (Noda, 2011 p. 18)

Item	N	Mean	SD	1	2	3	4
1 Oral presentation	72	3.46	0.79	4.2	5.6	30.6	59.7
2 Leading whole class discussions	72	2.96	0.91	6.9	22.2	38.9	31.9
3 Leading small group discussions	72	3.04	0.93	6.9	19.4	36.1	37.5
4 Participating in whole class discussions	72	3.32	0.78	1.4	15.3	33.3	50.0
5 Participating in small group discussions	72	3.39	0.76	1.4	12.5	31.9	54.2
6 Asking questions during class	72	3.10	0.75	2.8	15.3	51.4	30.6
7 Answering questions during class	71	3.00	0.91	5.6	23.9	35.2	35.2
8 Oral interactions with native speakers	71	3.46	0.75	2.8	7.0	31.0	59.2
9 Oral interactions with international students	72	3.25	0.87	5.6	11.1	36.1	47.2
10 Oral interactions with professors	71	3.46	0.73	1.4	9.9	29.6	59.2
11 Participating in debates	71	3.06	0.94	8.5	15.5	38.0	38.0
12 Taking notes during the lectures	72	3.35	0.81	2.8	12.5	31.9	52.8

Note: Survey Part B-3, items 1–12. There was no response to item 13. 1 = not at all important; 2 = not very important; 3 = somewhat important; 4 = very important. There were some participants who skipped this part because they were not attending non-ELI courses. Percentages may not total to 100 because of rounding. Question numbers correspond to the order they appear in the questionnaire.

was 0.79, and 4.2 percent selected 1, 5.6 percent chose 2, 30.6 percent, picked 3, and a whopping 59.7 percent decided on 4. The associated prose description might examine which items had the highest or lowest means and which had the highest or lowest standard deviations, as well as any other features of the results that stand out. When describing such a table in prose for many audiences, you may want to consider helping the readers by telling them how to read the table and explaining what information in the table you think they should pay particular attention to. For examples of other tables that present quantitative results, see Tables 5.2 and 5.3 in Chapter 5.

Qualitative results tend more often to be described and explained in words, but can also be presented quite profitably in tables or figures. For example, in Chapter 5, I argued that various types of matrices can be used to help you analyze, understand, and present your qualitative results. More precisely, I explained how researchers can use matrices to discover general, specific difference, and specific similarity patterns in qualitative data. Recall that the definition I supplied in Chapter 5 for a *matrix* is something like "a table, grid, or array" with one set of categories labeled across the top and another categories labeled down the left. For example, the matrix I show in Table 5.4, labels Curriculum Issues across the top (including objectives, tests, and materials) and Groups down the left side (including ESL teachers at McNamara Adult Ed School, KPIS Center for Adult Ed, and McKinley High night school).

A quick glance back at Table 5.4 will reveal that the cells within the matrix/ table describe the views of the three groups on each of the three issues – all of which is very qualitative and derived from qualitative data. Another example of a table that presents qualitative information is Table 5.5 in Chapter 5. Examples of figures that present qualitative information in Chapter 5 include Figure 5.4 onward, all of which are used to present some qualitative information. Indeed, I would be remiss if I did not point out that I have used many if not most of the tables and figures in this book to present qualitative information. Perhaps it would be useful to take a look back at how I did that in various ways.

Mixed-methods results can also be described in prose, tables, figures, or all three. In fact, because of the complexity of MMR results, visual representations of those results in tables and figures are often very helpful to readers. For example, consider the very abridged version of a table from the section on presenting mixed-methods research results in Brown (2014, pp. 167–170) shown in Table 7.7.

Notice in Table 7.7 how the observations made in the study are shown in the first column and that they are categorized with separate headings for Teaching, Materials, Syllabus/Curriculum, and Testing. Over to the right, the different data-gathering tools and groups are listed including: classroom observations (of students, teachers, and inspectors, who were administrator/coordinators), materials, meetings (again with students, teachers, and inspectors), and questionnaires (again for students, teachers, and inspectors).

Clearly, multiple types of triangulation were going on in this study and the layout of Table 7.7 allowed me to show what the source, or sources, were for each observation. Thus a very complex set of analyses were explained visually in such a way that sources for each observation were easy to see and understand. This not only helped me to discern useful patterns, but also to present my results to readers. So for example, it became clear to me that the observation 1 under Teaching (that is, that "Enormous amounts of material must be covered in the little time allowed") was a pervasive view because all groups and data-gathering techniques revealed the same thing. In contrast, the view in observation 1 under Testing that the "Diploma and Baccalaureate tests are not 100% representative of what is taught" only surfaced in the Inspector Group Meetings. Thus, I had to wonder how widespread this view really was, or how important it might be to students and teachers.

Figure 7.1 shows how a figure can be used effectively in a mixed-methods study (Kletzien, 2011). Notice that the author was able to show his two studies and the relationships between them as well as the various data-gathering techniques he applied to teachers and students. (For more on how he created this figure, see Brown, 2014, pp. 165–166.)

Table 7.7 Abridged summary of observations and multiple data sources in Brown (2014, pp. 167–170)

Categories Observations	Classroom obs. of students	Classroom obs. of teachers	Classroom obs. of inspectors	Materials	Student meetings	Teacher meetings	Inspector group meetings	Student questionnaires	Teacher questionnaires	Inspector group questionnaires
Teaching										
1 Enormous amounts of material must be covered in the little time allowed.	×	×	×	×	×	×	×	×	×	×
2 Because of the short amount of time and large amount of material, the coverage is cursory.	×	×	×		×	×	×	×	×	
3 More time and practice to help students assimilate the material.					×	×				
…										
Materials										
1 Materials seem to be more than can be covered in the time allowed.	×	×			×	×	×	×	×	×
2 Coverage of objectives presents the language points, but gives very little reinforcement, review, and spiraled recycling.	×	×			×	×	×	×	×	
3 No workbook for the textbooks.				×	×	×		×		
…										

(Continued)

Table 7.7 (Continued)

Categories Observations	Classroom obs. of students	Classroom obs. of teachers	Classroom obs. of inspectors	Materials	Student meetings	Teacher meetings	Inspector group meetings	Student questionnaires	Teacher questionnaires	Inspector group questionnaires
Syllabus/curriculum										
1 English not given much importance within the whole educational system in terms of hours per week and coefficient.					×	×	×	×	×	×
2 Huge and daunting numbers of objectives.				×						
3 Rationale for selection and sequencing of objectives not clear within or between textbook levels.				×		×			×	
...										
Testing										
1 Diploma and Baccalaureate tests are not 100% representative of what is taught.							×			
...										
6 Reliability (internal consistency, interrater reliability, etc.) and validity (content, construct, criterion-related) are not studied and reported publicly for each test.						×	×		×	×
7 One rater is used for writing samples.							×			

Study 1 - Survey of PEP students and teachers

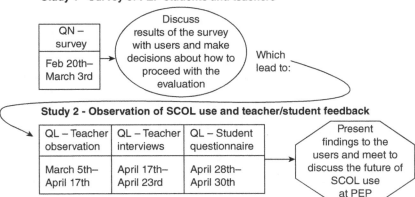

Study 2 - Observation of SCOL use and teacher/student feedback

QL – Teacher observation	QL – Teacher interviews	QL – Student questionnaire
March 5th– April 17th	April 17th– April 23rd	April 28th– April 30th

Figure 7.1 Design and simplified timetable (Kletzien, 2011, p. 57). QN = quantitative; QL = qualitative.

Table 7.8 The ELI 80 advanced listening and speaking course SLOs (Noda, 2011, p. 6)

By the end of the course students will be able to:

1 Demonstrate effective use of strategies for comprehending advanced academic lectures in English
2 Critically evaluate speakers perspectives, techniques, and arguments
3 Make academic presentations (individually or in group or panel contexts) with a high degree of formal accuracy and cultural and stylistic appropriacy
4 Autonomously lead academic discussions using academic English
5 Demonstrate excellent use of advanced strategies for participation in academic discussions with expert users of English
6 State a range of strategies for using listening/speaking opportunities to develop academic vocabulary (in English) and specify which they have an active command of in their repertoire
7 State a range of strategies for developing academic English and specify which they have an active command of in their repertoire
8 Self-assess their strengths in terms of listening/speaking abilities, as well as identify areas for continued development

Reporting SLOs in an NA report

One other aspect of an NA report that might benefit from some examples is the presentation of the SLOs that an NA is recommending. Consider, for example, the SLOs presented in Table 7.8 from Noda (2011, p. 6), which simply lists fairly formal SLOs complete with the usual beginning: "By the end of the course the students will be able to."

Table 7.9 Target tasks for business English in Korea (Huh, 2006, p. 27)

Target task types	Target tasks
Getting a job	Writing a resume and cover letter, job interviews, translation, free talking, presentation
Correspondence	Email, phone calls, faxes
Writing a document	Memorandum, proposal, report, contract/agreement, business letter, order, claim, annual report, evaluation form, international relations materials, summary of meetings
Order/customer satisfaction	Placing and receiving an order, purchasing, dealing with claims
Business meeting	Meetings, conferences, seminars, social meetings, briefing, presentation, Q&A, negotiations, video conferences, teleconferences, making a reservation, business meetings, sightseeing, finding directions, visiting other companies or factories, social meetings
Attending foreign guests	Pick-up, sightseeing guide, interpreting
Interpretation	Business meetings, company ceremonies
Translation	Documents, booklets, brochures, books
Market research	Visiting other companies' homepages, asking questions using Q&A board
Reading	Reading articles and magazines related to job
Others	Social talks with foreign colleagues or foreign guests, making an English homepage, proofreading, making presentation materials

In contrast, what appear to be SLOs in Table 7.9 are a bit more abbreviated (though no less useful) perhaps because they are more numerous. The SLOs in this case are called Target Tasks, and they are grouped into Target Task Types, which helps make the relationships among them clearer.

Table 7.10 shows the Health Care English Course SLOs (reproduced here as shown in the original) from Freihat and Al-Makhzoomi (2012, p. 145). Like those in Table 7.8, these are rather formal. In addition, they are described in terms of the course units in which they appear (in the first column).

On some occasions, an NA may span several courses, levels, or skills. In such cases, it may prove useful to connect SLOs across those dimensions in a single table as shown in Table 7.11. Notice that this table shows the goals and their relationships for two EAP listening courses at different levels. Each of those goals was then expanded into precisely defined SLOs elsewhere in the NA documentation.

Table 7.10 Specific health care course objectives (Freihat & Al-Makhzoomi, 2012, p. 145)

Course unit title	Specific objective no.	Course specific objectives
		By the end of the course, the study participants will be able to:
1 Assertive Communication	1	– distinguish between passive, aggressive, and assertive communication;
	2	– demonstrate positive, assertive communication in role-plays;
2 Therapeutic Communication and	3	– identify, define, and generate appropriate examples of therapeutic communication and information-gathering techniques;
3 Information-Gathering Techniques	4	– demonstrate appropriate therapeutic communication and information-gathering techniques in role-plays;
	5	– understand the role of culture in health care communication settings;
4 The Role of Culture in Health Care Communication	6	– identify the cultural knowledge, values, and assumptions implicit in certain countries' health care settings, and compare and contrast with participants' own culture;
5 The Role of Non-Verbal Communication in Health Care Communication Settings	7	– understand the role of non-verbal communication in health care settings;
	8	– demonstrate appropriate gestures, facial expressions, and eye contact, and appropriate tone, rate and volume of speech in role-plays

Task 7.1 Planning the organization and content of your ESP NA report

1   Individually, write out an outline of headings for the organization of an ESP NA report that you would like to write.
2   Then, after each heading, jot down what content you think you should include in each section.
3   When you are finished, find a partner and give each other feedback on both the outline and the content in each section.
4   Revise your outline.
5   Is the outline improved by the feedback that you got? Would you be comfortable at least starting to write you ESP NA based on this outline?

Table 7.11 Goals for EAP listening courses at UHM (Kimzin & Proctor, 1986)

ELI 70 goals	ELI 80 goals
#1 Students will be able to follow the basic ideas of a lecture	#1 Students will be able to synthesize arguments within a lecture

A Lecture organization
    B Cohesion
    C Vocabulary
    D Lecturer's style	

#2 Students will be able to use effective note-taking skills	#2 Students will be able to devise and reference a note-taking system compatible with their academic needs
A Taking notes B Using notes	
#3 Students will be able to effect learning by actively participating in academic situations	#3 Students will be able to develop coherent arguments in class discussions and in oral presentations

A Classroom discussions
    B ELI 70: Student–teacher conferences
       ELI 80: Oral presentations	

Publishing an NA report

Careful examination of the references in this book will reveal a number of published NA papers. Most of these papers are no doubt reports of local NA efforts that are themselves rewrites of larger reports produced at the institutional level. Such reports can certainly serve as models (in addition to the examples given in this chapter) for how such reports should be organized and written, as well as how prose, tables, and figures can be used to present NA results and the SLOs that stem from those results.

However, it is important to recognize that all published NA reports are not equal in quality. Some journals are probably more trustworthy than others. For example, I generally put more faith in the articles I find in *TESOL Quarterly*, *English for Specific Purposes*, *Foreign Language Annals*, the *Journal of English for Academic Purposes*, and *System* than in some of the other online journals. I also am more likely to trust NA papers found in books published by respected publishers, than in other corners of the profession.

It also appears that only some journals are interested in publishing locally generated curriculum work including NAs. The editors of journals that refuse to publish NA reports seem to feel that NAs are too local in focus and not generalizable to their readership who work outside of the institutions in which they occurred. That belief can certainly be challenged, but such debate is unlikely to change the journals' policies, at least not in the short term. One alternative way to deal with this issue would be to locate your NA in the broader research literature and emphasize what the results of the NA have to say to people working throughout the field and in other parts of the world. In any case, the five journals listed in the previous paragraph are clearly willing and able to publish NA studies.

I should mention that no journal is perfect and hence the articles found in journals I listed above are not likely to be perfect, or even necessarily trust-worthy. Nor am I willing to say that articles found online in some of the other journals are poorly done. Hence, you will have to judge the quality of each NA report for yourself.

Nonetheless there are two concepts that may help readers and budding authors to know which journals are more prestigious and trustworthy: peer review and pay-to-publish. *Peer review* is a process whereby articles are reviewed by experienced researchers and either accepted, rejected, or recommended for revision and resubmission by the journal editors based on those reviews. This process is not foolproof because reviewers are human and may not themselves have critical knowledge important for reviewing some papers. It is also important to consider who the *peers* are that are doing the reviews. Clearly even when there are peer reviewers, the *peers* reviewing for a prominent international journal like the *TESOL Quarterly* will be quite different from the *peers* reviewing for a small, local, online journal.

Pay-to-publish journals are ones that require authors to pay a fee to have their articles included. In many fields this is common practice (to cover print-ing costs), but in language teaching and learning, this practice may make the publication suspect in the minds of many, especially if there are no printing costs (as in online journals) and/or there is no system of peer review.

All of this means that readers need to carefully analyze published NA papers and make judgements for themselves as to the trustworthiness of what they read. It also means that authors of NA reports who want to publish their work or a revised, shorter version, should consider these fac-tors in deciding where to submit that work. (For articles on publishing in academic journals in our field, see Benson, 1994; Brown, 2005c; Holmes and Moulton, 1995; LoCastro, 1988, or Richards, 1988. For a book length treatment, see Paltridge and Starfield, 2016.)

However, I also feel duty bound to point out that even a badly done NA report may contain useful information like (a) interesting research questions, (b) ideas for variables to consider, or (c) items to put on a questionnaire. This is especially true if the article is focused on the type of English germane to a particular NA. For example, even a poorly done NA on nursing English may be interesting and useful in some ways to those doing their own nursing English NA.

Personal reflection – Would you like to publish your ESP NA?

Think about an NA report that you might write for a group of ESP students that you teach (or some you would like to teach). Would you like to publish it? Where do you think it should be published? How might you go about improving your chances of getting it published? How can you tell if a publication is trustworthy?

Accounting for various views expressed in an NA

In many places in this book, I have stressed the importance of gathering information, analyzing that information, and using it. In ending this book, I would like to stress one other aspect of this process that is often forgotten: NA in ESP is about people, especially about getting people to cooperate and do things, that is, getting people to reveal information, understand, and act on information about their needs and the ESP needs of their students. To address the issues involved in getting people to cooperate, support, and use NA results, I focus on answering four questions:

- How should we deal with various attitudes toward an NA?
- What is the truth about learning needs?
- How important are teachers in the NA scheme of things?
- How can all of the above be accomplished?

Dealing with various attitudes toward an NA

A number of years ago, I found myself working on the nationwide junior and senior high-school English curricula in Tunisia with a group of about 29 English *inspecteurs* (each of whom was responsible for the English teaching and teachers in one area of the country). We were discussing NA and the need to gather data from students about things like their ideas, opinions, and preferences. One very dignified and greying inspector stood up and interrupted me to ask: "Don't you think we teachers really know what the students need to learn?" I have run into this attitude in many countries in the world, an attitude generated by well-meaning language-teaching professionals, who quite obviously believe that there is some true way to go about language teaching that they are privy to. My answer to such people is always "no" because I believe that there is no single true way to teach or learn languages. Yes, most of us teachers do think we know what the students need based on the fact that we are older and perhaps wiser than our students. What we are really saying is that our preferences and beliefs are more correct than those of the students.

Indeed, those teachers who have sound training and have kept up with developments in the field do know what the literature and theory have to offer with regard to the language learning needs of our students. However, such teachers typically disagree among themselves about what that literature and theory means in the everyday classroom. For example, within the group of inspectors that I just mentioned, I found three distinct factions that seemed to sort themselves more or less by age and then sat together most of the time; these groups clearly held very different belief systems about what and how the students needed to learn.

Such differences probably result from the fact that teachers are trained in a wide variety of institutions that are promoting different ideas about what and how students need to learn English. Moreover, since such theories tend to change over time, variations in when teachers were trained can lead to very real differences in their views on language teaching and learning. Thus, in any group of teachers, it is probable that disagreements will surface about the relative value of the various language teaching and learning theories, and by extension, about what and how students need to learn in the teachers' classrooms. What are needs analysts to do? Where in all this confusion of beliefs and preferences are they to find the truth? More importantly, whose truth is it that should triumph? In my view, the only way for an NA to survive is for the needs analysts to realize from the beginning that *no single truth exists in any language-teaching situation*. Instead, views will differ considerably from person to person and even from moment to moment.

The truth and learning needs

The central problem with many NAs is that they have focused solely on the learners' *language needs* often based on some *truth* that the needs analysts believed from the beginning about those needs from a very specific theoretical viewpoint. When I was helping to set up the EST program in China, we made that very mistake. We analyzed the students' communicative needs because we held it as self-evident that communicative language teaching was exactly what the students needed (based on what the latest ESP theory in the literature was telling us). As a result, we focused on the language needs of the students especially in terms of functions, general and specific notions, and exponents. Then, low and behold, we found what we were looking for. So we created communicative materials, teaching strategies, and assessments based on our NA information.

When we started implementing this curriculum, we were stunned to find that the students reacted negatively. They did not like at all what we had so lovingly created for them. They listed a number of reasons why our new curriculum was bad. For example, they generally felt that group and pair work were a waste of time. Their reasoning was that "we cannot learn from other students." Instead, the students wanted us to lecture to them and provide detailed explanations of the vocabulary and grammar in a written paragraph as they followed along and took notes. The reason they gave for wanting to learn more grammar and vocabulary was that "we have been learning languages this way for thousands of years in China, and it works." The real reason was probably that they had always learned languages that way and were comfortable with that method. Regardless of their reason for believing as they did, theirs was a fairly compelling argument. And, we were nine foreigners arguing with a billion Chinese.

We eventually resolved this issue by respecting the students enough to gather information on their points of view, carefully consider those views, and gather further evidence on the students' relative strengths and weaknesses. In the process, we realized, based on the testing we were doing when the students first arrived, that we had strong evidence supporting our point of view: their grammar and vocabulary scores were uniformly very high, while their reading, writing, listening, or speaking scores were generally relatively low. It appeared to us that the last thing they needed was more grammar and vocabulary knowledge. Instead, we wanted to work on activating that already strong knowledge of grammar and vocabulary so they could actually use their knowledge to communicate when they arrived in an English-speaking country a few months down the road. Thus we concluded that they needed to practice, practice, and then practice some more while using their extensive knowledge to read, write, listen, and speak in English. We called this practice *fluency development*.

To make a long story short (or at least shorter), we had (a) gathered additional NA information from them, (b) looked at what the test scores were telling us, (c) thought about our views and theirs, and only then, (d) decided that the weight of the evidence supported our ideas. Thus we decided that we were right: the last thing they needed was more grammar and vocabulary and our communicative language teaching ideas would ultimately be better for this particular group of students. We were not abandoning accuracy or disrespecting their beliefs in the importance of accuracy in grammar and vocabulary. However, we were emphasizing the importance of improving their fluency in all four skills, at least some of the time.

Naturally, we needed to explain all of this to the students and respect them enough to develop strategies we could use to convince them that our ways trumped thousands of years of Chinese experience, at least for the purposes of this group of students who were all headed abroad in a few months. We also took the trouble to monitor their attitudes toward all of this through questionnaires that we administered at the end of every term, and we saw large shifts in their attitudes toward what we were doing as time went by. Thus, the NA had continued and widened to respect and include the ideas of our students, that is, we were dealing with some of the political realities of our program.

Yet, I find that many of the published NA reports that I encounter, most of which I have cited in this book, focus exclusively on the language needs of the ESP programs involved. As I hope I have illustrated in the paragraphs above, viewing needs through such a narrow tunnel is too limited because it disregards the realities that: (a) students, teachers, administrators are people; (b) people seldom agree about anything; indeed, (c) people hold very different views on what should be learned, on what language teaching strategies should be used, and on what successful language learning is; and (d) people need to be shown the respect of including them in the NA discussion.

Once you accept that the stakeholders in an ESP program are likely to have views that differ, it is difficult to escape the obvious conclusion that you need to know what those stakeholders are thinking and need to include their thinking in the strategies you use to deal with all aspects of the resulting curriculum. NA is the perfect way to explore what stakeholders are thinking, and how the views of various groups are similar or different. I am not saying that all stakeholders are right, nor am I arguing that all stakeholders should get what they want, or think they want. I *am* saying that it is important to know what all the stakeholders are thinking so that their views can be included in the decision making that will come out of the NA. Naturally, it is important to use the best available knowledge and theory about ESP learning and teaching, but it is also crucial to include the political aspects of curriculum if a *defensible curriculum* is ever to result.

From the above example, you might reasonably conclude that the NA process is never really finished, and that is true. It seems to me that any program needs to use strategies and tools (like the attitude questionnaires used each term in the above example) to constantly monitor opinions and criticisms from all important stakeholder groups while doing the initial NA, but also during all subsequent curriculum development stages. At some unidentifiable point in the ESP curriculum development process, the ongoing NA simply morphs into ongoing program evaluation. My guess is that ongoing NA becomes ongoing program evaluation at that point where the program has been fully developed and the information being gathered is being used to improve the existing curriculum rather than to develop new curriculum. Thus *program evaluation*, at least of the *formative type* I am describing here, might be defined as a sort of ongoing NA (with a wider array of information sources than the usual NA) of an existing program with the goal of determining if the needs of the students and teachers are still the same and continue to be met.

How important are teachers in the NA scheme of things?

If my experience has taught me anything, it is that the teachers absolutely must be involved in all aspects of any NA and all resulting curriculum activities because such projects will require:

- teachers to change their ways of doing things;
- teachers to do additional work that they did not have to do previously;
- teachers to relinquish a portion of their sovereignty and independence in their classrooms.

And it is crucial to bring them on board in such a project because:

- Teachers are the individuals who must deliver the curriculum.
- Teachers have to live with the curriculum on a daily basis even after any group of current students has been replaced by new students.
- Teachers, like any other group of people, need to be taken seriously and feel respected.
- Teachers can easily doom to failure any NA or curriculum development project if they feel ignored or disrespected, or even if they simply do not like the project for other reasons.

In short, failing to involve the teachers and consider their needs will almost always prove fatal to any NA project.

How can all of the above be accomplished?

In Brown (2009), I summarized some NA information-gathering steps that should help in accounting for the views of different stakeholder groups and effectively using that information to create a defensible curriculum:

1 discover what the options (in perceived student needs with regard to approaches, syllabuses, objectives, etc.) are and what people think about those options;
2 decide which options are most likely to serve as a defensible basis for curriculum (i.e., options that might lead to a sort of average or consensus "truth");
3 marshall information and formulate arguments (sometimes alternative arguments) for the most viable options in perceived student needs with regard to approaches, syllabuses, objectives, etc.;
4 work to get all stakeholders to come to agreement, to form a consensus, or to at least compromise on those perceived needs;
5 work to accommodate the views of those who disagree with perceived needs, if possible;
6 try to change the views of those stakeholders who disagree with the perceived needs, when necessary;
7 show respect for all participants by listening and taking their views seriously (even if there is ultimately no intention of doing what they want).

(p. 287)

Personal reflection – How can I account for the various points of view in an NA?

Go back through the section above on accounting for the various stakeholder views in an ESP NA and highlight those considerations and strategies that you think might help account for the various points of view you are likely to cover in any NA that you conduct. Can you think of other ways to accomplish the same things?

Summary and conclusions

This chapter described options that you have in organizing and writing an NA report. Those options included: (a) ideas about how you can organize your NA report; (b) who you should write the NA report for; (c) how you can describe the NA process itself; (d) different ways you might want to report quantitative, qualitative, and mixed-methods results; and (e) ways you might consider to format the SLOs that the NA recommends. The chapter also considered some of the issues you need to consider in publishing your NA report so that others in the field might also learn from it. The chapter ended with a discussion of key ideas that should help you to account for the various points of view expressed in your NA, including some thoughts on the inutility of the notion of *truth* in needs analyses. As I summed up in Brown (2009):

> [A]n obsessive focus on language needs that seeks the "truth" is probably destined to fail; a NA designed to investigate what bits of language the students "really need" to learn is doomed to collapse from the weight of its own single-minded focus. In contrast, a needs analysis that gathers information about what options are available (approaches and syllabuses) and what various groups of stakeholders (students, teachers, administrators, future employers, etc.) think about those options necessarily recognizes that there is no single truth, that NA is political act and a process, and therefore, that the goal is a "defensible curriculum."
>
> (p. 286)

Note

1 Important: if you want to publish your NA in a journal or book, most journals and some book publishers nowadays will want assurances from you that the project had ethics or human subjects approval from your institution (which typically needs to be done before beginning the NA) and, if it didn't, they may refuse to publish it.

References

Abbott, G. (1981). Encouraging communication in English: A paradox. *English Language Teaching Journal, 35*(3), 228–230.

Abdellah, A., & Ibrahim, M. (2013). Towards developing a language course for Hajj guides in Al-Madinah Al-Munawwarah: A needs analysis. *International Education Studies, 6*(3), 192–212.

Afzali, K., & Fakharzadeh, A. (2009). A needs analysis survey: The case of tourism letter writing in Iran. *ESP World, 8*(1), 1–10. Retrieved from http://www.esp-world.info/Articles_22/PDF/A%20needs%20analysis%20survey.pdf

Akyel, A. S., & Ozek, Y. (2010). A language needs analysis research at an English medium university in Turkey. *Procedia Social and Behavioral Sciences, 2*, 969–975.

Alderson, J. C., & Beretta, A. (Eds.). (1992). *Evaluating second language education.* Cambridge: Cambridge University Press.

Alexandrou, R. L., & Revard, D. M. (1990). A task-based needs analysis for ELI listening courses. Unpublished paper. Honolulu: University of Hawai'i at Mānoa.

Altschuld, J. W., & Witkin, B. R. (2000). *From needs assessment to action: Transforming needs into solution strategies.* Thousand Oaks, CA: Sage.

Anthony, E. M. (1965). Approach, method, and technique. In H. B. Allen (Ed.), *Teaching English as a second language: A book of readings.* New York: McGraw-Hill.

Anthony, L. (2017). *Introducing English for specific purposes.* Abingdon, UK: Routledge.

Asahina, R., & Okuda, J. M. (1987). Lecture skills for foreign teaching assistants: Goals, microskills and objectives. Unpublished paper. Honolulu: University of Hawai'i at Mānoa.

Asahina, R., Bergman, M., Conklin, G., Guth, J., & Lockhart, C. (1988). ELI 82 curriculum development project. Unpublished paper. Honolulu: University of Hawai'i at Mānoa.

Atai, M. R., & Ogholgol, N. (2011). Exploring reading comprehension needs of Iranian EAP students of health information management (HIM): A triangulated approach. *System, 39*(1), 30–43.

Barbara, L., Celani, A., Collins, H., & Scott, M. (1996). A survey of communication patterns in the Brazilian business context. *English for Specific Purposes, 15*, 57–71.

Barrett, T. C. (1972). *Taxonomy of reading comprehension. Reading 360 Monograph.* Lexington, MA: Ginn.

Basturkmen, H. (2006). *Ideas and options in English for specific purposes*. New York: Routledge.

Basturkmen, H. (2010). *Developing courses in English for specific purposes*. London: Palgrave Macmillan.

Belcher, D. (Ed.) (2009). *English for specific purposes in theory and practice*. Ann Arbor: University of Michigan Press.

Belcher, D., & Lukkarila, L. (2011). Identity in the ESP context: Putting the learner front and center in needs analysis. In D. Belcher, A. Johns, & B. Paltridge (Eds.), *New directions for English for specific purposes research* (pp. 73–93). Ann Arbor: University of Michigan Press.

Belcher, D., Johns, A. M., & Paltridge, B. (Eds.) (2011). *New directions in English for specific purposes research*. Ann Arbor: University of Michigan Press.

Benesch, S. (1999). Rights analysis: Studying power relations in an academic setting. *English for Specific Purposes, 18*(4), 313–327.

Benesch, S. (2001). *Critical English for academic purposes: Theory, politics, and practice*. Mahwah, NJ: Erlbaum.

Benson, M. (1994). Writing an academic article: An editor writes… *English Teaching Forum, 32*(2), 6–9.

Berkowitz, S. (1996). Using qualitative and mixed-method approaches. In R. Reviere, S. Berkowitz, C. C. Carter, & C. G. Ferguson (Eds.), *Needs assessment: A creative and practical guide for social scientists* (pp. 110–120). Washington, DC: Taylor & Francis.

Bernbrock, C. W. (1977). Determining English-language needs for curriculum planning in a Thai business college. Unpublished master's thesis, University of California at Los Angeles.

Berwick, R. (1989). Needs assessment in language programming: From theory to practice. In R. K. Johnson (Ed.), *The second language curriculum* (pp. 48–62). New York: Cambridge University Press.

Bloch, J. (2013). Technology and ESP. In B. Paltridge & S. Starfield (Eds), *The Handbook of English for specific purposes* (pp. 385–401). Malden, MA: Wiley-Blackwell.

Bloom, B. S. (Ed.) (1956). *Taxonomy of educational objectives, book 1: Cognitive domain*. London: Longman.

Bosher, S., & Smalkoski, K. (2002). From needs analysis to curriculum development: Designing a course in health-care communication for immigrant students in the USA. *English for Specific Purposes, 21*(1), 59–79.

Bosuwon, T., & Woodrow, L. (2009). Developing a problem-based course based on needs analysis to enhance English reading ability of Thai undergraduate students. *RELC Journal, 40*, 42–64.

Bowles, H., & Seedhouse, P. (Eds.) (2007). *Conversation analysis and language for specific purposes*. Bern, Switzerland: Peter Lang.

Braine, G. (2001). Twenty years of needs analysis: Reflections on a personal journey. In J. Flowerdew & M. Peacock (Eds.), *Research perspectives on English for academic purposes* (pp. 195–207). Cambridge: Cambridge University Press.

Brecht, R. D., & Rivers, W. P. (2005). Language needs analysis at the societal level. In M. H. Long (Ed.), *Second language needs analysis* (pp. 79–104). Cambridge: Cambridge University Press.

Brindley, G. (1984). *Needs analysis and objective setting in the adult migrant education program*. Sydney, Australia: Adult Migrant Education Service.

Brown, J. D. (1989). Language program evaluation: A synthesis of existing possibilities. In K. Johnson (Ed.), *The second language curriculum*. Cambridge: Cambridge University Press.

Brown, J. D. (1995). *The elements of language curriculum: A systematic approach to program development*. Boston: Heinle and Heinle.

Brown, J. D. (1997). Designing surveys for language programs. In D. Nunan & D. Griffee (Eds.), *Classroom teachers and classroom research* (pp. 55–70). Tokyo: Japan Association for Language Teaching. Also available from ERIC: ED 415 700; FL 025 008.

Brown, J. D. (2001). *Using surveys in language programs*. Cambridge: Cambridge University Press.

Brown, J. D. (2004). Research methods for Applied Linguistics: Scope, characteristics, and standards. In A. Davies and C. Elder (Eds.), *The handbook of applied linguistics* (pp. 476–500). Oxford: Blackwell.

Brown, J. D. (2005a). *Testing in language programs: A comprehensive guide to English language assessment* (New edition). New York: McGraw-Hill.

Brown, J. D. (2005b). Second language studies: Curriculum development. In K. Brown (Ed.), *Elsevier encyclopedia of language and linguistics* (2nd ed., completely new). Oxford: Elsevier.

Brown, J. D. (2005c). Publishing without perishing. *Journal of the African Language Teachers Association, 6*, 1–16.

Brown, J. D. (2009). Foreign and second language needs analysis. In M. H. Long & C. J. Doughty (Eds.), *The handbook of language teaching* (pp. 269–293). Malden, MA: Wiley-Blackwell.

Brown, J. D. (2011). Statistics Corner. Questions and answers about language testing statistics: Likert items and scales of measurement. *Shiken: JALT Testing & Evaluation SIG Newsletter, 15*(1), 10–14. Also retrieved from http://www.jalt. org/test/bro_34.htm

Brown, J. D. (2012a). EIL curriculum development. In L. Alsagoff, S. McKay, G. W. Hu, & W. A. Renandya (Eds.), *Principles and practices for teaching English as an international language* (pp. 147–167). London: Routledge.

Brown, J. D. (Ed.) (2012b). *Developing, using, and analyzing rubrics in language assessment with case studies in Asian and Pacific languages*. Honolulu, HI: National Foreign Languages Resource Center.

Brown, J. D. (2014). *Mixed methods research for TESOL*. Edinburgh, UK: Edinburgh University.

Brown, J. D., Chaudron, C., & Pennington, M. (1988). Foreign teaching assistant training and orientation pilot project. In *Report on the Educational Improvement Fund 1987/1988*. Office of Faculty Development and Academic Support, University of Hawai'i at Mānoa, Honolulu, HI.

Buckingham, T. (1981). *Needs assessment in ESL*. Washington, DC: Center for Applied Linguistics.

Byrd, P. (Ed.). (1995). *Material writer's guide*. Boston: Heinle & Heinle.

Cai, D. Y. (2012). Teaching nursing English based on needs analysis in Chinese context: Problem-situated instruction for EOP in a non-English speaking country. *2012 International Symposium on Information Technology in Medicine and Education: Proceedings of a meeting held 3–5 August 2012* (pp. 186–190). Hokodate, Hokkaido: Japan.

Cameron, R. (1998). A language-focused needs analysis for ESL-speaking nursing students in class and clinic. *Foreign Language Annals, 31*(2), 203–218.

Carr, N. T. (2008). Using Microsoft Excel to calculate descriptive statistics and create graphs. *Language Assessment Quarterly, 5*(1), 43–62.

Carr, N. T. (2011). *Designing and analyzing language tests.* Oxford: Oxford University Press.

Casanave, C., & Hubbard, P. (1992). The writing assignments and writing problems of doctoral students: Faculty perceptions, pedagogical issues, and needed research. *English for Specific Purposes, 11*, 33–49.

Cathcart, R. L. (1989). Authentic discourse and the survival English curriculum. *TESOL Quarterly, 23*, 105–126.

Chan, V. (2001). Determining students' language needs in a tertiary setting. *English Teaching Forum, 39*(3), 16–27.

Charles, M., & Pecorari, D. (2016). *Introducing English for academic purposes.* Harlow, UK: Longman.

Chaudron, C., Doughty, C. J., Kim, Y., Kong, D-K., Lee, J., Lee Y-G., Long, M. H., Rivers, R., & Urano, K. (2005). A task-based needs analysis of a tertiary Korean as a foreign language program. In M. H. Long (Ed.), *Second language needs analysis* (pp. 225–261). Cambridge: Cambridge University Press.

Cheng, A. (2011). ESP classroom research: Basic considerations and future research questions. In D. Belcher, A. M. Johns, & B. Paltridge (Eds.), *New directions in English for specific purposes research* (pp. 44–72). Ann Arbor: University of Michigan Press.

Chew, K.-S. (2005). An investigation of the English language skills used by new entrants in banks in Hong Kong. *English for Specific Purposes, 24*(4), 423–435.

Chia, H. U., Johnson, R., Chia, H. L., & Olive, R. (1999). English for college students in Taiwan: A study of perceptions of English needs in a medical context. *English for Specific Purposes, 18*(2), 107–119.

Clark, J. L. (1987). *Curriculum renewal in school foreign language learning.* Oxford: Oxford University.

Coleman, H. (1988). Analyzing language needs in large organizations. *English for Specific Purposes, 7*, 155–169.

Conseil de la Coopération Culturelle. (2000). *Un cadre Européen commun de référence pour les langues: Apprendre, enseigner, évaluer.* Strasbourg, France: Conseil de la Coopération Culturelle, Comité de l'Éducation, Division des Langues Vivantes. Also viewed August 23, 2014 at http://www.coe.int/t/dg4/linguistic/Source/Framework_FR.pdf

Coombe, C., & Davidson, P. (2016). Constructing questionnaires. In J. D. Brown & C. Coombe (Eds.), *Cambridge guide to second language research* (pp. 217–223). Cambridge: Cambridge University Press.

Council of Europe (2001). *Common European framework of reference for languages: Learning, teaching, assessment.* Cambridge: Cambridge University Press. Also viewed August 23, 2014 at http://www.coe.int/t/dg4/linguistic/Source/Framework_EN.pdf

Courtney, M. (1988). Some initial considerations for course design. *English for Specific Purposes, 7*, 195–203.

Cowling, J. D. (2007). Needs analysis: Planning a syllabus for a series of intensive workplace courses at a leading Japanese company. *English for Specific Purposes, 26*, 426–442.

Craig, M. (1994). *Analysing learner needs.* Aldershot, UK: Gower.

Crosling, G., & Ward, I. (2002). Oral communication: The workplace needs and uses of business graduate employees. *English for Specific Purposes, 21*(1), 41–57.

Decamps, S., & Bauvois, C. (2001). A method of computer-assisted language learning: The elaboration of a tool designed for an 'un-schoolable' public. *Computer Assisted Language Learning, 14*(1), 69–96.

Deutsch, Y. (2003). Needs analysis for academic legal English courses in Israel: A model of setting priorities. *English for Academic Purposes, 3,* 123–146.

Dibakanaka, A., & Hiranburana, K. (2012). Developing an e-learning competency-based English course module for chief flight attendants. *International Journal of Scientific and Research Publications, 2*(8), 1–14. Accessed March 13, 2015 at http://www.ijsrp.org/research-paper–0812.php?rp=P07106

Donna, S. (2000). *Teach business English: A comprehensive introduction to business English.* Cambridge: Cambridge University Press.

Douglas, D. (2000). *Assessing languages for specific purposes.* Cambridge: Cambridge University Press.

Douglas, D. (2013). ESP and assessment. In B. Paltridge & S. Starfield (Eds.), *The handbook of English for specific purposes* (pp. 368–383). Malden, MA: Wiley-Blackwell.

Dovey, T. (2006). What purposes, specifically? Re-thinking purposes and specificity in the context of the 'new vocationalism'. *English for Specific Purposes, 25*(4), 387–402.

Downey Bartlett, N. J. (2005). A double shot 2% mocha latte, please, with whip: Service encounters in two coffee shops and at a coffee cart. In M. H. Long (Ed.), *Second language needs analysis* (pp. 305–343). Cambridge: Cambridge University Press.

Dubin, F., & Olshtain, E. (1986). *Course design.* Cambridge: Cambridge University Press.

Dudley-Evans, T., & St. John, M. J. (1998). *Developments in English for specific purposes: A multidisciplinary approach.* Cambridge: Cambridge University Press.

Edwards, N. (2000). Language for business: Effective needs assessment, syllabus design and materials preparation in a practical ESP case study. *English for Specific Purposes, 19,* 291–296.

Eggly, S. (2002). An ESP program for international medical graduates in residency. In T. Orr (Ed.), *English for specific purposes* (pp. 105–115). Alexandria, VA: TESOL.

English, F. W., & Kaufman, R. A. (1975). *Needs assessment: A focus for curriculum development.* Washington, DC: Association for Supervision and Curriculum Development.

Ferris, D. (1998). Students' views of academic aural/oral skills: A comparative needs analysis. *TESOL Quarterly, 32,* 289–318.

Ferris, D., & Tagg, T. (1996a). Academic listening/speaking tasks for ESL students: Problems, suggestions, and implications. *TESOL Quarterly, 30*(2), 297–320.

Ferris, D., & Tagg, T. (1996b). Academic oral communication needs of EAP learners: What subject-matter instructors actually require. *TESOL Quarterly, 30*(1), 31–58.

Finocchiaro, M., & Brumfit, C. (1983). *The functional-notional approach: From theory to practice.* Oxford: Oxford University Press.

Flowerdew, J., & Peacock, M. (Eds.) (2001). *Research perspectives on English for academic purposes.* Cambridge: Cambridge University Press.

Flowerdew, L. (2011). ESP and corpus studies. In D. Belcher, A. M. Johns, & B. Paltridge (Eds.), *New directions in English for specific purposes research* (pp. 222–251). Ann Arbor: University of Michigan Press.

Freihat, S., & Al-Makhzoomi, K. (2012). An English for specific purposes (ESP) course for nursing students in Jordan and the role a needs analysis played. *International Journal of Humanities and Social Science, 2*(7), 129–145.

Freudenstein, R., Beneke, J., & Ponisch, H. (Eds.) (1981). *Language incorporated: Teaching foreign languages in industry.* Oxford: Pergamon.

Garcia, P. (2002). An ESP program for union members in 25 factories. In T. Orr (Ed.), *English for specific purposes* (pp. 161–174). Alexandria, VA: TESOL.

Gass, J. (2012). Needs analysis and situational analysis: Designing an ESP curriculum for Thai nurses. *ESP World, 36*(12), no page numbers. Accessed August 31, 2014 at http://www.esp-world.info

Gee, J. P. (2011). *An introduction to discourse analysis: Theory and method* (3rd ed.). New York: Routledge.

Gilabert, R. (2005). Evaluating the use of multiple sources and methods in needs analysis: A case study of journalists in the Autonomous Community of Catalonia (Spain). In M. H. Long (Ed.), *Second language needs analysis* (pp. 182–199). Cambridge: Cambridge University Press.

Glendinning, E. & Holmström, B. (2008). *English in medicine* (3rd ed.). Cambridge: Cambridge University Press.

Glendinning, E., & Howard, R. (2009). *Professional English in use: Medicine.* Cambridge: Cambridge University Press.

Goldstein, I. L., & Ford, J. K. (2002). *Training in organizations: Needs assessments, development, and evaluation.* Belmont, CA: Wadsworth.

Gravatt, B. D., Richards, J. C., & Lewis, M. (1997). *Language needs in tertiary studies: ESL students at the University of Auckland.* University of Auckland, Institute of Language Teaching and Learning.

Graves, K. (2000). *Designing language courses: A guide for teachers.* Boston: Newbury House.

Gronlund, N. E., & Brookhart, S. M. (2009). *Gronlund's writing instructional objectives* (8th ed.). Upper Saddle River, NJ: Pearson.

Grosse, C. (2004). English business communication needs of Mexican executives in a distance-learning class. *Business Communication Quarterly, 67,* 7–23.

Gupta, K., Sleezer, C. M., & Russ-Eft, D. F. (2007). *A practical guide to needs analysis* (2nd ed.). San Francisco, CA: Pfeiffer.

Hale, G., Taylor, C., Bridgeman, B., Carson, J., Kroll, B., & Kantor, R. (1996). *A study of writing tasks assigned in academic degree programs.* Princeton, NJ: Educational Testing Service.

Harding, K. (2007). *English for specific purposes.* Oxford: Oxford University Press.

Harper, A., Gleason, A., & Ogama, A. (1983). *A needs assessment and program design for an academic listening comprehension course.* Honolulu: Department of English as a Second Language, University of Hawai'i at Mānoa.

Hilferty, A. G., & Brown, J. D. (1982). *E = MC²: English modern conversation course* (Student Book). Unpublished textbook. Guangzhou, Guangdong: Guangzhou English Language Center.

Holden, S. (Ed.) (1977). *English for specific purposes*. Basingstoke, UK: Modern English.

Holliday, A. (1995). Assessing language needs within an institutional context: An ethnographic approach. *English for Specific Purposes, 14*(2), 115–126.

Holme, R., & Chalauisaeng, B. (2006). The learner as needs analyst: The use of participatory appraisal in the EAP reading classroom. *English for Specific Purposes, 25*, 403–419.

Holmes, J. (2005). When small talk is a big deal: Sociolinguistics challenges in the workplace. In M. H. Long (Ed.), *Second language needs analysis* (pp. 344–371). Cambridge: Cambridge University Press.

Holmes, V., & Moulton, M. (1995). A guide for prospective authors. *TESOL Journal, 4*(4), 31–34.

Hsu, C.-C., & Sandford, B. A. (2007). The Delphi technique: Making sense of consensus. *Practical Assessment, Research & Evaluation, 12*(10), 1–8.

Huang, L.-S. (2010). Seeing eye to eye? The academic writing needs of graduate and undergraduate students from students' and instructors' perspectives. *Language Teaching Research, 14*(4), 517–539.

Huh, S. (2006). A task-based needs analysis for a business English course. *Second Language Studies, 24*(2), 1–64.

Huhta, M., Vogt, K., Johnson, E., Tulkki, H., & Hall, D. R. (2013). *Needs analysis for language course design: A holistic approach to ESP*. Cambridge: Cambridge University Press.

Hussin, B. (2002). An ESP program for students of nursing. In T. Orr (Ed.), *English for specific purposes* (pp. 25–39). Alexandria, VA: TESOL.

Hutchinson, T., & Waters, A. (1987). *English for specific purposes*. Cambridge: Cambridge University Press.

Hyland, K. (2002). Specificity revisited: How far should we go now? *English for Specific Purposes, 21*, 385–395.

Hyland, K. (2008). *English for academic purposes: An advanced resource book*. London: Routledge.

Ibbotson, M. (2009). *Cambridge English for engineering*. Cambridge: Cambridge University Press.

I-Tech (2010). *Writing good learning objectives: I-Tech technical implementation guide #4*. Seattle, WA: Department of Global Health, University of Washington. Retrieved February 28, 2015 from http://www.go2itech.org/resources/technical-implementation-guides/TIG4.WritingLrngObj.pdf/view

Janssen, G., Nausa, R., & Rico, C. (2012). Shaping the ESP curriculum of an English for PhD students program: A Colombian case study of questionnaire research. *Colombian Applied Linguistics Journal, 14*(2), 51–69.

Jasso-Aguilar, R. (1999). Sources, methods, and triangulation in needs analysis: A critical perspective in a case study of Waikiki hotel maids. *English for Specific Purposes, 18*(1), 27–46.

Jasso-Aguilar, R. (2005). Sources, methods, and triangulation in needs analysis: A critical perspective in a case study of Waikiki hotel maids. In M. H. Long (Ed.), *Second language needs analysis* (pp. 127–158). Cambridge: Cambridge University Press.

Johns, A. M., & Makalela, L. (2011). Needs analysis, critical ethnography, and context. In D. Belcher, A. Johns, & B. Paltridge (Eds.), *New directions for*

English for specific purposes research (pp. 197–221). Ann Arbor: University of Michigan Press.

Johnson, D. E., Meiller, L. R., Miller, C. L., & Summers, G. F. (Eds.) (1987). *Needs assessment: Theory and methods.* Ames: Iowa State University.

Johnson, R. B., Onwuegbuzie, A. J., & Turner, L. A. (2007). Toward a definition of mixed methods research. *Journal of Mixed Methods Research, 1*(2), 112–133.

Johnson, R. K. (1989). *The second language curriculum.* Cambridge: Cambridge University Press.

Jordan, R. R. (1997). *English for academic purposes: A guide and resource book for teachers.* Cambridge: Cambridge University Press.

Kaewpet, C. (2009). Communication needs of Thai civil engineering students. *English for Specific Purposes, 28,* 266–278.

Kaufman, R., Rojas, A. M., & Mayer, H. (1993). *Needs assessment: A user's guide.* Englewood Cliffs, NJ: Educational Technologies.

Kaur, S., & Khan, A. B. M. A. (2010). Language needs analysis of art and design students: Considerations for ESP course design. *English for Specific Purposes World, 9*(2), 1–15. Available at http://www.esp-world.info/index.html

Keller, E., & Warner, S. (1979a). *Gambits 1 conversational tools: Openers – the first of three modules.* Hull, Quebec: Canadian Government Printing Office.

Keller, E., & Warner, S. (1979b). *Gambits 2 conversational tools: Links – the second of three modules.* Hull, Quebec: Canadian Government Printing Office.

Keller, E., & Warner, S. (1979c). *Gambits 3 conversational tools: Responders, Closers and Inventory – the third of three modules.* Hull, Quebec, Canada: Canadian Government Printing Office.

Kellerman, E., Koonen, H., & van der Haagen, M. (2005). "Feet speak louder than the tongue": A preliminary analysis of language provisions for foreign professional footballers in the Netherlands. In M. H. Long (Ed.), *Second language needs analysis* (pp. 200–222). Cambridge: Cambridge University Press.

Kikuchi, K. (2001). *Analysis of the listening needs for EFL learners in a Japanese college.* Unpublished master's thesis. Honolulu: University of Hawai'i at Mānoa.

Kikuchi, K. (2004). Triangulating perceptions of learners' needs: An alternate way of conducting needs analysis. *2004 JALT Pan-SIG Proceedings.* Tokyo: JALT.

Kim, S. (2006). Academic oral communication needs of East Asian international graduate students in non-science and non-engineering fields. *English for Specific Purposes, 25*(4), 479–489.

Kim, Y., Kong, D.-K., Lee, Y.-G., Silva, A., & Urano, K. (2003). A task-based needs analysis for the English Language Institute at the University of Hawaii at Mānoa. *Korean Journal of Applied Linguistics, 19*(2), 93–114.

Kimzin, G., & Proctor, S. (1986). An ELI academic listening comprehension needs assessment: Establishing goals, objectives, and microskills. Unpublished paper. Mānoa: University of Hawai'i at Mānoa.

Kletzien, J. A. (2011). On the merits of mixed methods: A language program evaluation. *Second Language Studies, 30*(1), 49–94.

Koh, P., Michaelis, K., & Wichitwechkarn, J. (1990). Goals and objectives based on a needs analysis for ELI 83: Writing for foreign graduate students. Unpublished paper. University of Hawai'i at Mānoa, Honolulu, HI.

Krathwohl, D. R. (2002). A revision of Bloom's taxonomy: An overview. *Theory into Practice, 41*(4), 212–218.

Krathwohl, D. R., Bloom, B. S., & Masia, B. B. (1956). *Taxonomy of educational objectives, Handbook 2: Affective domain*. New York: David McKay.

Lambert, C. (2010). A task-based needs analysis: Putting principles into practice. *Language Teaching Research, 14*(1), 99–112.

Lehtonen, T., & Karjalainen, S. (2008). University graduates' workplace language needs as perceived by employers. *System, 36*, 492–503.

Leki, I. (1995). Coping strategies of ESL students in writing tasks across the curriculum. *TESOL Quarterly, 29*(2), 235–260.

Lepetit, D., & Cichocki, W. (2002). Teaching languages to future health professionals: A needs assessment study. *Modern Language Journal, 86*(3), 384–396.

Lett, J. A. (2005). Foreign language needs assessment in the US military. In M. H. Long (Ed.), *Second language needs analysis* (pp. 105–124). Cambridge: Cambridge University Press.

Litticharoenporn, P.-P. (2014). Oral and aural English as a foreign language needs at an international school. *Second Language Studies, 32*(2), pp. 26–75. Accessed January 10, at http://www.hawaii.edu/sls/wp-content/uploads/2014/08/ Litticharoenporn1.pdf

LoCastro, V. (1988). Academic writing: The author's point of view. *The Language Teacher, 12*(13), 8–10.

Long, M. H. (2005a). Methodological issues in learner needs analysis. In M. H. Long (Ed.), *Second language needs analysis* (pp. 19–76). Cambridge: Cambridge University Press.

Long, M. H. (Ed.) (2005b). *Second language needs analysis*. Cambridge: Cambridge University Press.

Louhiala-Salminen, L. (1996). The business communication classroom vs. reality: What should we teach today? *English for Specific Purposes, 15*, 37–51.

Lund, R. J. (1990). A taxonomy for teaching second language listening. *Foreign Language Annals, 23*(2), 105–115.

Lynch, B. K. (1997). *Language program evaluation: Theory and practice*. Cambridge: Cambridge University Press.

Mackay, R., & Mountford, A. J. (Eds.) (1978). *English for specific purposes*. London: Longman.

Mackay, R., & Palmer, J. D. (Eds.) (1981). *Languages for specific purposes: Program design and evaluation*. Rowley, MA: Newbury House.

Marcia, E. A., Cervera, A. S., & Ramos, C. R. (Eds.) (2006). *Information technology in language for specific purposes: Issues and prospects*. New York: Springer.

Master, P., & Brinton, D. M. (Eds.) (1998). *New ways in English for specific purposes*. Arlington, VA: TESOL.

Matsuda, M. (2010). *Designing course guidelines for language communication of the faculty of environmental studies: Part II – needs analysis*. Nagasaki, Japan: Nagasaki University's Academic Output SITE. Accessed September 2, 2014 at http://naosite.lb.nagasaki-u.ac.jp/dspace/handle/10069/24575

Matsuda, P. K., Saenkhum, T., & Accardi, S. (2013). Writing teachers' perceptions of the presence and needs of second language writers: An institutional case study. *Journal of Second Language Writing, 22*, 68–86.

McClelland, S. B. (1995). *Organizational needs assessments: Design, facilitation, and analysis*. Wesport, CT: Quorum.

McKay, S. (1978). Syllabuses: Structural, situational, notional. *TESOL Newsletter, 12*(5), 11.

McKay, S. L., & Brown, J. D. (2016). *Teaching and assessing EIL in local contexts around the world.* New York: Routledge.

McKillip, J. (1987). *Needs analysis: Tools for the human services and education.* Newbury Park, CA: Sage.

Miles, M. B., & Huberman, A. M. (1984). *Qualitative data analysis: A sourcebook of new methods.* Beverly Hills, CA: Sage.

Miles, M. B., & Huberman, A. M. (1994). *Qualitative data analysis: An expanded sourcebook* (2nd ed.). Beverly Hills, CA: Sage.

Miles, M. B., Huberman, A. M., & Saldaña, J. (2014). *Qualitative data analysis: A methods sourcebook* (3rd ed.). Beverly Hills, CA: Sage.

Moreno, A. I. (2003). Análisis de necesidades para el aula de lengua inglesa en filología inglesa: Un estudio de caso. *Barcelona English Language and Literature Studies, 12* (no page numbers). Downloaded August 25, 2006 from http://www.publications.ub.es/revistes/bells12/PDF/art10.pdf

Munby, J. (1978). *Communicative syllabus design: A sociolinguistic model for defining the content of purpose-specific language programs.* Cambridge: Cambridge University Press.

Nation, P., & Macalister, J. (2010). *Language curriculum design.* New York: Routledge.

Nickerson, C., & Planken, B. (2016). *Introducing business English.* Abingdon, UK: Routledge.

Noda, K. (2011). *Needs analysis in an academic listening and speaking course: An approach to English L2 learners' difficulties.* Scholarly Paper for the Department of Second Language Studies at the University of Hawai'i at Mānoa. Accessed March 13, 2015 at http://scholarspace.mānoa.hawaii.edu/bitstream/handle/101 25/27142/NodaKazuyo.pdf?sequence=1

Noden, P. (2002). An ESP program for a home-cleaning service. In T. Orr (Ed.), *English for specific purposes* (pp. 189–204). Alexandria, VA: TESOL.

Norris, J. M., Davis, J. McE., Sinicrope, C., Watanabe, Y. (Eds.) (2009). *Toward useful program evaluation in college foreign language education.* Honolulu, HI: National Foreign Language Resource Center.

Nunan, D. (1985). *Language teaching course design: Trends and issues.* Adelaide, Australia: National Curriculum Resource Centre.

Nunan, D. (1988). *The learner-centered curriculum.* Cambridge: Cambridge University Press.

Nunan, D. (1990). Using learner data in curriculum development. *English for Specific Purposes, 9,* 17–32.

Nunan, D. (1991). *Syllabus design.* Oxford: Oxford University Press.

Orr, T. (Ed.) (2002). *English for specific purposes.* Alexandria, VA: TESOL.

Orsi, L., & Orsi, P. (2002). An ESP program for brewers. In T. Orr (Ed.), *English for specific purposes* (pp. 175–188). Alexandria, VA: TESOL.

Paltridge, B. (2013). Genre and English for specific purposes. In B. Paltridge & S. Starfield (Eds.), *The Handbook of English for specific purposes* (pp. 348–366). Malden, MA: Wiley-Blackwell.

Paltridge, B., & Starfield, S. (Eds.) (2013). *The handbook of English for specific purposes.* Malden, MA: Wiley-Blackwell.

Paltridge, B., & Starfield, S. (2016). *Getting published in academic journals: Navigating the publication process*. Ann Arbor: University of Michigan Press.

Parker, G., & Reuben, C. (Eds.) (1994). *Languages for international scientists*. London: Centre for Information on Language Teaching and Research.

Patton, M. Q. (1987). *How to use qualitative methods in evaluation*. Newbury Park, CA: Sage.

Peck, S. (1979). Recognizing and meeting the needs of ESL students. In M. Celce-Murcia & L. McIntosh (Eds.), *Teaching English as a second or foreign language* (pp. 261–269). Boston: Newbury House.

Pennington, M. C. (Ed.) (1991). *Building better English language programs: Perspectives on evaluation in ESL*. Washington, DC: NAFSA.

Pierce, S. (2012). Utilization-focused evaluation for program development: Investigating the need for teaching experience within the Bachelor of Arts Program in Second Language Studies. *Second Language Studies, 30*(2), 43–107. Accessed June 30, 2012 at http://www.hawaii.edu/sls/sls/?page_id=135

Pierce, S. (2016). Conducting focus groups. In J. D. Brown & C. Coombe (Eds.), *Cambridge guide to second language research* (pp. 224–230). Cambridge: Cambridge University Press.

Poon, W. (1992). *An analysis of the language needs of accountants and company administrators in Hong Kong. Research report no 21*. Hong Kong: City Polytechnic of Hong Kong.

Pratt, S. (Ed.) (1982). *English in the workplace*. Toronto: Ontario Ministry of Citizenship and Culture.

Pugh, A. K., & Ulijn, J. M. (Eds.) (1984). *Reading for professional purposes: Studies and practices in native and foreign languages*. London: Heinemann Educational.

Purpura, J. E., Graziano-King, J., Chang, J., Cook, K., Kim, J. W. Krohn, N., & Wiseman, C. (2003). An analysis of the foreign language needs of SIPA students at Columbia University. Unpublished Technical Report submitted to the Mellon Foundation through the Arts and Sciences at Columbia University, New York.

Queeny, D. S. (1995). *Assessing needs in continuing education*. San Francisco, CA: Jossey-Bass.

Richards, J. C. (Ed.) (1976). *Teaching English for science and technology*. Singapore: RELC.

Richards, J. C. (1983). Listening comprehension: Approach, design, procedure. *TESOL Quarterly, 17*(2), 219–240.

Richards, J. C. (1988). Writing for academic journals. *The Language Teacher, 12*(13), 5–7.

Richards, J. C. (2001). *Curriculum development in language teaching*. Cambridge: Cambridge University Press.

Richards, J. C., & Rogers, T. (1982). Method: Approach, design, and procedure. *TESOL Quarterly, 16*(1), 153–168.

Richards, J. C., & Schmidt, R. (2010). *Longman dictionary of language teaching and applied linguistics* (4th ed.). London: Longman.

Richterich, R. (1980). Definition of language needs and types of adults. In J. R. Trim, J. R. van Ek, & D. Wilkins (Eds.), *Systems development in adult language learning* (pp. 29–88). Oxford: Pergamon.

Richterich, R. (Ed.). (1983a). *Case studies in identifying language needs*. Oxford: Pergamon.

Richterich, R. (1983b). Introduction. In R. Richterich (Ed.), *Case studies in identifying language needs* (pp. 1–13). Oxford: Pergamon.

Richterich, R. (1984). Identifying language needs as a means of determining educational objectives with the learners. In J. A. van Ek & J. L. M. Trim (Eds.), *Across the threshold: Readings from the modern language projects of the Council of Europe* (pp. 29–33). Oxford: Pergamon.

Richterich, R. (1985). *Besoins langagiers et objectifs d'apprentissage.* Paris: Hachette.

Richterich, R., & Chancerel, J.-L. (1977). *L'identication des besoins des adultes apprenant une langue étrangère.* Strasbourg: Conseil de l'Europe.

Richterich, R., & Chancerel, J.-L. (1987). *Identifying the needs of adults learning a foreign language.* Englewood Cliffs, NJ: Prentice-Hall.

Robinson, P. (1980). *ESP (English for specific purposes).* Oxford: Pergamon.

Robinson, P. (1991). *ESP today: A practitioner's guide.* New York: Prentice Hall.

Rossett, A. (1982). A typology for generating needs assessments. *Journal of Instructional Development, 6*(1), 28–33.

Sawyer, R. (2001). An ethnographic approach to needs analysis for international graduate students of science in Japan. In E. F. Churchill & J. W. McLaughlin (Eds.), *Temple University Japan working papers in applied linguistics: Qualitative research in applied linguistics: Japanese learners and contexts* (pp. 102–117). Tokyo: Temple University Japan.

Seedhouse, P. (1995). Needs analysis and the general English classroom. *ELT Journal, 49*(1), 59–65.

Shamsudin, S., Manam, A. A., & Husin, N. (2013). Introducing engineering corpus: A needs analysis approach. *Procedia Social and Behavioral Sciences, 70,* 1288–1294.

Shing, S. R., Sim, T. S., & Bahrani, T. (2013). EGAP or ESAP? Towards meeting the academic English language needs of undergraduates. *The International Journal of Language Learning and Applied Linguistics World, 2*(1), 31–44.

Singh, R. K. (1983). ESP: Communication constraints. *System, 11*(2), 155–158.

So-mui, F. L., & Mead, K. (2000). An analysis of English in the workplace: The communication needs of textile and clothing merchandisers. *English for Specific Purposes, 19,* 351–367.

Soriano, F. I. (1995). *Conducting needs assessments: A multidisciplinary approach.* Thousand Oaks, CA: Sage.

Spence, P., & Liu, G.-Z. (2013). Engineering English and the high-tech industry: A case study of an English needs analysis of process integration engineers at a semiconductor manufacturing company in Taiwan. *English for Specific Purposes, 32,* 97–109.

St. John, M. (1996). Business is booming: Business English in the 1990s. *English for Specific Purposes, 15,* 3–18.

Strain, S. S. (2006). *A friendly approach to English for academic purposes.* Tokyo: Shohakusha.

Stufflebeam, D. L., McCormick, C. H., Brinkerhoff, R. O., & Nelson, C. O. (1985). *Conducting educational needs assessments.* Hingham, MA: Kluwer-Nijhoff.

Sugrue, B. (2013). A learning science alternative to Bloom's taxonomy. *Learning Solutions Magazine,* 1–4. Available at http://www.learningsolutionsmag.com/articles/1116/a-learning-science-alternative-to-blooms-taxonomy

Swales, J. (1985). *Episodes in ESP.* Hemel Hempstead, UK: Prentice-Hall.

Tanaka, H. (2001). English communication needs of an international advertising company: An ethnographic appraisal. In E. F. Churchill & J. W. McLaughlin (Eds.), *Temple University Japan working papers in applied linguistics: Qualitative research in applied linguistics: Japanese learners and contexts* (pp. 143–163). Tokyo: Temple University Japan.

Tarone, E., & Hanzeli, V. (Eds.) (1981). *English for academic purposes: Studies in honor of Louis Trimble*. Washington, DC: Newbury House.

Tarone, E., & Yule, G. (1989). *Focus on the language learner: Approaches to identifying and meeting the needs of second language learners*. Oxford: Oxford University Press.

Teng, H. (1999). Needs analysis of EFL listening by Taiwanese college students. *KOTESOL Proceedings of PAC2* (pp. 169–177). The Second Pan Asian Conference, Seoul, Korea.

Tickoo, M. L. (Ed.) (1987). *Language syllabuses: State of the art* (Anthology series 18). Singapore: RELC.

Tobey, D. (2005). *Needs assessment basics*. Alexandria, VA: ASTD.

Tomlinson, B. (Ed.) (1998). *Materials development in language teaching*. Cambridge: Cambridge University Press.

Tomlinson, B. (Ed.) (2003). *Developing materials for language teaching*. London: Continuum.

Trace, J., Hudson, T., & Brown, J. D. (Eds.) (2015). Developing courses in languages for specific purposes (NetWork #69) [PDF document]. Honolulu: National Foreign Language Resource Center. Accessed June 9, 2015 at http://hdl.handle.net/10125/14573

Trim, J. L. M. (1973). *Système d'apprentissage des langues vivantes par les adultes: Un système européen d'unités capitalisables*. Strasbourg: Conseil de la Coopération Culturelle du Conseil Européen.

Trim, J. L. M. (1978). *Developing a unit/credit scheme of adult language learning*. Oxford: Pergamon.

Trim, J. L. M. (1980). *The place of needs analysis in the council of Europe modern language project. Foreign language teaching: Meeting individual needs*. Oxford: Pergamon.

Trim, J. L. M., Richterich, R., van Ek, J. A., & Wilkins, D. A. (1980). *Systems development in adult language learning: A European unit/credit system for modern language learning by adults*. Oxford: Pergamon.

Trimble, L. (1985). *English for science and technology: A discourse approach*. Cambridge: Cambridge University Press.

Trimble, M. T., Trimble, L., & Drobnic, K. (Eds.) (1978). *English for specific purposes: Science and technology*. Corvalis, OR: Oregon State University.

Uvin, J. (1996). Designing workplace ESOL courses for Chinese health-care workers at a Boston nursing home. In K. Graves (Ed.), *Teachers as course developers* (pp. 39–62). Cambridge: Cambridge University Press.

van Ek, J. A. (1975). *Threshold level English in a European unit credit system for modern language learning adults*. Oxford: Pergamon.

van Ek, J. A. (1984). Foreign language learning needs in schools. In J. A. van Ek & J. L. M. Trim (Eds.), *Across the threshold: Readings from the modern language projects of the Council of Europe* (pp. 67–72). Oxford: Pergamon.

van Ek, J. A., & Alexander, L. (1980). *Threshold level English*. Oxford: Pergamon.

van Ek, J. A., & Trim, J. L. M. (1998a). *Threshold 1990*. Cambridge: Cambridge University Press.

van Ek, J. A., & Trim, J. L. M. (1998b). *Waystage 1990*. Cambridge: Cambridge University Press.

van Ek, J. A., & Trim, J. L. M. (2001). *Vantage*. Cambridge: Cambridge University Press.

van Hest, E., & Oud-De Glas, M. (1990). *A survey of techniques used in the diagnosis and analysis of foreign language needs in industry*. Brussels, Belgium: Lingua.

Walker, J. (1977). *The flying circus of physics (with answers)*. New York: Wiley & Sons.

Waters, A. (1996). *A review of research into needs in English for academic purposes of relevance to the North American higher education context*. TOEFL monograph series #6. Princeton, NJ: Educational Testing Service.

West, R. (1994). Needs analysis in language teaching. *Language Teaching, 27*, 1–19.

White, R. V. (1988). *The ELT curriculum: Design, innovation and management*. Oxford: Blackwell.

Widdowson, H. G. (1981). English for specific purposes: Criteria for course design. In M. Selinker, E. Tarone, & V. Hanzeli (Eds.), *English for academic purposes: Studies in honor of Louis Trimble* (pp. 1–11). Rowley, MA: Newbury House.

Wilkins, D. (1976). *Notional syllabuses: A taxonomy and its relevance to foreign language curriculum development*. London: Oxford University Press.

Winn, M. (2005). Collecting target discourse: The case of the US naturalization interview. In M. H. Long (Ed.), *Second language needs analysis* (pp. 265–304). Cambridge: Cambridge University Press.

Witkin, B. R. (1984). *Assessing needs in educational and social programs*. San Francisco, CA: Jossey-Bass.

Witkin, B. R., & Altschuld, J. W. (1995). *Planning and conducting needs assessments*. Thousand Oaks, CA: Sage.

Wozniak, S. (2010). Language needs analysis form a perspective of international professional mobility: The case of French mountain guides. *English for Specific Purposes, 29*, 243–252.

Wu, Y. (2012). An empirical study of needs analysis of college business English course. *International Education Studies, 5*(2), 216–221.

Yalden, J. (1987). *Principles of course design for language teaching*. Cambridge: Cambridge University Press.

Zhu, W., & Flaitz, J. (2005). Using focus group methodology to understand international students' academic language needs: A comparison of perspectives. *TESL-EJ, 8*(4), 1–11.

Index

Note: Page numbers in **bold** indicate figures or tables. The following abbreviations are used in the index: ESP, English for specific purposes; NA, needs analysis.